Danny Samson and Tom Bevington

IMPLEMENTING STRATEGIC CHANGE

MANAGING PROCESSES AND
INTERFACES TO DEVELOP
A HIGHLY PRODUCTIVE
ORGANIZATION

Implementing Strategic Change

Managing processes and interfaces to develop a highly productive organization

Tom Bevington and Danny Samson

KoganPage

LONDON PHILADELPHIA NEW DELHI

First published in Great Britain and the United States in 2012 by Kogan Page Limited

120 Pentonville Road	1518 Walnut Street, Suite 1100	4737/23 Ansari Road
London N1 9JN	Philadelphia PA 19102	Daryaganj
United Kingdom	USA	New Delhi 110002
www.koganpage.com		India

© Tom Bevington and Danny Samson, 2012

The right of Tom Bevington and Danny Samson to be identified as the authors of this work has been asserted by them in accordance with the Copyright, Designs and Patents Act 1988.

ISBN   978 0 7494 6554 4
E-ISBN 978 0 7494 6555 1

**HD
58.8
.S259
2012**

British Library Cataloguing-in-Publication Data

A CIP record for this book is available from the British Library.

Library of Congress Cataloging-in-Publication Data

Samson, Danny.
  Implementing strategic change : managing processes and interfaces to develop a highly productive organization / Danny Samson, Tom Bevington.
     p. cm.
  ISBN 978-0-7494-6554-4 — ISBN 978-0-7494-6555-1 1. Organizational change—Management.
2. Organizational effectiveness. 3. Strategic planning. I. Bevington, Tom. II. Title.
  HD58.8.S259 2012
  658.4'06—dc23
                              2011038486

Typeset by Macmillan Publishing Solutions
Printed and bound in India by Replika Press Pvt Ltd

CONTENTS

FOREWORD

In my decades as General Manager, CEO and Chairman of the board of a large bank, large manufacturer and the world's largest mining/resources company, I was acutely aware of the need to effectively link operational excellence to overall business strategy. In working for a decade with one of this book's co-authors, it became clear that the high level principles outlined in this book provide guidance of how to create great organizations. The ultimate challenge of any leader is to create a world-class organization, one that is highly productive and able to withstand competitive assault. Yet as pointed out in this book, the rubber does not hit the road unless the organization has a sound operational base to proceed from.

The statistics given in the book ring true, for example that one-third of organizational work is noise, or waste in my terms. Various organizations that I have been in have tried to implement Lean, Total Quality Management or Six Sigma approaches with mixed success. This book lights up the reasons as to why this happens: the 'hidden in plain sight' interfaces preclude progress, and they must be identified and eliminated. The devil is really in the detail when it comes to implementing change.

To implement business strategies effectively, an organization's managers must know where they are starting from. They must engage in outcome thinking which imagines and implements the doable and creates results.

I heartily endorse this book: this approach can create a real cut-through on connecting top down strategies to bottom-up process excellence.

Don Argus AC
(Retired) Chairman BHP Billiton,
Group CEO National Australia Bank, Chairman Brambles

PREFACE

When we first discussed writing this book we both felt constrained by the accepted frameworks used for deployment of business strategy, which we knew we were about to challenge and challenge hard. The approaches to determining business strategy are taught in every business school and are widely practised. Further, the mechanisms for deployment, such as business process re-engineering (BPR), are more than familiar to every manager and business consultant in the world. Yet from our many observations we see that there is a huge chasm between the refinement of the well-researched and documented business strategy as formulated and the incompleteness of the design and deployment of the changes needed to enact it. Every change seems to take longer than expected and the 'settling in' and 'debugging' goes on forever, leaving organizations exposed to attack from competitors and consumers. Business strategies are often sensibly formulated and sensible in content, yet they often fail in implementation. This is due to poor implementation approaches, not usually due to flaws in the conceptual elements of the strategy.

This chasm between strategy formulation and effective deployment, with a few notable exceptions in organizations such as Toyota and GE, results from using judgement, guesses and experience and tools that are more aligned with the analogue estimates of the sextant than the digital precision of GPS. Indeed, taking this GPS analogy further, we felt that we had in the palm of our hand a new way of thinking about deployment of strategic change, and a new tool, which could easily be used by staff, managers and change practitioners to take advantage of every bit of driving experience they already possessed to reach the organization's goal. And the result of its use would be acceleration in the pace of change while gaining step increases in performance – often at no cost.

This missing piece of the strategic deployment jigsaw puzzle lies in the understanding and managing of the interfaces between the always carefully defined functional activities every organization documents in order to deliver its strategy. Interfacing activities are those activities that occur between defined process steps. They include many forms of adjustment and rework necessary to get items processed, and they exist because of the lack of process control and standardization in those business processes. The surprise, when the importance of interfacing activities is understood, is that not one of the hundreds of organizations we have worked with had ever documented their interfacing activities comprehensively and most had never even tried. We show that undocumented interfacing activities outnumbered the well-documented (functional) activities by 3:1. This is to recognize the enormous complexity that really exists in the full set of activities that is going on in every organization, way beyond what is documented. The cost of these myriads of interfacing activities is high, and many of them can be eliminated, using little more than common sense management. However, this common sense management must be applied by the right people in the right ways and places to take effect. In other words, managing interfacing activities should be central to the management effort.

These interfacing activities occur everywhere in every organization. Failure to document means there is no visibility of the mass of resource devoted to the gaps and weaknesses that show up as poor customer service, employee dissatisfaction and massive productivity shortfalls. We do therefore spend a considerable amount of time in organizations on raising the understanding of the behaviour of interfacing activities, but we obviously needed to do more. Making people aware of interfacing activities and how to map them very quickly was, in our minds at least, not enough. We had to prove their worth and expose their pivotal role in strategy deployment.

We have been extremely fortunate to have two sets of research at our disposal. Our international literature searches confirm that there is no more comprehensive, peer-based research into the management principles that drive success in the best organizations in the world than the research to which we already had ready access. Further, no one has ever attempted consistently to 'map' so many businesses at such a detailed level and then use the data to drive performance gains. We were therefore easily able to assemble a uniquely detailed database of over 100 organizations, many being household names, that furnished material in a consistent way to show how their business processes functioned. We are therefore able to support every one of our conclusions with rock solid evidence, as well as plenty of anecdotes to bring them to life.

When we had completed the analysis and integration of the two sets of material, our early inhibitions and reservations fell away. Our material allowed us to describe the management principles that characterize the best organizations in the world. We were able to demonstrate that by analysing interfacing activities, the incidences of non-compliance with these principles stand out. Further, the quantification inherent to interface mapping allowed priorities to be established with unheard-of ease and speed. We had thus uncovered the key to the linkage between strategy and business processes that lies hidden in plain sight in every organization.

In summary, our book shows how 'top-down' strategies can best be fitted with precision to 'bottom-up' processes and process improvements. When this link is absent, strategy fails in deployment. When it is clear and present, strategy has every chance of being implemented correctly. This book explores two connected ideas. The first is the core management capability of the organization defined by the management principles that are common to excellent organizations. The second is the necessary process management capability to use these principles to implement strategy and change successfully.

Chapter 11 contains useful definitions of some of the key terms used in this book.

We are grateful for the support and encouragement of both our families. Particular acknowledgement is due to members of the Department of Management and Marketing at the University of Melbourne who gave so freely their advice and input. And we are grateful to Stephen Bungay for his assistance on historical accuracy. Our thanks are also due to the Bevington Group and in particular to Diana Perry for her insightful comments and to Andrew Shiels for his help with the assembly and analysis of the database. We are also appreciative of the guidance given by Iain McLaren.

Tom Bevington and Danny Samson

Introduction

After waiting in a long queue at the supermarket you get to the front only to find that the scanner cannot read any of the barcodes on your goods. You wait while someone checks the scanner. It still doesn't work. You're asked to move to another checkout. You gather up your goods, load them back into your trolley and wheel them over to yet another long queue before finally you can pay for your goods.

All the activities you had to do to move to a new checkout were unanticipated interfacing activities that delayed and probably frustrated you, leaving you with an impression of poor customer service. The implications might not end there. Perhaps this has caused you to overstay your time on a parking meter and you leave the store to find that your car has been towed away. Now how long will it take to get home? How much will it cost to get your car back? Will you miss your doctor's appointment? Do you have to cancel a critical meeting at work?

In this instance, poorly managed interfacing activities could have wasted a lot of your time and money. But it was, after all, only a one off, wasn't it? Just a bit of bad luck.

But to those working in the supermarket the perception is likely to be very different. What might happen to you once a year is a much more regular occurrence there. It's just business as usual! Of course, the interfacing difficulties don't apply to all transactions but when they do happen, they can have an equally toxic effect, causing major disruption and delays downstream in the business if they are not dealt with expeditiously. They distract staff from doing the job they are supposed to be doing and thus cause a great deal of frustration within the organization. Bad luck for one individual customer translates to a huge amount of frustration throughout the business. We will show that such 'exception' activities are actually not unusual or exceptional at all in most organizations, but that, as one senior banking executive recognized, they 'happen all the time'. How often do mortgage application processes not go 'to plan', having some irregularity occur that requires some form of exception work, chasing documents that are not in place when and where they should be? The answer is that irregularities happen often, and in some organizations and on some transactions, far too often. They occur primarily because business processes are poorly specified or poorly connected. This can be fixed, but first it needs acknowledgement, efficient identification and sensible economic decisions about which flaws to fix. Of course, we advocate prioritizing the vital few, not the trivial many. But first they need to be correctly held up to the light. Once this is done, the organization can actually run like a well-oiled, smooth machine, and not with the creaky, capricious and sometimes sputtering systems that some of us have, sadly, become accustomed to. Whether your organization is a sputterer, or just could do with a tune-up, the way to do so with more power than ever thought previously possible is to identify all the interfacing activities efficiently and then eliminate those 20 per cent that cause 80 per cent of the problems. The total amount of waste in organizations that currently averages some 33.6 per cent of activity can be halved with precision and efficiency, and it is possible to go even further.

Organizational impact of toxic interfaces

As you can see from the example of the supermarket checkout process, understanding and managing interfaces is critical in a business environment. Everything in business is magnified. Business processes are created to handle enquiries, book appointments, give advice, process orders, process payments, handle complaints, assemble a product, design a service, assess a risk, develop a policy, etc. We will use the word 'stuff' generically to encompass all of these various types of transactions.

First, the volume of product or 'stuff' being handled will be much greater so these disruptive interfacing activities will inevitably occur regularly. Second, there are constant changes at the interfaces – changes to products, procedures, equipment, new staff, temporary staff, new instructions, legislation, etc. These changes bring a continual stream of new issues that have to be resolved. With so much variation to deal with in our fast-moving world, it's no wonder that staff so often resist change, as they have more than enough change to handle without someone introducing even more. The thing about these toxic interface activities, described as 'unusual routines' by Rice and Cooper (2010), is that they are not actually unusual at all. They account for over 50 per cent of what everybody does in every one of the organizations we have studied!

The failure of strategic change

Based on rigorous international research, this book seeks to develop a new understanding of how organizations work. It presents managers with a once in a lifetime opportunity to deliver huge performance gains because it:

- universally applies to all organizations;
- always delivers an enormous bottom-line benefit;

- can be implemented quickly;
- delivers the world's best practice.

The opportunity arises from combining two factors which at first sight make strange bedfellows. These are the top-level management principles that distinguish the best organizations in the world; and the ubiquitous myriad of interfacing activities which are enacted every day to enable 'stuff', transactions and products, to be passed from one person to the next in every single one of our business processes.

Detailed analysis of data from over 400 organizational applications of interface mapping has shown that interfacing activities, rather simplistically documented as the connecting lines on a business process map (see Figure 3.2 on page 67), are the primary drivers of poor customer service, low sales growth, employee dissatisfaction and inflated costs. The failure to manage the interfacing activities means that it is impossible for any organization consistently to achieve its key strategic goals or build strategic capabilities. These interfacing activities, rendered invisible by widespread failure to document them, distract people from the real job because, as we will demonstrate, they absorb almost two days out of the working week of every member of staff and management.

These interfacing activities are never understood because they are never properly documented. Consequently, they cannot be analysed and understood. Every day these overlooked activities continue to grow unchecked in number and complexity as organizations feverishly build strategic partnerships and outsource elements of manufacturing and services, which keeps on expanding the number of interfaces needed to do business. No wonder some organizations are terminating their outsourcing deals and bringing the work back under their direct control.

Interfaces are not the problem

There is nothing inherently bad in having interfacing activities. They are steps that occur at a multitude of points in a process in order to pass 'stuff' – products, services, items, transactions – from one person, step or entity to another. Well-planned and executed interfacing activities are necessary and routine in every endeavour. There is nothing more natural in the way humans deal with each other than to conduct interfacing activities. For example, when you buy items in a supermarket, the checkout assistant hands you your purchases and you hand over money. The assistant then gives you your change and receipt. These are such simple and straightforward interface activities that they hardly seem worthy of our attention – so not bothering to document them is an easily won argument. However, when staff doing the job are given the tools and support to document all that they routinely do, fundamental issues are suddenly exposed because of the cumulative impact of unmanaged interfaces.

Best practice using interface mapping

In Chapter 2 we establish the 14 best-practice management principles that are always found in the world's leading organizations. Many are commonly-held truths. Who would dispute that the principles of: wanting to be 'out front', focusing on customer needs, having shared common objectives and being time-based, are essential ingredients to organizational success? However, since Samson and Challis documented these principles (1999) we have become increasingly aware of the difficulties in implementing any one of them, not to mention all of them. Until now even the best attempts have been hit or miss.

Take one of the most common principles on which many organizations work – the building of shared objectives. Organizations usually tackle this by arranging off-site workshops for groups of managers and/or staff at which the attendees collectively develop a set of business objectives. Without doubt the participants will leave the sessions with a clear understanding of the shared objectives for their business, but how does each of them approach implementation? What happens if the objectives are not accepted by their peers, other staff or their immediate manager? Can this be measured and understood, as reality of what people do, not just what they say? What happens if implementation feels like it is just too hard? How do managers detect conscious or unconscious failure to implement the principle?

Until now by our observation there has been no practical way to close this open loop. Implementation is left to the individuals as infringements go unnoticed, appear not to be important or are even actively encouraged by those with power and a different agenda. If it is not measured, it won't get done.

Combining principled implementation with interface mapping will close this loop efficiently and quickly. This is because infringements, if they have business relevance, result in 'stuff' being delayed or otherwise affected. This causes people to have to invent extra interfacing activity in order to keep everything moving. Interface mapping not only makes all infringements obvious, it puts a cost to each of them so that priorities are easily set and addressed. Through exploring and addressing the relationship between infringement of, or non-compliance with, best-practice principles and the interfacing activities, one can directly build towards the achievement of world's best practice.

Too good to be true?

Perhaps you feel another expensive and long lead time three-letter acronym like BPR (business process re-engineering), SBUs (strategic business units) or BSC (Balanced Scorecard, first presented by Kaplan and Norton) creeping up on you? Please discard the thought. At the very minimum we will show you that, by simply documenting the interfacing activities, you can grow your existing Six Sigma, Lean or BPR initiatives by achieving better targeting, yield realization and prioritization. But better still you will be able to deliver your organization's goals by using the opportunity to implant the world's best-practice management principles in the business and thus build the sustainable competitive advantage your strategy has targeted.

This is not another treatise on Six Sigma, the Lean approach, BPR or Total Quality Management (TQM), although every bit of in-house experience your people have gained from using these approaches will be put to good use. Nor are we saying that you need to acquire these types of skills. This book is about something quite different. It is about building and sustaining competitive advantage through the way you use your resources – how you should strategically align your end-to-end business processes using the management principles found in the top-performing organizations in the world. This book will enable you first to build and then to maintain your organization's strategic capabilities with precision. This precision will eliminate the trial and error approach to strategy implementation. It will reduce your organization's reliance on judgement, guesswork and experience in determining change needs and priorities and speed up delivery of benefits while lowering the effort involved.

How much will this cost?

You may perhaps be wondering how much mapping interfacing activities will actually cost. Please don't – it will not 'cost' at all. A high level of waste in an organization is simply not newsworthy today. Back in the 1970s the quality guru Philip Crosby asserted that there was a waste level of 2½ per cent to 20 per cent deeply embedded in every organization and we know that intuitively many managers feel that the waste is still there. Interface mapping will confirm in just three weeks the level of waste in your organization as well as precisely where it is (see Table 7.1 on page 139). Indeed, in most cases an interface mapping programme will reveal a quantified waste percentage which exceed Crosby's level in spite of today's highly competitive global climate and the huge efforts made by every organization to eliminate it. The information provided by interface mapping will enable you to pinpoint and free up between half and two thirds of the waste quickly with little or no capital investment. The time released will create a capacity of about one day per week per person in your organization, and another result will be to lift customer service and employee satisfaction dramatically.

Many people argue that there can be no organizational gain without pain. These people believe, perhaps from bitter experience, that staff and managers really have to suffer to make any progress. Well, again, no! Interface mapping, of necessity, involves just about everyone in a firm. Staff always tell us that their job descriptions, their procedures and the process maps only contain a fraction of the activities they routinely undertake to do their jobs, and interface mapping will demonstrate that they are right. Interface mapping does two important things – it truly engages staff, and it requires those actually doing the work to 'certify' that everything that is done is documented. Of course, on the first day of a routine three-week interface mapping programme, real concern will be in evidence. Everybody will recall the last change programme – the wasted effort, the long hours, the often disappointing outcomes. But by the end of the first week cautious excitement followed by outright enthusiasm will be in evidence, summed up by often heard remarks such as: 'We have never documented everything we have to do before, especially all the rubbish we have to work with,' and 'Now we have documented it, why can't we fix it?' The risk after interface mapping is not that change will not occur but that people will rush in and try to fix interface issues on an ad hoc basis. The management job will change radically. It will become one of harnessing the energy generated by using the real data to achieve beneficial change. This is quite a departure from trying to agree change based on a knowledge of just one quarter of what is really happening, followed by cajoling the unwilling to do the unnecessary.

Don't make the mistake either that interface mapping only applies to small businesses. Detailed mapping of 5,000 staff will be achieved in three weeks even though, if you ask us, we would recommend that first-time users start with a more compact scope. Interface mapping really is very different from the more superficial process mapping that nearly everyone has some familiarity with.

Does it work in practice?

We had been aware for a long time that most businesses ignore interfacing activities in the various forms of documentation they use. We have compiled a database of organizations where the staff have been trained in the last five years to map their interface activities. The organizations include banks, hospitals, insurance companies, manufacturers, regulatory bodies, public policy units, call centres, not-for-profit organizations, professional societies, airports, transport companies and utility companies. It includes two of the world's best-known businesses, two businesses in Australia's listed top ten and includes representatives from four continents.

This database contains all of the activities undertaken by all of the 13,657 staff and managers in 117 different organizations. These 13,657 people used interface mapping to document the 395,832 activities they routinely undertook. They were also able to quantify the time each activity absorbed. The total was 1,775,377 hours per month – equivalent to almost US $1.45 billion per annum in salary costs.

The database shows that the largely unreported interfacing activities account for three out of every four activities routinely undertaken when compared to the pre-existing information in the organizations. Most of the interfacing activities never appear in job descriptions, procedures or even complex process maps.

Analysis of this interfacing data showed that, on average across all 117 organizations, 33.6 per cent of everyone's time is spent on interface activity noise. Interfacing activity noise includes correcting errors and omissions and chasing missing information as well as dealing with the downstream consequences of the errors and delays. We refer to waste as interface activity noise because, like the noise in electronic circuits, it is interference. It interferes with the ability of business processes to deliver required outcomes. The average noise amounts to a staggering one and two third days each week for each person employed, or around US $25,000 per person employed per annum (based on an average cost of employment). The data also demonstrated that interfacing activity and these levels of noise were present in all businesses in all sectors (see Table 5.3 on page 98).

The noise embedded in the usually unrecorded interfacing activity increases the cost of every business transaction by about 50 per cent. Businesses therefore pay the 50 per cent overhead and destroy customer service and staff satisfaction at the same time. In addition to the 50 per cent increase in cost, the noise reduces customer service because chasing missing information and correcting errors and omissions means delays, and your own experience would confirm that these delays can last days or weeks until the right person can be tracked down. Further, no one enjoys checking, chasing, correcting or dealing with the angry customers who are affected by this noise, so many staff leave if they can. Noise in poorly managed interfacing activities frustrates the staff and managers who stay and have to deal with it. Critically, noise distracts them and often prevents them from doing their real job of sustaining and increasing the value of the business. This staff dissatisfaction, lowering of morale and staff engagement, and turnover of staff is also costly.

As managers, unlike your staff and team leaders, you can ignore interfacing activities day after day. In contrast, staff have to receive the incomplete and incorrect 'stuff' within the business process and they absolutely have to find a way to deal with it. To do this they will define interfacing activity elements of your business processes on the spur of the moment with little knowledge of the strategic intent. They will be held back by the authority and levels of influence inherent to their status in the organization and so will tend to do what is expedient, not what is required. They will have to pass on many errors because they do not have the wherewithal to address them. These errors and omissions will, like a virus, continue, wreaking havoc further on in the process. The staff will delay things because they have to wait for something they need but cannot influence its provision. They will thus continue, unknowingly or because they have no other option, to compromise your customer service imperatives. They will be bound by their immediate boss's priorities which may not align with those of the company, thus wasting resource and causing further impact to customer service levels. Staff satisfaction will consequently remain below the level you would like to achieve. Staff will even try to please customers who have been adversely affected by poor interfacing activity management by doing something extra – such as not charging for every service, conducting extra research, crediting accounts to reduce charges, giving discounts on bills, changing delivery priorities, re-arranging appointments – all downstream noise impacts – which will only in the end cause more disruption and destroy further value.

You can also ignore interfacing activities when investing in new systems and organizational changes. The professional staff engaged will design the new system, or changes, on the assumption that your interfacing activity is clean and that hand-offs are error free, as mostly shown in the process maps. That is because process maps are generally incapable of handling the detail needed to show the interfacing activities. Then there will be the prolonged period termed euphemistically 'settling in' and 'bug fixing'. The settling-in period with its inherent disruption is actually needed to allow the staff and junior managers the time they need to work out new interfacing activities to address the issues which have been ignored. Most of the inevitable bugs arise from the design staff being unaware of what was really happening in the first place. As a result, the designers have been unable to configure the system properly to meet the real needs.

This book has therefore been written for two groups of people. The first are the many board members or managers who feel that their organization has exhausted the traditional strategy agenda but intuitively know that the organization could do a lot better. You will know your organization has a well-articulated business strategy and understands its competitive differentiators. Your organization will have made investments in the tools such as key performance indicators (KPIs) and the Balanced Scorecard, or approaches to customer needs assessment and business process alignment, such as BPR, Six Sigma or Lean. You just know that the business needs something to exploit these investments to the fullest extent and lift the business to the next level. You might even suspect that the business is wasting its resource from weak management of interfacing activity and you will be confident that some, but not all, of the best-practice management principles are embedded in current practices.

Alternatively, you may have been handed the reins of a once good business that has lost its way. You are looking for something to galvanize action to make up the years of lost ground. You have a team of people, many very experienced, who have been worn down by the routine grind. You have tried to push people on but you get the same answers every time: 'We have tried that, but it didn't make the impact promised,' or 'We don't have that issue.' You need something, and you need it now. It has to deliver a shock, demonstrate unambiguously that there is a real opportunity that will lead to real impact to the bottom line. It needs to provide quickly unarguable opportunities and delivery of them has to begin quickly. You might suspect that the interfacing activity noise in your business is absorbing 30 per cent or even 40 per cent of your people resources. You will know that there will be a low level of compliance to the management principles found in excellent organizations. You really need the 'swept under the carpet' horrors to be exposed to the light of day quickly and indisputably.

If either of these caps fit and you really want your business to be out front (that is, be the best in class) you are, with the interface mapping process, now just three weeks away from uncovering the nature and extent of your interface management gold seam – costs, customer service, staff satisfaction and performance. The choice, as ever, is yours.

Business strategy

Rigorous formulation, routine under-achievement

Objectives

This chapter will present the core ideas of why efforts at implementing new strategies and significant change usually fail to deliver to expectations. It will explore the fact that conventional strategy formulation typically focuses on only half of what is needed to drive improvement. The focus of conventional strategy is on the 'what' of strategy, what resource and market position is needed. It glosses over the 'how', how the functional activities that need to be undertaken are linked together or interfaced. This key element for implementing strategy has been largely overlooked by researchers and consultants, and has been often poorly implemented by even the most professional of managers. Hence even the most sensible-sounding strategies as formulated often underperform in real-time implementation. The reason is that implementing efficient and effective business process change is very difficult if the interfacing activities between functional process steps are ignored.

This chapter will explain that interfacing activities usually comprise a large proportion of total activity in the firm and hence account for large chunks of cost and elapsed time in processes. They are the very things that cause customer and employee frustration. They inhibit change and strategy implementation when left unchecked. And in most organizations, they are hidden and ignored!

This chapter will show that these problems can be overcome by identifying and standardizing not just the process steps that are usually visible, but also the often hidden interfacing activities that junior staff have to invent when things (inevitably) do not go exactly to plan, and need 'spur of the moment' adjustment, which we also call 'fettling'.

Introduction

Our peer-reviewed research of over 200 international organizations has enabled us to describe with a high degree of precision the 14 management principles for excellence, which together are strongly associated with business success, longevity and value creation. These principles, as you might expect, reaffirm the value of investing in developing a business strategy and organizing to implement it, hard. They highlight the need to align both intra-organizational and inter-organizational resources with the business strategy and customers' priorities at the same time as achieving high levels of efficiency. They also underscore the need to manage some of the well-researched factors that enable episodic and ongoing change to be effected. These management principles are described thoroughly in Chapter 2.

The key question is why have these principles (described by Samson and Challis, 1999) not been universally adopted by the private and public sectors to deliver outstanding business performances? The problem is actually quite simple and clear to understand: it is quite feasible to formulate good business and business improvement strategy rationally, and much harder to implement it well. Most companies that fail to move forward fall into the cracks of poor implementation more than poorly conceived strategies.

We must therefore start by examining both parts of strategic management processes: formulation and then implementation. We will be going into the nuts and bolts of why an otherwise excellent strategy fails to live up to expectations. There will be discussion about how to make the whole organization and its partners into a watertight single delivery mechanism in every respect (top-down strategy meeting bottom-up business processes, across the whole extended enterprise). First though, we propose to consider the context this book addresses. We therefore briefly examine the development of business strategy over the past four decades, how the environment in which a business operates has changed and how this change has affected the role of managers and team leaders, especially with respect to strategic resource management. In particular, we explain why an organization should understand and manage its interfacing activities, those ubiquitous activities needed to allow 'stuff' (meaning transactions, information, goods and services) to flow freely through extended organizations to deliver value to customers, in order to deploy strategy effectively. The 'seam of gold' in an organization becomes accessible to all once these interfacing activities are revealed and examined properly.

We do need to visit strategic theory, though, to show where to look for the seam of gold that is just under the surface in your organization, waiting to be uncovered. We begin by hypothesizing why it has taken so long for such a glaring opportunity to be recognized.

Only half a solution?

Since the 1950s the dominant business strategy mindset has been focused on the tangible or hard assets a business possesses, such as the scale and scope of facilities; distribution coverage and brand equity (Jones and Butler, 2000). Military analogies have often been used. For example, in the bloody trench warfare that characterized the World War 1 Battle of the Somme, the possession of a particular, strategically positioned asset (a well dug-in, heavy Maxim machine gun with commanding height over the opposing trenches), virtually guaranteed unassailability. Millions died waiting for someone to invent the tank to break the stalemate of the strategic advantage of that machine gun.

The best known proponent of business structural or asset-based strategy approaches is the respected academic, Michael Porter. His theory of competitive forces has provided many, if not all, businesses with a framework and an approach that helps them to plan to achieve market 'unassailability' or dominance, or the achievement of at least industry attractiveness. It is the most widely known and practised example of the genre with its underpinning principles being based in achieving cost leadership or market differentiation (Porter, 1990). This approach is without any doubt one of two essential components of a sustainable competitive advantage.

The emphasis placed on tangible or hard assets in Porter's approach is hardly surprising. At the end of World War 2 there was a pressing need to rebuild and refocus organizations. Much of Europe's industry had been destroyed and what remained had been subverted to focus on war material. Millions of people were dying from starvation. Infrastructure, equipment and people skills needed to be rebuilt or replaced in as short a time as possible. Some big bets had to be placed because this task was far more complex than the other, albeit daunting, task of just replacing everything that had been destroyed. New technologies and materials had been developed during the conflict, for example electronic computing; telecommunications and radar; the jet engine; new weapons, such as cruise and ballistic missiles; major advances in hydraulic, electrical and pneumatic controls; and streamlined techniques for mass production. These held the promise of vast, new commercial opportunities and access to new markets. The issue was picking the winners and putting at risk as little of the scarce capital as was possible.

The sheer scale of the investments required, and the wide range of technologies in which to invest thus demanded the development of tools and techniques to formulate strategy and to minimize the associated commercial risks. The need was for a better definition of what to focus on – what markets, what technologies and what resources. Academic research led ultimately to development of concepts of competitive forces and related theories. The international management consultancies and business schools evolved and grew largely by capitalizing on the need for these new theories to be communicated to and understood by managers, and then by providing managers with assistance and training to enable them to implant the approaches in their businesses.

Over the period of 40 years since then the situation has inevitably changed. Highly competitive global markets have supplanted post-war austerity, with the result that physical resources and specialist skills can be readily acquired by any organization with the wherewithal so to do. From shortages of post-World War 2, we now have many industries in overcapacity. This development has reduced the opportunity to gain competitive advantage just from the tangible assets and 'things' a business possesses. Further, governmental consumer and competition regulation has made it illegal to collude with or to engage in anti-competitive activities and this has eroded the benefits from a strategy based on position. And, more recently, globalization means that structural competitive advantage can be quickly eroded these days. Something else is needed.

Two parts to the strategy – an uncomfortable truth

Something else is clearly required. After all, the Maxim machine gun would have been useless without a focus on how to use it – in effect the business processes required to set it up, maintain it, supply it with ammunition and trained operators, and obtain access to deep underground bunkers to protect it and its crew during enemy artillery barrages.

In our view, and for far too long, the management of internal resources to achieve strategic alignment has been viewed as being unimportant. Resource management, including the development of business processes, has been left in the hands of functional managers. The importance of the strategic alignment of internal resources only began to be acknowledged by top managers and business consultants at the end of the century. Ireland and Hitt, respected management researchers, enunciated the situation in a research paper (1999) where they wrote 'in the 1960s and 1970s the [external] situations facing the firm were thought to be the primary determinant of organizational outcomes… managers were believed to have little ability to make decisions that would affect the firm's performance.' The subject of our own international research has uncovered the 14 management principles that characterize leading organizations. These 14 principles are, almost exclusively, concerned with how a firm's resources are managed to achieve strategic alignment of business processes. The 'what' is just no longer enough to gain advantage in most industries.

The over-reliance on structural strategy approaches became evident and was demonstrated, sometimes spectacularly, by the demise of market dominant firms in Australia and in the United States. This has contrasted with the unstoppable growth of other companies, such as Toyota. Toyota's success is made even starker by looking at what should have been impregnable structural advantages that were held in the US market by GM. GM had the advantage of a market share of over 50 per cent in the United States at its peak, yet it went into provisional bankruptcy in 2009. This was despite its structural advantages, which were massive according to the theory, and included its established dealerships, supplier base and manufacturing facilities, its trained workforce, its knowledge of the market and its well-established brands (including Cadillac, Pontiac, Chevrolet, Vauxhall, Holden, Opel). Can anyone seriously argue that Toyota went from a zero market share to being the largest supplier of vehicles in the world, including in the United States, by exerting structural advantages? Rather, it was because its organization works so smoothly, and with relatively few 'gaps': that is, it effectively managed its interfaces.

These are dramatic events, representing not some small and insignificant changes in market share, profitability and industry leadership, but large differences indeed, leading to large changes in the fortunes of large organizations and all their stakeholders. So why is the 'other half' of the strategic agenda largely neglected in too many organizations? And why haven't all the investments we have been making in BPR or Lean or Six Sigma put us on a par with Toyota and General Electric?

This missing bit in the business strategy approach has, as one might expect, become a focal point for academic research, as was the case for the structural aspects of business strategy just after World War 2. The obvious need for something beyond the structural theory spurred much academic research into radically different and complementary approaches to business strategy. The first murmuring surfaced in the 1950s when Penrose proposed, speculatively, a strategic role for resource management. Her theory, the resource-based view (RBV), was subsequently supported by Tranfield and Smith (1998). They saw that Penrose proposed an argument to counterpose the dominant competitive forces theory. Her RBV theory was claimed to recognize the potential to achieve competitive advantage from the close management of internal resources.

In 1983 Schroeder explored distinctive competencies and internal resources. Then Wernerfelt (1984) linked internal resources to strategy and postulated how strategic advantage would accrue from what he termed attractive resources, such as in-house knowledge of technology and efficient procedures. He proposed a direction for the development of the RBV, and potentially for strategic business process management. It is instructive to examine his conclusions: '... much needs to be done on the implementability of the strategies suggested... nothing is known about the practical difficulties involved in identifying resources... or about to what extent one in practice can combine capabilities across operating divisions... or... set up a structure and systems which can help a firm execute these strategies' (Wernerfelt, 1984:180). Unfortunately, while Wernerfelt's 1984 questions remain pertinent today for both academics and business managers, proffered answers from research are far from achieving universal acceptance, let alone practical usability. Wernerfelt referred to the possible need to combine capabilities across operating divisions in order to create strategically focused business processes or strategic capabilities. He gave guidance about how he envisaged these cross-functional capabilities would deliver the business benefits to achieve significant competitive advantage in areas such as superior utilization of equipment, more effective customer relationships or more efficient production – exactly those benefits Toyota consistently demonstrates. Staggeringly, as late as 2008, Simon, Gove and Hitt admitted that the conundrum of strategic management of resources has yet to be solved. They said that there is an urgent need to understand how to achieve 'the idiosyncratic bundling and deployment choices that optimize the use of the firm's resources' (Simon, Gove and Hitt, 2008).

A need for a change in thinking

Even though the assumption of the low impact from the management of internal resources was first challenged in the 1950s, positional, or structural, strategic thinking still retained the high ground in the minds of many senior managers. In the pursuit of gaining cost advantage these companies investigated whether they should transfer significant portions of their value chain to lower-wage economies. Undeniably the companies achieved lower costs, but often at the expense of longer supply chains resulting in reduced service levels. This often opened their markets to competitors.

Why did the well-respected management teams follow this path? We have to conclude that structural analysis was being applied, illogically to those who understand interfacing activity, to try to understand and then replicate the success of organizations such as Toyota. The companies either tried to emulate some of these organizations' observed business practices or concentrated on copying the organizational development approaches it found the leading organizations were using.

The companies that tried emulation copied some (but never all) of the business practices found in high-performing companies. High-performing organizations were first identified by benchmarking and then visiting and researching to pick out different (best) practices the researcher concluded were associated with success. The identified elements were widely promoted at the time and will be familiar to many managers. The practices included: just-in-time production, Kanban, machine cells, employee empowerment and supplier quality control. Many companies then invested a great deal of time and resource in establishing one or more of these practices in their business only to find the changes did not deliver the expected level of improvement. The companies, in our view, 'bought' just a component of a business process – a 'solution' – without understanding its relationship and dependence on the other elements of the process. They had not targeted the interfacing activities that would have pinpointed their ills and had only addressed some of them by implementing the change by good luck. They had used a structural assessment approach such as they would have used to select a new lathe, weaving machine, retail branch location or truck. Perhaps they did not have the right analytical tools and approaches but they did not appear to try to understand the end-to-end process or the management principles that would have led to the development of aligned resources. They then simply installed their new purchase and sat back to wait for the benefits to accrue. Most are still waiting. Most times, they never achieved as Simon, Gove and Hitt put it (2008, quoted above) – 'idiosyncratic bundling' – choices that optimize the use of the firm's resources. Hence the business benefits were either not accrued at all, or at best were temporary, and most of such change and improvement initiatives did not last more than a year or two.

Other organizations were persuaded to copy the organizational development tools that were being used by leading companies. The size of the resulting investments was staggering and resulted in the terms BPR, TQM, Lean and Six Sigma entering everyday business language. In this wave the management consulting majors did much of the analysis of successful organizations such as General Electric and Motorola. They concluded that it was change tools, not specific bits of business processes, that were the key drivers of success. So tool kits for Six Sigma and Lean approaches were quickly assembled and sold to a market only too ready and willing to purchase. This was because managers could now analyse and compare the different offerings, select the one with the 'best' fit and features and deploy it within their organization. Again, they made their decisions, paid the money and sat back to watch the benefits flow in. Most, again, are still waiting.

Managers, without any doubt, would have chosen the best offering and hired and trained the most appropriate people to use their new-found approaches. But expectations were largely not met. This is because they only did the first part of the job in selecting the best tool and the right people. The missing piece was ensuring that the key changes needed in their business processes were identified and then deployed to achieve the required strategic alignment of the processes. This analysis and deployment required organizations to understand business processes at a level that made the change needs obvious and allowed them to use the best practice management principles to guide the formulation of the change. They needed to understand their interfacing activities. Only through this detailed understanding can the end-to-end implications of changes and improvements be understood and effectively managed. And without it, the unanticipated impacts of piecemeal initiatives will surely lead to them coming undone, which corporate history of initiatives such as TQM has proven. The powerful set of ideas TQM comprises is worth exploring briefly as a specific case of 'great ideas, poor implementation'. Most companies that tried TQM did not make a lasting go of it, but a few have really made it pay. Is it that the ideas were poor, or that the ideas were indeed rich, but implementation was poorly orchestrated and hence ineffective. Consider the core and essential ideas of what was TQM, listed below, and judge whether these are generally sound business ideas. Our view is that they were and indeed still are very powerful and sensible:

1 Focus the whole organization on the customer's requirements.

2 Eliminate waste in all forms: get it right the first time.

3 Achieve the above through processes that are 'in control' and 'capable', meaning able robustly and consistently to produce to the specification.

4 Drive all the organization's processes forward through continuous improvement.

5 Engage all employees in process control, customer focus, waste reduction and improvement work.

It is impossible to argue with the above business ideas, which we called TQM in the 1980s and 1990s, because they are compelling and valuable, yet most companies made a mess of their execution. How did this happen and why? The tools used for business process analysis – primarily process mapping – overlooked the most critical elements in achieving strategically aligned business processes – the interfaces – and interfacing activities make up three out of every four activities routinely carried out in organizations of all types.

Many managers believed that they were focusing on their businesses' interfaces. But we will show that most merely deployed their new tool (whether TQM or any other type of approach) into an existing framework. They did not change the framework, including the way that they identified the change needs, and thus as managers they unknowingly abdicated their responsibility, effectively leaving the members of their new teams to fend for themselves. The new teams, often operating in a new and unfamiliar industry, had to market their skills to whoever was willing to listen. This is reminiscent in our mind of selecting the best performance car available, perhaps a Ferrari, then using it only to pick up the groceries from the local supermarket.

We place the fault line in business strategy approaches right here, as few organizations who invest in these approaches or tools have reaped the promised benefits. The core question is: how should an organization link its bottom-up resource management to the top-down strategic needs to achieve strategic alignment of business processes? The next step is therefore to understand business processes and how they are actually being influenced by external factors.

Increasing criticality of managing interfaces

Consumerism and globalization have driven huge changes in business operations, all of which have occurred since the widespread use of Porter's theory of competitive forces for generating business strategy. Perhaps the greatest challenge these developments have imposed on management is the increase in complexity and scale of the coordination task to develop, deliver to the customer and support contemporary products and services. Vertically integrated and unitary managed firms have been replaced by complex supply chains. Many of these supply chains consist of multiple, independent organizations each with their own managers who, without careful management and coordination, could well have conflicting objectives. Consequently, a much greater amount of time has to be spent on interfacing activities carried out to enable the many personnel involved in any business process to work together on the functional activities the strategy calls for.

Obviously, this has led to a dramatic scope increase in the middle management role. Middle managers have needed to set up and manage each element of the supply chain so that transactions pass smoothly between the personnel in each business in order to meet customers' needs. They have needed to manage both the inter- and intra-firm transactions to deliver these customers' needs, and many have recognized that the goal posts have been moving as customers' expectations have scaled new heights each and every year. And this 'new' requirement on middle managers has occurred while organizations have become more complex (requiring more and more effective coordination), yet while middle management ranks were dramatically thinned out to reduce costs.

Consumerism, industry overcapacity and globalization have put downward pressure on costs and this in turn has made managing business processes much harder. These pressures require the many involved teams to work together without buffers. For example, the adoption of a just-in-time approach in manufacturing and distribution militates against the previous, more error tolerant, inter-stage inventory practices. The adoption of time-based competition has reduced the flexibility of service teams to deploy elapsed time, or waiting time, to allow issues to be resolved. The mantra of doing everything 'faster, better and cheaper' has exposed the cracks, the interfacing problems, in organizations like never before. We will show in this book that enormous amounts of value flows continuously into those cracks, on a 24/7 basis, such that even when those cracks are individually small, they are in aggregate very large destroyers of value.

To add further to the management difficulty, products and services have become much more complex. Few people today acquire a simple product. We are more likely to purchase one of many options of a complex product with various service and performance obligations delivered through a network of partner organizations. Purchasing a camera, for example, used to involve only the retailer who sold the body and suitable lenses and that usually concluded everything. Today the retailer's role is riddled with interfacing activity. The retailer supplies the camera, has to explain the merits of the different lens options and coaches the purchaser on the selection criteria for software from another supplier. This software in turn will inevitably require an upgrade to the configuration of the purchaser's home computer and possibly the selection of a more suitable printer and a larger mass storage device. When the purchaser gets home and it all doesn't quite work out as expected the retailer conducts more interfacing activities to resolve the issues.

Undocumented interfacing activities make up over 50 per cent of routine work steps

So the achievement of Simon, Gove and Hitt's 'idiosyncratic bundling and deployment of resources to gain sustainable competitive advantage' (2008) has become much more taxing for managers as progressively more time and effort is devoted to coordinating the often disparate groups who have to work together, and thus, of necessity, to perform the required enabling interfacing activities. Chapter 3 examines the rich field of interfacing activities, which in Chapter 4 it is shown will supply the base information needed to plug the strategy gap referred to above. To do this we provide our in-depth research into interfacing activities that link the tasks carried out by both the individuals and the inter- and intra-organizational teams. This book shows that without these interfacing activities firmly and correctly in place, business processes would simply never operate. It shows how the failure to understand errors and omissions revealed in interfacing activities allows something akin to viral attacks downstream, which in turn prevents the achievement of strategic goals. This book also demonstrates how a full knowledge of these interfacing activities vastly simplifies the management task of achieving alignment of resource with strategy to create strategic capabilities.

Obviously, a detailed knowledge of processes and activities routinely conducted in a business would be a prerequisite to assessing where change is needed. This is because we need to answer a number of fairly obvious questions:

- What does the new strategy call for?
- How does this differ from what we are doing at present?
- What are we doing at present?
- Which routine activities are affected?
- How do these specific routine activities need to change?
- What change is needed to each and who will be responsible for making each change happen?

The first question must be: what documentation is available to enable organizations to work on these questions? Every single one of the 200 organizations we have encountered in the 400 interface mapping exercises we have been intimately involved in has developed, over time, extensive documentation on what it does, who does it and how it is done. This documentation includes job descriptions, policies, procedures, standing instructions and process maps. Nonetheless, every time we have ever interviewed employees about the content of their jobs, they all make it very clear that they feel that many, even most, of the activities they routinely carry out never appear in their job descriptions, the company procedures or the often extensive process maps. We have to agree with them: they are right. The job descriptions usually catalogue the functional activities (such as receive a claim, receive an order, check a claim is complete, enter details into a computer system, authorize payment) which the job holder is rather obviously required to carry out to satisfy the strategy. What is never properly documented is the interfacing work, the activities required to put the transactions they receive into a form that the person receiving them can process. This preparatory work all too often includes elements of finding, chasing, reformatting, dealing with omissions and correcting errors. Typical process documentation found in organizations assumes that these transactions are always smooth, without problems or are so small in nature that they can be ignored. In reality, this is always far from the truth.

Most of these problems are interfacing activities that are undocumented. We therefore investigated whether the 'missing' interfacing activities were to be found elsewhere. Process maps were often given to us as the most comprehensive and up-to-date documentation available. These process maps were not at all helpful. The interfacing activities were missing from them as well. Most of the interfacing activities were represented in exactly the same most unhelpful way they were the lines drawn to link functional activities together (see case study beginning on page 55). The ubiquitous lines convey neither indication of the nature of the interfacing activities, nor who does them, the amount of effort involved or their downstream impact. Why then, would anyone ever rely on process maps as a base for strategically realigning business processes, the most common source of information used to determine change needs? Such process maps, that assume that business processes always nicely link to each other, are missing so much of what employees actually do, and that causes frustration, cost and delay, that they are actually quite useless as the guide for improvement they were supposed to be.

Our search continued into the procedures and standard instructions. Again there was a strong bias to the functional tasks similar to those found in the job descriptions, and the interfacing activities were massively under-represented.

A later chapter shows how detailed data on all activities undertaken by all of staff can be quickly obtained and validated by using interface mapping, as we have done in more than 200 organizations across four continents. We show that when we compare this new, detailed data with the activity documentation that already exists within the companies (usually in their procedures, standing instructions, job descriptions and flow charts) we uncover something quite startling: no business documents more than half of the activities their staff routinely perform. Table 3.1 (see page 69) shows that the ratio of documented to undocumented activities is actually close to 1:3.

This goes back to the issue of process control mentioned above: most organizations do not document the bulk of their processes, the interfacing activities, and they are therefore not in control. If these interfacing activities are not identified as such, and hence remain uncontrolled, how can a business be capable of delivering consistently to customers' requirements? Obviously, it cannot.

To get a feel for what these interfacing issues are, consider your role as a consumer. When you contacted your bank, travel company or IT department with anything but the most trivial request, did the company or department have standard processes, well in control, to respond? The answer is probably 'No'. For most of us, the service supplier has to rely on undocumented personal expertise rather than standard process that has been documented in the organization. How many times do untidy and expensive hand-offs occur during these processes, often leading to unsatisfying experiences for consumers and expensive repeated work for service suppliers?

Our analysis may reveal the reason why most organizations find it difficult to link top-down strategic intent to the bottom-up activities carried out in business processes. The omitted data, primarily the interfacing activities, is where as much as 80 per cent of the steps to correct process failure (error and omission correction and chasing and the viral downstream consequences) undertaken by staff are to be found. This omission, or blindness, is the reason that most attempts to build strategic capabilities into the organization's business processes must, by definition, always fall well short of expectations and make it impossible for an organization to create or sustain strategic capabilities.

Worryingly, the result of ignoring interfacing activities is that business process documentation and process maps provide a record only of what staff are supposed to do. Indeed, one of the organizations we worked with, a large national company, had developed criteria for selecting a tool to document its business processes as the first step in its transformation programme. A specific criterion for tender evaluation was to exclude the ability to record all elements of process failure, as the evaluating committee felt that recording every instance of business process failure in the interfacing activities would be too complex and confusing. This organization was classified in our international survey as one of the benchmark-lagging organizations and continues, with unerring consistency, to underperform on the stock market.

It's worth repeating the key question here. How can managers or specialists be expected to align business processes strategically if process information does not describe what their staff teams are actually doing? More specifically, how can managers align business processes strategically if process information does not describe most of the activities that waste money, distract managers and reduce customer service levels? In fact, in getting involved in this documentation of required tasks and interfacing activities we encountered what looked to us like staggering ineptitude in the teams undertaking work on business process transformation on an international scale.

For example, one truly international organization we encountered was engaged in re-engineering its key business processes in its 4,000 person US business. It was using an analysis process based on process mapping by interviewing staff in 14 roles to re-engineer the business process from receiving orders to receiving cash. Members of the organization's transformation team were completely unaware of the 69 other roles carried out in the process they were focusing on.

Far worse was to emerge. The act of re-engaging with the staff and adding in all the activities each staff member routinely carried out, including the interfacing activities, demonstrated that the team members had overlooked 54 per cent of the activities routinely carried out on a daily or weekly basis by those they had interviewed. The omitted activities were, in the main, the interfacing activities already referred to that dealt with routine process failure – the very process failures the new system was expected somehow to address. The company was being rather foolhardy, we thought, basing its worldwide business re-engineering initiative on a knowledge of less than 14 per cent of the activities routinely carried out in its current business process. Imagine what could have happened if this company engaged in an expensive computer-based support system to support what turned out to be only 14 per cent of the activities carried out in its real processes. It would have been in for a major disappointment and a lot of 'fixing up' in terms of what both the process analysis and the investment in automation provided.

Automation of business processes that contain large measures of interfacing activity 'noise' just enshrines or even amplifies the gaps and weaknesses in the business. The percentage of productivity expected by the automation will never be achieved because the 'hidden' and hence unaddressed interfacing activities are likely to continue to be needed to prepare the transaction before the automation can take over. Further, unknown errors and omissions allowed to enter and remain in the system will often be more efficiently transferred on, so their downstream viral impact may well be amplified. Could this be why so many IT and automation processes disappoint those who invest in them? Most IT projects come in late and usually do not perform fully or deliver their promised performance improvements, and quite a few are abandoned altogether. CEOs have been known to say things such as 'It just got too hard.' The amount of money that has been wasted on ineffective IT projects, advanced technology and equipment is actually staggering when considered as a percentage of most companies' profit margin.

Seeing how some highly respected businesses re-engineered their business processes led us to conclude that it is not surprising to read that the outcomes of many major re-engineering and system implementations do not meet expected goals and are often accompanied by major disruptions.

Interfacing activities' invisibility

So why are more than 50 per cent of activities routinely performed, mainly the interfacing activities, so rarely documented, you might ask? We would like to talk about 'stealth technology' and its insidious and growing impact on business. The reasons why interfacing activities are invisible is, however, much more prosaic. The first and most obvious reason is that the tools and approaches used are unsuited to the task of collecting this data (as demonstrated later in this book). However, the substantive answer to the question lies more in the nature of how organizational processes are planned and deployed. Most interfacing activities are generally defined and implemented after the design, approval and documentation stages for a new process have been completed. This occurs for three reasons:

- First, specification of activities to be carried out tends to focus on the functional, the so-called value-adding content, rather than the interfacing tasks.
- Second, interfacing activities are difficult to envisage at the design stage because they are always highly situational. They are, for example, often needed because of simple physical differences in the sites where the activities are carried out.
- Third, changes in the business environment such as competitors' activity, customers' needs, new technology or staffing changes occur continuously and these affect the way 'stuff' is received (and passed on) by each team.

When processes are specified, professional staff (usually managers or appropriate HR or IT staff) draw up job descriptions and procedures by defining the activities that need to be carried out to meet the strategic goal. They design the organizational processes. They spend most of their time on functional activities – such as receiving an order, preparing a patient for an operation, assessing an insurance claim or processing a term deposit – which they envisage are needed to deliver the strategy. They also define the activities needed to handle the interfacing issues they are able to anticipate will occur – they will, for example, in an order-processing environment, specify how to receive and check, say, an insurance proposal.

However, when the new procedure is implemented there will be variations to the way things are received by a particular staff member that could never be anticipated. Take the example of the junior customer service officer (CSO) who receives an insurance proposal. The procedure sets down how CSOs should receive the paper-based or electronic proposals at the start of each day and how they should process them. However, in the real world, few are found to arrive on the desk or in a CSO's electronic in-tray at the beginning of the day. So what happens next, in this example, is a hurried discussion with the team leader, when it is agreed that one CSO should go down to the post room to check for mail and all the other CSOs without work should get on the phone to their assigned group of insurance brokers to chase up their day's work. This adds an hour of undocumented interfacing activity for the whole team, and it gets repeated every day thereafter.

Of course, we encountered the same type of thing in every function we collected data from. Take for a second example receiving orders for goods. The anticipated interfacing activities included that staff check on receipt of order that the goods are in stock. The unanticipated interfacing activities included having to compensate for the product options being out of date as a result of an omission in the product specification by the marketing department. So the quick fix, in consultation with the team leader, was to phone the customer to understand what the person wanted and then phone the warehouse to get the code. We followed it through further. Apparently a phone call to ask the marketing department to fix the problem elicited an all too common answer – staff there would get on to it as soon as they could and, of course, in the meantime the new work around practice became the routine.

These unanticipated needs keep arising time after time after time so within a few months the invisible but routine interfacing activities outnumber the documented functional activities. We have termed the development and implementation of these essential process workarounds as 'business process fettling'. Fettling is a term we have resurrected from early engineering practices. In the days before Henry Ford and the wide application of quality management, it was common practice for manufactured items to be made only to broad size tolerances. As a consequence, it was common practice for an artisan fitter to have to rework, for example file (or fettle), the item so that it would fit where needed. Software engineers refer to this process as 'bug fixing', somehow hoping to imply that it is an inherent computer technology problem rather than something more honestly described as correcting errors resulting from inadequate analysis of inadequate data.

Taking into account that these 'of necessity designed' process activities ultimately make up over 50 per cent of an organization's routine activities, one can only conclude that more than 50 per cent of an organization's activities are designed on the spur of the moment by people at the most junior levels, and are not visible to most of the organization. This is perhaps one more reason why strategic alignment initiatives are not always as successful as might be expected or promised.

Interfacing activities and strategic impact

These largely undocumented interfacing activities have four worrying and strategically fascinating characteristics. They militate against cost effectiveness, customer service and employee satisfaction and they distract managers from conducting their performance-driving activities. Let's explore these in turn:

- Cost effectiveness. Poorly managed interfacing activities inflate transaction costs in the best companies (see Figure 5.1 on page 96). The undocumented interfacing activities generally arise because some event happening somewhere else in the organization, or in a partner firm, needs to be adjusted (that is, aligned) in order to eliminate an otherwise unnecessary series of activities. Unnecessary activity by its very nature adds unanticipated and unnecessary cost – and globalization has made cost and productivity such a key strategic issue for most businesses. So more than 50 per cent of activities being undocumented promises real opportunity to all businesses if they are able to identify them and then address them through their in-house change capability.

- Customer service. Unnecessary activity brings in unnecessary delays by increasing lead times, often a hundredfold, and in almost every case negatively affecting customer service. As many businesses compete on service, making these activities visible and understanding them in relation to customer service needs holds further strategic promise.

- Employee satisfaction. The required adjustment to the process is usually outside the span of authority of the team leader or manager directly responsible for inventing and implementing the interfacing activity in question. This is because the 'virus' will have entered the organization elsewhere. The people affected therefore will be unable to exercise control over the required change to achieve the alignment. So, for example, in most businesses the affected person will try to get a fix made, but having no authority, the individual will soon give up trying. Instead, he or she may well knuckle down to do the extra work every day and potentially go home late and frustrated. A high proportion of the businesses we became involved with set employee satisfaction and achieving a particular work–life balance as one of their highest strategic priorities. Yet the constant 'fettling' makes the achievement of employee satisfaction merely a pipe dream.

- Strategic distraction. This means diversion of effort away from performing core, value-driving activities. Most managers, team leaders and staff place the achievement of achieving the expected transactional throughput as their highest priority and their KPIs generally underpin this focus. This means that the effort focuses on the routine not on driving performance. For example, our analysis reveals that sales teams in pharmaceuticals, travel, business banking, insurance, fashion retailing, hardware, domestic appliances, packaging, etc spend much of their 'face-to-client' time dealing with product and service failure and product return issues (see Figure 6.4 on page 127). The result is that there is little or no time left to be spent on core sales activities and promoting margin growth.

The importance of having complete documentation of interfacing activities in order to manage business processes properly is illustrated in the extreme in hazardous industries such as surgery, the maintenance of petrochemical plants and railway signalling, where the lack of visibility of the interfacing activities introduces unmanaged risks that can actually kill people. Take for example case study 1.1 below, from the health industry.

In this instance the surgical team was entirely dependent on the staff themselves actually carrying out one or more of the undocumented interfacing activities:

- Admissions staff were to check from the notes and the patient consent form that the completed admissions slip stated the correct side for surgery.
- The surgeon had to check that the patient's notes and consent form were correct, waking the patient up if necessary.
- A second team member was to check that the surgeon had put the X-ray into the light box the right way round.
- The specialist registrar had to check vital signs were consistent with the notes before the operation started.
- All comments and observations were to be considered by the team, with regard to the observing student.

CASE STUDY 1.1   Operate on a patient

A patient was admitted for right nephrectomy in Carmarthenshire. Due to a clerical error the admission slip stated 'left'. The operating list was transcribed from the admissions slip. The patient was not woken from sleep to check the correct side on the pre-operative ward round. The side was not checked from the notes or the consent form.

The side was questioned by the consultant surgeon on the patient's arrival in theatre but was not confirmed. The consultant surgeon instructed the specialist registrar to carry out the operation. The consultant surgeon mistakenly put the correctly labelled X-rays on the viewing box back to front. The consultant surgeon supervised the positioning of the patient. The specialist registrar did not check the side and was not alerted to this being the wrong side by noticing the normal pulsating in the renal artery of the kidney he was removing.

A medical student observing the operation suggested to the specialist registrar that he was removing the incorrect kidney but was told by the specialist registrar that she was wrong.

The mistake was not discovered until two hours after the operation.

The patient died.

Source: Based on wrong-side surgery, 'The leadership and management of surgical teams', The Royal College of Surgeons of England, June 2007: 13

Analysis of interface maps of health business processes identifies all of the activities the medical staff have to do, including those when patients have the wrong medicine administered or the wrong limb operated on. Knowing that these interfacing activities actually occur places managers in a powerful position, they are informed for their decision on what must be controlled. They can then require particular activities to be done much in the way that airline pilots are required to use checklists.

Century-old practices abound

The practice of ignoring most of the interfacing activities when planning business changes closely resembles manufacturing practice before the manufacturing breakthroughs pioneered by Remington and deployed extensively by Henry Ford 100 years ago.

Before Ford, vehicles were built by highly skilled artisans. This was because component parts were manufactured without paying attention to how each part would fit together, ie interface, with the other parts in the vehicle. This, in our eyes, is no different from the common practice in organizations of defining the functional activities staff are required to carry out without specifying how all the various activities will work together, or interface, with each other. As we have already described, a line on a process map is hardly a definition of what staff should do in the various different situations they face.

The consequence, before Ford, of not specifying the interfacing for manufactured parts was that the mating of two parts usually required 'fettling'. Perhaps the end of a car's steering track rod would not mate with the axle casting because it had been cast and machined dimensionally 1 millimetre too large. The artisan then had to decide what to do. He might decide to file (fettle) the track rod carefully to fit into the axle casting while his colleague, encountering a similar problem while working on the next vehicle, might decide to fettle the axle casting. The fettling, and the variations in everything produced, made the track rod non-standard as well as absorbing a lot of time of a relatively costly, highly skilled person (it perhaps should have taken 30 seconds to mate the two parts together compared with 15 minutes to file the excess metal away carefully). To illustrate, in today's automotive plants it takes about 8 person hours to assemble a complete motor vehicle.

Ford's genius was to revolutionize manufacturing by focusing on design and manufacturing on the interfaces between components to ensure that every component was manufactured to specific tolerances so that they fitted together and worked together first time, every time. The result of his thinking is often described as introducing precision into parts manufacture. Its real significance has apparently not been understood by practising managers or change agents. It was to enable much faster, error-free assembly by widely available, largely unskilled line operatives by eliminating interfacing activity noise. This delivered massive time reductions as well as enormous savings on the costs of materials and manpower.

Tranfield and Smith (1998) noted that an organization can achieve competitive advantage from the close management of its internal resources by building strategic capabilities. They argue that advantage accrues because these capabilities, once established, become difficult to copy or emulate.

From our direct observations fettling is alive and thriving in most businesses. The 21st century fettler is easy to identify. He or she is engaged in determining and implementing change. He or she typically uses a large slab of judgement to compensate for having little or no knowledge of interfacing activities and can be observed spending many weeks of efforts surmounting the unexpected (to this person) consequences of change. Everyone who has been involved in implementing a new IT system, or significant changes to business processes, knows it will be followed by a period of consolidation to provide time to make things actually work. There will have been no precision in specifying how clean hand-offs will be assured, just as there was no precision in parts manufacture prior to Henry Ford. The only thing the person implementing change can anticipate is that there will be lots of unanticipated problems.

Among the worst cases we have seen were two organizations who implemented enterprise resource planning (ERP) systems only to see customer service levels fall from over 95 per cent to below 50 per cent. Later in this book we will show that much of this fettling pain would be avoided by documenting and analysing interfacing activities before undertaking the change.

Have you been a customer in such a situation? How many times do we experience frustration when the CSO serving us says sorry and blames the process he or she has to follow, or even worse, tells us that the computer doesn't allow for what we want but the CSO wishes he or she could deliver? This, while not reducing our frustration, does build some understanding of the CSO's constraints and sympathy for his or her difficulties. At this point perhaps you would care to go one step further and think yourself into the role of the CSO having to deal with you, the frustrated customer. Is it at all that surprising that the person will usually strive to make changes to processes in order to deliver what you want? CSOs fettle to please you if they can. You will be pleased if they fix the problem for you and you will not be concerned if they satisfy you by inventing new activities. They will 'invent' interfacing activities that will not be documented, will soon become routine and will invisibly add to the costs of doing business. The CSO will be fettling the process in front of your very eyes. Now imagine that, because of all this activity he or she has invented to overcome weaknesses in the process, the CSO has to work overtime to get through the day's work. This is noticed by diligent management who leap into action and hire a trainee CSO to relieve the pressure. Then the new person joins. Can you now see in your mind's eye the CSO telling the trainee, 'When xxxx occurs it will really upset some customers, so this is what you have to do to…'.

This is further compounded because in the organization, there is usually more than one CSO, and in large organizations there can be hundreds or thousands. When they 'fettle to please' they don't all do it the same way, so the organization develops lots of process variance, meaning many ways of doing ostensibly similar things. Then when the time comes for a major or formal change, the huge opening question of 'What are we changing from?' cannot, in the absence of an understanding of interfacing activity, be answered.

Customers notice that different CSOs do things differently, because they have invented different 'workarounds'. For example, in one international professional services firm commercial customers complained that they had to prepare and deliver their documentation quite differently depending on which of the firm's offices they were dealing with. The customer in this instance bore the cost and inherent delays of handling the interfacing activity noise. Such an organization is on its way to 'process hell' with endemic deficiencies in productivity, customer service, employee satisfaction and performance. Fortunately, it can always be brought back, with an understanding of the real activities undertaken in the business. Indeed, the further it has gone towards 'process hell', the more is the potential for improvement.

The people planning and executing change are usually unaware of the importance of interfacing activities and:

- how much time they absorb;
- the size of the direct cost burden they imply;
- their direct and long-lasting impact on strategic issues such as service, delivery speed and reliability;
- the frustration they cause to employees, directly driving up staff turnover and the consequent recruitment and training costs;

- the level of unreliability they bring to the organization;
- the all-absorbing distraction that militates against the ability of an organization to focus on core activity.

Summary

We argued at the beginning of this chapter that every organization's strategy is made up of two component parts. The first component is the written strategy, a statement of intent. It is a specification of the nature of the organization; the resources it needs; its position in the value chain of the chosen industry sector and the performance goals set for it. The second component of the strategy is its achievement; that is, the re-alignment and maintenance of its business processes to build and maintain strategic capabilities. We have argued that by definition strategy will not and cannot be fulfilled without understanding what is really happening in the business and this means engaging the staff and management to forensically align the organization's resources strategically. This latter component is the focus for this book.

This component has until recently been the poor, distant cousin for very good reasons. First, consultants, academics, business schools and managers have only comparatively recently, and as late as the 1980s, begun to acknowledge the pivotal role that resource management plays in strategy deployment, so they have not seen any need to examine the way resources are managed strategically. The second reason is a consequence of this blindness that has created a major data deficiency. Every organization we have ever worked with has demonstrably failed to document over 50 per cent of the activities their staff and managers routinely undertake. These missing activities, mainly interfacing activities, are the ones that by definition ensure that the strategically defined functional activities can be interfaced efficiently with each other. A multitude of hand-off problems are evident in every organization and some of these problems wreck performance.

Part of the reason for non-documentation lies in the nature of the common mapping tools used which are ill suited to the task. However, the main reason is that the importance of the undocumented interfacing activities has never been understood or acknowledged.

These interfacing activities have some interesting and worrying characteristics:

- Undocumented interfacing activities numerically far outnumber the functional activities, which are always well documented.
- Interfacing activity noise defines the work carried out as a result of routine process failure. This information must therefore be a

vital input to designing efficient interfaces within and between organizations.

- Interfacing activities are in the main designed and implemented by junior staff on the spur of the moment. They tend to increase in number with every passing year as a result of product and service extension, business regulation and the growth in outsourcing and partnering.

Achieving 'best practice' is impossible without managing these interfaces. The prize for doing so is large: major improvements in cost, speed, service, employee satisfaction and managerial focus are waiting to be achieved.

Strategic outcomes from best-practice management principles

Objectives

This chapter has two main objectives. The first is to describe the five management principles (the excellence principles) derived in our international research that enable leading organizations, in addition to being ahead of the game, to analyse their business processes strategically. The second is to begin a dialogue that will ultimately demonstrate the pivotal role interfacing activities play in achieving best-practice resource management.

Introduction

We are reminded of the old joke about the man who dropped his keys when getting out of his car on a dark night. 'Where did you drop the keys?' asks a passer-by who has offered to help with the search. 'Over there, behind you,' replies the driver. 'Then why are you looking for them here?' says the passer-by. 'Because the light is better under the street lamp!' By the end of this book we will have convinced you that analysis of business processes to plan their strategic alignment must be based on interface mapping in order to reveal the pertinent issues. Using process maps, the most common approach to process analysis, is looking where the light is best – not where the problems afflicting the organization are to be found.

This chapter begins with a review of all of the management principles (also referred to as excellence principles), segmenting them into four groups for clarity. Then the group of principles focusing on strategic intent is described in some depth and the implications of non-compliance are illustrated with case examples that draw out the critical linkage with interfacing activities.

A complete set of management principles

In 1996 the need to define and understand the complete set of factors necessary to achieve sustainable gains in the bottom line was recognized by one of this book's authors, Danny Samson. This need, the prevalence of over-reliance on anecdotal evidence and the paucity of rigorous research is discussed in the appendix to this chapter.

Samson promoted and led a research project designed to deliver a comprehensive and complete set of management principles. The research team first identified all the factors that had been linked by others to influencing business performance and these were used to develop a comprehensive questionnaire. The team identified 1,000 international companies with longitudinally consistent levels of performance, covering a broad spectrum of industry sectors. Over 200 of these companies responded to the survey. The outcome of the research was the derivation and validation of a set of 14 management principles that, when installed in a business, will yield class leading performance. We have termed businesses with these management principles 'best-practice businesses'. The management (or excellence) principles, taken from Samson and Challis (1999), are listed in Table 2.1.

Understanding the management principles

After reading through these principles you could be forgiven for saying 'So what?' While every one of these principles appears to be sensible, many managers would reasonably claim that elements of these principles are already well embedded in their organizations. The question in their mind might more importantly be why their business is not achieving best-practice performance. What is so different about this list of management principles? What do the principles actually mean and what are the essential differences to what is being done at present? Clearly some method of examining, evaluating and instituting them was required.

The first thing we realized we needed to do was to decide where an organization should start. Which of the principles should one think about implementing first? A potentially useful prioritization of the principles was

TABLE 2.1 General principles common to the world's best companies

	Principle	Description
1	Gaining alignment	There is good alignment of employee behaviour with stated company values and direction at all levels in the organization
2	Supporting distributed leadership	Individuals and work teams are assigned, and accept, responsibility for operational decision making and performance improvement
3	Ensuring integration of effort	The organization is focused on value creation and process management, not functional needs and hierarchies
4	Having the desire to be out front	The organization strives to lead the pack in all industry standards and practices: safety, customer service, product and process design, environmental management etc
5	Being up front	All employees demonstrate integrity and openness in all areas of their work and dealings with others. Relationships are highly valued
6	Resourcing for the medium term	The business is able to balance effectively short-term operational and medium- term development, and growth, issues and requirements
7	Being time-based	Time is developed as a critical organizational value. The business practises the principles of time-based competition
8	Embracing change	All employees demonstrate a willingness to embrace and accept change as an essential part of doing business. The organization excels in implementing new ideas

(Continued)

TABLE 2.1 General principles common to the world's best companies (*Continued*)

	Principle	Description
9	Establishing a learning culture	All employees demonstrate a willingness to develop skills and knowledge and are involved in a learning/development programme
10	Being disciplined	The organization invests in policies, procedures and standards and applies a strong system perspective in everything it does
11	Measuring and reporting	The business measures and reports to all employees the financial and non-financial performance information needed to drive improvement
12	Creating customer value	All employees understand the set of order winners and actively strive to enhance creation of customer value
13	Creating strategic capabilities	Business and organizational capabilities are defined and prioritized and drive critical development and investment decisions
14	Relating the micro to the macro	All employees know how their particular activities and individual efforts contribute to the 'big picture' of business success.

SOURCE Adapted from Samson and Challis, 1999: 30

suggested by the research itself. Four of the fourteen management principles correlated much more strongly with bottom-line success and longevity than the others (Samson and Challis, 1999: 34) so we opted to begin with them. The principles were ensuring integration of effort, creating customer value, ensuring alignment and having a bias for action through desire to be out front. Stating the obvious, business managers have to want to be best and therefore have to have a bias for action, have to focus the business on its customers and achieve strategic alignment of its processes.

Second, and equally obviously, the managers would need to know which of the thousands of activities in their business to change. They would clearly need to analyse the activities the staff undertake forensically, so that they could pinpoint the ones that needed to be changed in order to achieve strategic alignment of processes and create customer value. Third, once having determined which activities need to be changed in an organization they would need to foster an environment to ensure that the change happens. Finally, there would be a need to tackle the changes in such a way as to establish a framework to maintain and sustain the new order of things. In other words, establish a medium- or long-term horizon.

This broad grouping of the principles is supported by the other peer-reviewed research programme undertaken at the same time as our research, by Guimaraes in 1999. His work stood out for two reasons. First, he tested a large number of change factors, some 26 in all. Second, he tested them against two criteria: achieving bottom-line gains and achieving an organizational change outcome. His analysis supported the conclusion that bottom-line gains correlated with a small subset of focusing factors and achievement of change correlated with a larger 'cultural' group of factors. The factors that correlated with achieving bottom-line gains were being driven by customer demand, experiencing competitive pressure and eliminating non value adding activity. These were consistent with those discovered by Samson and Terziovski, 1999).

We therefore grouped the 14 management principles into segments as shown in Table 2.2:

- Segment 1: Having the desire to be out front – managers wanting their business to be the best.
- Segment 2: Focusing on strategic intent – the management team establishing a clear definition of the activities staff and managers need to carry out routinely to achieve the organization's strategy, and a clear definition of the changes needed to achieve strategic alignment of business processes.
- Segment 3: Driving the changes through – managers creating the environment and culture to foster change, thus enabling them to drive it through and to achieve continual strategic alignment of business processes.
- Segment 4: Resourcing for the medium term.

TABLE 2.2   Management principles regrouped

Segment	Principle	Description
1 Being out front	Having the desire to be out front	The organization strives to lead the pack in all industry standards and practices: safety, customer service, product and process design, environmental management, etc
2 Focusing on strategic intent	Ensuring integration of effort	The organization is focused on value creation and process management, not functional needs and hierarchies
	Being disciplined	The organization invests in policies, procedures and standards and applies a strong system perspective in everything it does
	Creating customer value	All employees understand the set of order winners and actively strive to enhance creation of customer value
	Being time-based	Time is developed as a critical organizational value. The business practises the principles of time-based competition
	Creating strategic capabilities	Business and organizational capabilities are defined and prioritized and drive critical development and investment decisions
3 Diving changes through	Gaining alignment	There is good alignment of employee behaviour with stated company values and direction at all levels in the organization. Employees are involved
	Embracing change	All employees demonstrate a willingness to embrace and accept change as an essential part of doing business. The organization excels in implementing new ideas
	Establishing a learning culture	All employees demonstrate a willingness to develop skills and knowledge and are involved in a learning/development programme

Segment	Principle	Description
	Relating the micro to the macro	All employees know how their particular activities and individual efforts contribute to the 'big picture' of business success
	Measuring and reporting	The business measures and reports to all employees the financial and non-financial performance information needed to drive improvement
	Supporting distributed leadership	Individuals and work teams are assigned, and accept, responsibility for operational decision making and performance improvement
	Being up front	All employees demonstrate integrity and openness in all areas of their work and dealings with others. Relationships are highly valued
4 Resourcing	**Resourcing for the medium term**	The business is able to balance effectively short-term operational and medium-term development and growth issues and requirements

Segment 1: Having the desire to be out front

Much has been written about ongoing change being driven by external events such as globalization, consumerism and government regulation. Our research shows that the first management principle is the determination to stay on top of, or even take advantage of, this level of market dynamism. A leading company's managers have to be determined that their company will be out front, that is, to lead in all the aspects that are strategically important. These aspects are:

- what the business delivers (its products and services, and thus the business processes by which these are specified and designed);
- how the business delivers its products and services (efficient business processes that are socially and environmentally responsible);
- employee policies (its management practices and processes for employees' development);
- business processes regarding investor relations;
- financial performance.

Segment 2: Management principles focusing on strategic intent

There are five principles in segment 2 that enable managers to define with precision which of the many activities undertaken by staff need to be changed to achieve strategic alignment of business processes. These five principles are:

- ensuring integration of effort;
- being disciplined;
- creating customer value;
- being time-based;
- creating strategic capabilities.

We describe each of these principles below, focusing on activity in organizations, and include, in each case, typical examples taken from our work to illustrate how organizations have failed to adhere to them and the consequences of this.

Ensuring integration of effort

Leading organizations that achieved this management principle were focused on value creation through managing their end-to-end business processes. The management in lagging organizations in contrast concentrated on functional needs within hierarchies. The leading organizations had a clear understanding of their key business processes and, by implication, had focused on ensuring that the activities undertaken by their teams, and the individuals in them, worked together to perform the activities that achieved the company's overall goals. They were, in relative terms, particularly good at managing their interfacing activities. Individual and functional goals directly supported the achievement of the corporate goals.

To illustrate the need for this principle, take the case of a fast-growing US-owned international company which was a major player in the international communications industry. The ambitious chief financial officer (CFO) in the UK plant, with an eye to his next promotion, was keen to demonstrate to his US headquarters that his finance function was under tight management. He chose to do this by ensuring that his monthly finance figures were published first in the worldwide group. He prided himself that his team always met this goal. At the latest the results were made available by the close of business on the first day of the new accounting period, even if this meant that close of business was well after midnight.

We used the fast techniques to map interface activity (which we explain in Chapter 3) to understand how the business was achieving this early close and to understand the impact it was having, if any, on the business as a whole.

It was immediately obvious from the data how this apparently stellar performance was being achieved – and so was the cost to the plant and the international business as a whole. The finance function broke all the rules of the principle of integration. The data showed that in the last week of the accounting period a very significant proportion of the direct and indirect workers' time, and that of their team leaders, was being deflected from running the equipment in the manufacturing plant to focusing on an unusually large amount of interfacing activity such as completing records, chasing missing data and checking accounting information. Valuable production resource was being channelled into carrying out overhead activities in the last week of the period and this practice had become business as usual. What it meant was that the direct workers were doing the accounting staff's work for them so that the finance department could get its figures out quickly. As a consequence, production in the last week of every accounting period was materially below normal achievement in the heavily loaded plant and significantly below plant capacity.

Even worse, the CFO was using his accounting staff to identify and expedite the delivery of product that could be completed, shipped and billed by month end in the mistaken belief that this would maximize revenue. For some customers this meant product was being delivered before it was expected, often incurring demurrage penalties on the docks waiting for transport or waiting for the export or import paperwork to catch up with it. Other product, delayed by the last minute rescheduling as a result of the finance function's meddling, was missing customer deadlines. This resulted in sales staff having to take time out, yet more interfacing activity, to placate unhappy customers and, all too frequently, authorize otherwise unnecessary discounts.

These actions, revealed by the interface mapping, demonstrably reduced the throughput of the heavily loaded plant. The lost revenue from the time wasted on changing over machines to handle the brought-forward items, and the unnecessary chasing of paperwork, clearly could never be recovered. Further, the customer service performance, a key element of the company's brand positioning, was being systematically debased because personal and functional objectives, rather than business objectives, drove staff activity. The organization was focused on functional needs and hierarchies, not on value creation and process management. Obviously, there was a real danger that the CFO would meet his personal goal and be rewarded by being promoted and then move on to pursue value destruction in other parts of the business.

Being disciplined

To be consistent with this principle the international research revealed that leading organizations had invested in policies, procedures and standards to create a living knowledge platform which they then used to manage by. This knowledge platform enabled these businesses to maintain their focus when potentially destabilizing personnel and policy changes occurred. These organizations also applied a strong system perspective to everything they did by planning and installing necessary changes using this knowledge base.

This principle is consistent with the teachings of the quality guru Philip Crosby, who said: '... tough does not mean beating up on people. It means sticking to the necessary policies and actions no matter how enticing the reasons for easing up.' We live in a society where every day we routinely adhere to rules, such as obeying traffic signals, which, while imposing constraints on us, benefit everyone by allowing the traffic to flow freely and safely.

The international research showed that the achievement of the discipline principle required two conditions to be met. The first was that the policies, procedures and standards needed to be available, up to date, understandable and complete. The second condition was that management and staff needed to follow or 'live' them. In Chapter 3 we provide the evidence to show that most companies fail to document over 50 per cent of the activities their staff perform routinely. Therefore full adherence to this important principle of focusing on strategic alignment of business processes is perhaps for most organizations an impossible goal.

Let's take a transport industry example to illustrate what happens when the principle of discipline is not adhered to in an organization. The Operations Director was concerned about two key elements that directly affected performance. The first was the ever-increasing cost of servicing crucial equipment, which his staff argued was due to the increasingly sophisticated equipment and age. The second was falling serviceability. As both cost and serviceability were strategic issues, he was tired of hearing the excuses trotted out by his subordinates and wanted to challenge them.

As with most equipment, there was a regular maintenance programme laid down by the various manufacturers. A business process for equipment maintenance is thus required to comply with the manufacturer's programme. For example, we take our cars in for service and the mechanic changes the oil, makes any adjustments required and replaces worn or failing components. To do this the mechanic keeps a stock of consumables and the lower-value parts and has a process in place to obtain any required part, not carried in his or her stock, from the manufacturer. When parts are used from the mechanic's store there is a process to replenish them so as to eliminate the need to hold any vehicle back waiting for spares.

This maintenance team operated on much the same lines. In this case there were four groups involved. One group operated the equipment and logged faults during operational usage; a team of maintenance fitters looked after the routine servicing as laid down; a supplies group managed the replacement of consumables, parts and the more expensive refurbished units and the many manufacturers were contracted to refurbish failed units and supply spares to order. The fitters were required to conduct routine maintenance, test equipment to identify faults and address them as well as act on the serviceability reports completed by the operational crews. When they used parts from store the procedures required them to complete documentation recording this on the maintenance team's computer system.

We used the same interface mapping techniques over a three-week period to help the staff document exactly what they were actually doing, including all interfacing activities between the four groups. In the first instance, the rigorous documentation confirmed that the functional activities set out in the procedures were being carried out as required, implying that all was well – a point that pleased the staff. However, the previously unrecorded interfacing activities uncovered why the operations director was rightly concerned. A large amount of time was being spent on previously undocumented interfacing activities associated with chasing the delivery of consumables, spares and refurbished units well before due dates, with this chasing occurring in both the supplies group and the fitter teams. The interface mapping data also showed significant time being spent getting records of the parts issued up to date by the supplies group (not their job) and even unanticipated interfacing time being spent by the fitters stripping out (cannibalizing) refurbished units to obtain parts needed.

What this interfacing activity revealed was that a great deal of time was being spent by the supplies group chasing the fitters to book out the parts they used, chase up deliveries of parts and consumables that were not behind schedule and spend excessive time with suppliers on refurbishment. The root issue was that maintenance fitters were not consistently booking parts out at the time they were taken from store – they were not adhering to the principle of discipline. As a result, replenishment needs could not be identified in the established processes in time so the organization frequently ran out of consumables and parts; hence the high level of activity devoted to chasing parts ahead of scheduled delivery. Worse still, because the fitters were required to keep the equipment serviceable, they sometimes resorted to cannibalizing refurbished units to obtain a part to get the job done and, by so doing, made unserviceable an expensively refurbished item.

Clearly, and as suspected by the operations director when commissioning the investigation, the staff and management did not operate to the principle of discipline. Who was blamed? Well, of course, the operational staff and the fitters said it had to be the supplies group and the manufacturers who were not doing their job. As they frequently said, 'How can the supplies group be doing their job when we are always chasing up orders for spare parts?' Obviously, the real issue was the lack of adherence to the management principle of discipline by the people who were suffering from the lack of spare parts.

The situation was rectified by instilling the needed discipline to ensure that key aspects of the procedures were being adhered to. Measures were put in place to ensure longevity of the changes made to operational practices. However, in order to instil the principle of discipline it was necessary to revisit and explain how the replenishment process depended on the fitters keeping records of the parts used up to date. As a result of the changes, maintenance costs fell to about 15 per cent below budget and serviceability increased markedly.

At this point it is worth noting that in this example both principles we have examined so far were actually being violated – being disciplined and ensuring integration of effort. The integration principle was being violated because the fitters were focused on their maintenance tasks, doing their record keeping only when they had time. This unmanaged delay had a se-vere impact on the overall performance of the business.

Creating customer value

The international research showed us that in leading organizations the prin-ciple of creating customer value required all employees to understand the set of order-winning activities they needed to do; that is, the things they rou-tinely should do to cause customers to transact with them and keep trans-acting. Further, it included the need for staff and managers continually to strive to enhance the creation of value for customers or clients. There were two key drivers that needed to be addressed for an organization to live by this principle. The first was that the needs of customers must be well under-stood by everyone. The second was that the staff and managers needed to know which of the activities they perform actually affect creation of cus-tomer value and ensure that these are consistently undertaken.

To illustrate some of the difficulties employees have in living by this prin-ciple let's take the example of a well-known international pharmaceutical company selling a well-known range of over-the-counter, branded products through retail pharmacies. We first spent three weeks with the staff of this company helping them to use interface mapping of their processes to under-stand how the processes worked, including therefore full details of all of the functional and interfacing activities.

During this work we discovered that the managers were also very con-cerned about the discipline principle as it applied to their sales force. Two sales people were frequently reported (incorrectly, as it turned out) as not following laid-down procedures. This was especially the case close to month end, when the monthly sales volume targets were obviously not going to be met. These two sales people always refused to obey specific instructions from their managers to break their call schedules and chase up extra busi-ness wherever it could be obtained.

The firm was on the verge of dismissing the two but was hesitating. The two sales people were outstanding on two counts – they were achieving the highest sales volume and margin growth in the country and they had the lowest rate of issuing credit notes (that is, none) for out-of-date prod-uct returns. Simply, they were by far the most profitable business getters.

So what did the quick interface mapping interlude reveal? Well, surpris-ingly in the circumstances, it confirmed that all the sales people were doing all of the functional activities they were charged to do. The differences in practices were only to be found outside the procedures and job descriptions in the hitherto undocumented interfacing activities. Of particular note were the interfacing activities covering the interaction between the sales people and the retail pharmacy managers and staff.

Most of the sales people obtained the current data on customers' stock to meet procedural requirements by counting the stock of their company's products on the pharmacy shelves themselves during their visit. This also allowed them to check for out-of-date items they were able to remove, and they also maintained that the pharmacy got a bonus in that the sales person generally tidied the display. The sales person then completed an order form on behalf of the pharmacy manager for all the items to be replenished and prepared a credit note for the out-of-date products that were to be returned. The sales person then met the pharmacy manager, talked about any new lines or changes if there was time, went through the paperwork and got the signatures required for the order and the out-of-date stock he or she was taking away.

The two, apparently ill-disciplined sales people did something rather different. They never counted stock themselves although the stock was still counted. They employed quite different interfacing activities. Two days before their scheduled visits they contacted the pharmacy and persuaded the pharmacy manager to take stock for them and e-mail it to them. This action obviously met the company's procedural needs to obtain the information on stock level. It also allowed more. The sales person was able to review the stock data the evening before the visit. He or she was thus able to work out sales volumes and compare them with the expectation for a pharmacy with similar demographics. He or she then identified what needed to be ordered, based on either sales volumes or demographics, and decided what new products or stock levels the pharmacy needed to have.

On the day of their visits, these two sales people handed the documentation to the pharmacist, discussed and agreed lines to be added and asked the pharmacy manager to do his or her own ordering. In each case the sales people then got down to interfacing with the pharmacy assistants who dealt directly with the real customers, the walk-ins. What these sales people were doing was training the assistants, as arranged on the previous visit, on the features and benefits of the firm's new products, major sellers or underperforming products. They thus equipped the pharmacy staff with the information they needed to recommend the company's products to address the walk-in customers' needs. This actually drove growth for the pharmacy and the pharmaceutical company. Later in the book we classify this activity as 'core' (value-driving) activity.

The two 'rogue' sales people had worked out the activities they needed to perform in conjunction with their own customers; that is, the activities they should do to increase sales volumes and profitability of their customers. They had therefore gained agreement with the pharmacy managers to train the pharmacy assistants on what to recommend. In fact, these two sales people had examined the total end-to-end business process including what a walk-in customer did, how the pharmacy assistants did their job and how sales people needed to interface with the pharmacy managers. They had concluded that what the pharmacy needed was advice, and help to increase volume and profitability, rather than the standard visit: as the pharmacy managers' rather mischievously said, 'There is not much value being created for us if the sales people merely visit to count and dust our stock.'

Why were there low returns of out-of-date stock? Well, the two rogue sales people, having on their previous visit arranged for off-duty sales staff to come in especially for the product training, were obviously reluctant to break their call pattern, potentially lose credibility and thus threaten their ability to get the pharmacy staff to do the stock counting for them. But, by adhering to the promises they had made, they were unable to mislead the pharmacist regarding the stock to order; that is, to oversell and over-stock pharmacies' shelves to meet the short-term business panic. They thus avoided the very overstocking that drove the high returns of their 'compli-ant' colleagues.

The whole sales force was retrained to reflect much of the practice pio-neered by the two 'rogues'. The result was a staggering 30 per cent lift in sales across the whole country's network of independent pharmacies, as well as significant savings from dramatically lowered product returns.

At this point perhaps it is worthwhile stating what should now be obvi-ous. This example of a pharmacy sales force illustrates failure to implement all three of the management principles focusing on strategic intent examined up to this point:

- First, let's look at the management principle of creating customer value. The rogue sales people rather impressively had discarded the outcome of a focus group workshop as a means to understand customers' needs. They had conducted their own research on how to add value to the pharmacy. To do this they had examined the total process – the walk-in customers' interface with the pharmacy assistants, their sales role and the pharmacy staff's role in the replenishment process, but taking into account the knowledge of product performance given to them by their organization for particular demographics, etc.

- Second, the two sales people fully met the discipline principle. Having redefined their procedures they stuck to them in the face of the powerful pressures being exerted on them by their managers when they were told: 'Break your call pattern and go and get any orders you can to meet our quota.' Disobeying a direct order is hardly an easy position to take, it took courage and discipline. However, demonstrably they got the benefits for their customer pharmacies and their company by sticking to the core value-adding activities they had pioneered. A derivative of their process was subsequently adopted by the company and everyone was measured on their adherence to it.

- Third, let's consider the management principle of ensuring integration of effort. The procedures the rogue sales staff developed were focused on the shared goals of the pharmacies and the pharmaceutical company – growth in sales and reduction in returns – not in meeting monthly sales targets at any cost in order to ensure that the sales managers achieved their targets so they would get their bonuses. In other words, the walk-in customers', the pharmacy's and the company's objectives were addressed in an integrated way. The walk-in customers' needs were considered and the sales managers' self-serving, functional focus was crushed.

Being time-based

Our international research revealed that this management principle was found in the leading organizations that used time as a critical organizing value. They were businesses that practised the principles of time-based competition.

When George Stalk and Tom Hout produced their acclaimed book on time-based competition (1990) the emphasis turned to helping clients to build strategic capabilities. To build strategic capabilities it is obviously critical to know which routinely performed activities directly drive business value; for example, the activities invented by the two rogue sales people above. It is equally important to know which activities destroy value, sometimes referred to as diversionary activities, so that these can be exorcized. Diversionary activities result in unnecessary increases in costs and response times and have a disproportionate impact on response time. For example, entering an order into a computer system might take three or four minutes. However, when there is an error (for example an unrecognized or incomplete delivery address) the ensuing interfacing activity could easily take an hour of the CSO's time to resolve and add several days of delay if, say, the originator of the order is on leave. Only after resolution can the information be correctly and completely entered and the order fulfilment is potentially significantly delayed.

Competing on time requires an organization to focus on its critical business processes and eliminate delays. This will improve customer service and reduce cost.

In manufacturing companies there are two common indicators of waste. The first is the presence of an inter-stage product buffer that incurs activity such as moving the work and accounting for the inventory as well as occupying valuable space. The second is rejecting or scrapping product, the physical evidence of failure and wasted cost in the manufacturing process. Administrative processes have few obvious indicators of waste, especially since most transactions are electronic and there are therefore no obviously full waste paper bins or pending trays crammed with delayed transactions. Cycle time was the proxy measure selected by Stalk and Hout to use to enable management to focus analysis and improvement effort as best they could on eliminating waste. We contend that measuring interfacing activity meets the need move quickly and without ambiguity.

Let's take a mortgage process as an example of failure to instil the management principle of being time-based. Most people at some time take out a mortgage and this can pose a problem to people wishing to make an offer on, or bid at auction for, a property. They need to know how much they can borrow. In the last financial cycle, competition from the rash of new, non-bank lenders drove changes to lending practices. One of the major banks had anticipated this change and had made considerable investments in streamlining its lending processes for home loans well ahead of its competition but found in the event that it was rapidly losing market share, not gaining it.

At the bank's head office managers were perplexed. Their revamped mortgage application process had eliminated the routine delays in their processes by streamlining the computer system, integrating back offices and revising their policies. This had allowed them to issue an offer very quickly to each applicant based on income and deposit capacity with caveats that made the applicant responsible for providing necessary proof of income before the loan could be drawn down. The applicant could then confidently proceed based on the knowledge of the amount he or she could borrow.

Unfortunately, the new process was just not working for the higher value, and therefore generally more profitable, loans. The bank's staff were therefore asked to spend three weeks on interface mapping all the activities they actually did in the branches, the regional centres and head office.

Two sets of formerly undocumented interfacing activity stood out – chasing insurance documentation and getting omitted insurance information from the applicant. For larger loans and those close to the income limit of the applicant, there was a need for the applicant to take out income protection insurance and so they had to complete an additional insurance proposal document. This insurance proposal was then submitted with the loan application documentation to head office for approval by the lending cell.

A review focused by knowledge of the interfacing activity quickly revealed a number of issues. For example, in the interest of cost, a diligent head office person was insisting that the branches should use up inexcusably high stocks of insurance application forms (two years' supply at the then ruling rate of usage) from which the question of whether the borrower was a smoker or non-smoker had been omitted. As a result of using this erroneous form, many applicants had to be asked to go back to the branch to complete another hastily designed form to collect the missing information. Needless to say, most of the applicants didn't bother. They had by that time already received an offer from a rival institution.

As with the example of the pharmaceutical company's sales force above, the case of this bank illustrates implementation failure in more than one management principle focusing on strategic intent. The failure was, and usually is, in all four best-practice principles, as itemized below:

- First, let's look at the management principle of creating customer value. The bank had failed to understand the absolute imperative of turnaround time to the customers who applied for a mortgage. As a consequence, managers had not put in place a cycle-time measure, a key performance indicator (KPI) that would have signalled the issue within a week of launch. Instead, they found out there was a problem several costly months later when the expected volume of higher quality business failed to materialize.

- Second, let's take the principle of being disciplined. The procedures issued with the launch of the bank's new mortgage application process may well have been appropriate. However, the bank then ignored its investment in policies, procedures and standards. It allowed a head office person to insist on using up incorrect, old application forms relating to income protection and then, almost unbelievably, allowed others to invent a further form to correct the error. The bank failed to maintain its focus when potentially destabilizing changes occurred and did not apply a strong system perspective to everything it did by planning and installing its necessary changes based on its documented knowledge base.

- Third, let's consider the management principle of ensuring integration of effort. The bank allowed the head office person to insist on satisfying a personal objective designed to cover his mistake at the expense of the laid-down goals.

- Fourth, the bank failed to adhere to the management principle of being time-based. There was simply no sense of awareness that the use of the old form and the extra work in chasing through the missing data militated directly against adherence to this principle.

Creating strategic capabilities

This is the last of the five management principles dealing with how leading organizations focus their resources strategically. Our research showed us that leading organizations understand how to build strategic capabilities and they use this understanding as their mechanism for documenting and driving the critical development and investment decisions for their business processes. These leading organizations demonstrated that their capability building occurs when the activities that make up their business processes are realigned in accordance with the four principles of ensuring integration of effort, being disciplined, creating customer value and being time-based (described above). The four organizations used as illustrations above needed to manage both their functional activities (which they were good at) and their interfacing activities (which they were unaware of) to achieve best practice.

We define a strategic capability as a business process in which the appropriate resources are strategically aligned through managing the process steps and interfaces to meet the organization's need. This involves managing closely both functional and interfacing activities. We have to conclude that the leading organizations in our worldwide research data demonstrate the state of the art, if not the mastery, of building strategic capabilities through managing their interfaces.

Link between best-practice principles and interfacing activity

The four examples used above illustrate how an organization's failure to comply with four of the management principles focusing on strategic intent, (ensuring integration of effort, being disciplined, creating customer value and being time-based) results in interfacing activity having to be carried out by the staff to compensate for the lapses. Looked at differently, the causal factor for much of the mapped interfacing activity is non-compliance to one or more of the management principles focusing on strategic intent. This means that the analysis of interfacing activity will pinpoint the need for, and the nature of, the change needed to install best-practice management principles. The four cases above also illustrate that best-practice organizations adhere to *all*, not a selection of, the management principles reviewed so far.

Using principles to achieve staff and management alignment

Table 2.2 (see page 36) shows a regrouping of the 14 management principles derived from our research. So far in this chapter we have delved into the first six of them. The remaining eight management principles deal mainly with creating and maintaining the staff and management culture needed to deploy strategic changes. The remaining eight principles are:

- gaining alignment;
- embracing change;
- establishing a learning culture;
- relating the micro to the macro;
- measuring and reporting;
- supporting distributed leadership;
- being up front;
- resourcing for the medium term.

These principles are discussed fully in Chapter 8.

Summary

This chapter has explored the nature of the management principles associated with defining the changes needed to achieve best practice and thereby full implementation of strategic intent. These principles are:

- having the desire to be out front – the determination to lead the pack in all strategically important business aspects;
- ensuring integration of effort, where all elements of the organization are focused unambiguously on achieving the organization's goal;
- being disciplined – requiring policies and procedures to be documented, up to date and used;
- creating customer value, delivering what the key customer segments need and going one step further – striving to work actively with customers to help them to meet their objectives;
- being time-based, eliminating waste of resources;
- creating strategic capabilities, building and maintaining strategically aligned business processes.

We have drawn three challenging conclusions:

- First, a piecemeal approach to implementing these six management principles will not deliver the required strategic alignment of business processes. An organization's business processes must comply with *all* six principles.
- Second, it is essential to identify and then rectify non-compliance with the six management principles discussed so far and this requires a full knowledge of interfacing activities. We cannot see how organizations can efficiently build and maintain strategic capabilities without mapping and analysing interfacing activities. Further, as we will show in the next chapter, because most organizations never properly map or measure interfacing activities, building true strategic capabilities can be only a dream for most organizations.
- Third, managers, by delegating the design of most of the firm's interfacing activities to the lowest levels in their organizations (who have little or no exposure to strategic thinking), are exposing the business to serious risk.

The next two chapters concentrate on the nature and value of interfacing activities.

Appendix

Our search for the set of management principles to achieve best practice

Before we started to write this book we conducted a thorough review of all the available research and published material on resource alignment to implement business strategy, strategically focused organizational change and organizational change achievement in general. We found, as you will be aware, that there is a huge volume of material on achieving change. However, there is little that establishes the relationship between business performance outcomes and the factors that enable organizations to achieve it. Much of the literature relies on anecdotal evidence and the experience of the author. Our international research is substantial and peer-reviewed and has been covered in depth in this chapter. The detailed data on how businesses operate is equally substantial and will be introduced beginning in Chapter 3.

The literature search into general change programmes allowed us to identify some 39 discrete factors that have been variously demonstrated to influence outcomes significantly. However, much of this research is probably only of fleeting interest to practising managers and change agents, for two reasons. First, much of this research has concentrated on investigating the relationship between just a small subset of these 39 factors and the achievement of outcomes. We contend that managers need to know about all the factors they need to manage in their situation before they commit the considerable resources needed to undertake a strategic change initiative. Second, it would be unrealistic to expect any manager to manage all 39 factors at the same time. Indeed, many organizations we have encountered have invested many person years of effort in creating an environment to establish just one of these enabling factors (for example the Balanced Scorecard, leadership or team working) in their business. Installing all 39 of them would be a gargantuan task.

Managers still need to know all the factors relevant to their situation that they need to manage in order to guarantee the achievement of the desired outcomes. There are just a handful of studies that address a wide selection of factors and relate them to business outcomes. These studies are: Samson and Terziovski (1999), Smith (2003), Antony and Banuelas (2002) and Guimaraes (1999). Samson and Challis (1999) usefully go a step further and group the factors into 14 management principles that should be applicable to all organizations.

Making the change needs obvious

03

The critical role of interfacing activities

Objectives

No organizational change programme should be undertaken, obviously, without first establishing a mechanism to identify forensically where the change is required. Ideally, the method used should make the opportunities visible to those who are planning the changes as well as engage those who have to put the changes into effect. This chapter will provide an understanding of interfacing activities as well as discuss how the knowledge gained from interface mapping will displace the use of pure guesswork or, at best, 'judgement' which is so often associated with defining major change initiatives.

The chapter will demonstrate how interface mapping speeds up and improves the delivery of outcomes by enabling the gaps and weaknesses in business processes to be pinpointed and quantified efficiently. The gaps include the non-compliance with the best-practice principles for focusing on strategic intent described in the last chapter. Finally, the chapter will explain why such a high level of engagement and enthusiasm is generated by the interface mapping approach.

How it all started

The decade from the mid-1970s onwards will have been purged from the minds of all managers and employees who were in the UK at the time. It was not a pleasant time to work in industry or commerce. Virtually every organization, private and public sector, seemed to be downsizing to reduce operating costs. In the manufacturing sector the focus for cost-down exercises had expanded to embrace the whole organization because management had recognized that the 'blue collar' areas then occupied an ever-shrinking proportion of the cost base. What had remained of the brass bands, tea ladies, chauffeurs and tiered dining facilities were being phased out. The scope of most cost reviews were expanded to include the 'white collar' and management areas and service industries, especially banking, finance and the public sector, were no longer exempted.

The change outcomes from these exercises affected everybody. Those who lost their positions were stunned by the suddenness of the decisions that affected them. Those who were 'lucky' and were retained were almost always dazed by the increased workloads and longer hours which were the inevitable consequence of ill-informed, and poorly planned 'downsizing' or 'right-sizing'.

It was against this backdrop that one of the authors was engaged on a project to raise productivity and define a new computer system for the downstream marketing operations of an international oil company. A team of six consultants was assigned to do the work using analytical tools which were much the same as those in common use today. The tools included process mapping to understand the physical goods and information flows and high-level timesheets to estimate resource allocations and costs.

An area of focus was the fuel depots or terminals where fuel bowsers were filled with the company's products for onward distribution to the petrol stations and commercial customers such as airlines, shipping lines and road fleet operators. The business processes in the terminals were apparently straightforward. For example, trucks arrived, were checked in, product was dispensed and volumes dropped were recorded and subsequently billed to the customer or the distributor. At first sight there was little complexity other than from the shared 'lifting' of product arrangements where competitors servicing that geographical area also obtained product from the company's facilities. Staff levels in each terminal were modest – three staff covering two shifts five days per week.

The inherently hazardous nature of the volatile petroleum products handled defined the culture. Procedures were seen by everyone as important and were carefully adhered to. This made the job of documenting the activities they carried out apparently straightforward. Process maps and resource allocations were developed well within schedule with excellent, if concerned, cooperation from the staff. A quick first analysis revealed a problem for the consultant. Virtually all of the activities which had been documented were easily reconciled back to the procedures and thus the business needs. There were few opportunities for improvement because the staff were doing what they were required to do. Nearly all the activities documented were value-adding activities and were being strictly adhered to. The only exception found was in the product replenishment process through the cross-country pipelines, where some procedures were unclear and therefore there was an opportunity to remove significant duplication of the work. However, the opportunity presented would be well below the expectation of senior managers, even though their own company benchmarking clearly showed that they were close to best in class on a world scale on customer service, safety and productivity.

A chance remark, made at what should have been the last meeting with three terminal staff to thank them for their input, turned upside down the orderly world in which the terminal staff apparently operated. The comment uncovered what was to become over the following 20 years for the consultant (and potentially the next 20 years for you) an almost bottomless pit of opportunity shallowly buried under the surface calm. One of the members of the terminal team was late so we were all sitting around waiting for him to arrive in the terminal meeting room. When he entered, he apologetically explained that he had been detained dealing with an issue that had arisen that morning. He was somewhat embarrassed by keeping everyone waiting and felt obliged to explain that a truck driver had not been able to produce his security pass and entry key. This had led to a series of phone calls to the driver's company and to the oil company's head office. This had been rather protracted as the person with the required authority was absent on a company training programme and it had taken an inordinate amount of time to track her down. The apparently unusual incident had obviously caused significant delays and extra work for the terminal, head office and the driver.

I, the author, casually asked whether these types of things occurred regularly. The terminal superintendent shocked me with his immediate answer. He said that these types of things occurred several times a day in almost everything they did. I blurted out the glaringly obvious question. 'Why on earth have we not documented these activities in the exercise we have just completed in the past week?' 'Just part of the job,' said the superintendent casually, 'and anyway they don't occur on every transaction, just a few of them, and they are not in the company procedures'. It was almost funny to see the lights go on for everyone in the room. What had been a relaxed meeting was electrified. They realized that significant opportunities had been missed in the documentation they had just developed. As a group, we excitedly and quickly revisited each functional task which we had so carefully documented over the past week adding what were later to be recognized and defined as interfacing activities.

The first tentative use of interface mapping had occurred. We used some simple questions for the terminal staff to ask. What do we do if the truck driver is late? What do we do if the driver does not have the right documentation or authority or equipment? What do we have to do if there is a malfunction in the equipment and then how do we get it rectified? What do we have to do for the customers when a problem happens? The tasks were the essential, absolutely undocumented tasks that were second nature to the staff. They had to do these interfacing activities to get through the day to enable them to do the tasks so precisely defined in their job descriptions and procedures.

I did my best in the next three days to complete the documentation we had started in the meeting by interviewing the team members. I was attempting to document the nature and impact on resources of every one of the interfacing activities we had talked about. There were so many interrelated tasks and dependencies that I quickly abandoned flowcharting when I reached connector 100 and moved to using hierarchical lists. The listing approach subsequently proved to be ideal for resource allocation. As before, I circulated the now much larger documentation packs to the terminal staff for their comment and sign off.

There was a nasty surprise in store for me at the review meeting – they were very, very disappointed by my efforts and were hardly shy in expressing their views. They felt that I had left out far too many things that routinely disrupted their working day. So, supported by the terminal superintendent, they spent a week changing it to their satisfaction. They then proudly (and I did not realize how critically important their change in attitude would prove to be) presented me with the catalogue of the real work they did every day. The number of tasks from the original had increased tenfold. Most of the additions were activities required to keep the system running smoothly by dealing with the all too frequent issues that occurred, so that the next step in the process could be executed. The result from the work was an almost indigestible amount of data laden with opportunities. The other outcome, which we were only to value much later, was the staff's change in attitude. If I had been more experienced I would have realized that something unusual had taken place. Fear and suspicion had been replaced by outright enthusiasm. At last they had made visible all the things they actually had to do. All I saw at the time was the quantity and quality of the data. What they now expected was to get in there and fix the problems.

However, at the time there were two far-reaching conclusions that we drew from this experience and we later found them to hold in all situations. First, the staff who do the work are the only people capable of documenting what really happens in the workplace – the activities we have defined as interfacing activities. An external agent, in this case a consultant, could simply not do the job to the satisfaction of the staff. Second, conventional process mapping tools are not suited to detailed and rigorous end-to-end mapping of all the activities undertaken.

Exploring interfacing activity

We have given several examples in the book so far to illustrate the role interfacing activity plays in organizations to enable 'stuff' to be passed from one person to another in a business process, enabling each person to apply their specific expertise and thus add value. We have also described a number of situations to demonstrate that where these interfaces have been poorly designed, or more commonly just left to chance, the nature and quantum of the interfacing activities starkly reveal process failure. One incident that gave rise to the idea to write this book was the experience one of the authors had as a result of an accident when he fractured his spine in Austria. The experience gives some unique insights into interfaces and interfacing activities. He was the 'stuff' which was to pass through the medical repatriation process. He was handed on from one person to the next benefiting progressively from each person's skills and the interfacing activities should have been managed to facilitate delivery back to his home in Australia. The contrast between the professional way the medical skills were expertly applied and the mayhem and distress caused by the poorly managed repatriation interfacing activities could hardly be starker. Case study 3.1 sets the scene so that you can share the experience and evaluate the various activities that made up the business process variously referred to as the 'patient's journey' by those who have studied medical processes in the past.

CASE STUDY 3.1   The patient's journey

First let's introduce the players in this case study, many of whom are among the most respected names in their field in the world. A top-ranked insurance company provided its top of the range travel insurance package and another international insurance company through its Australian office administered the scheme on the insurer's behalf. The service providers included several airlines, three airports, three ambulance services, two hospitals and two travel agents.

The accident was completely unexpected, it happened very fast and I was immediately totally incapacitated. I had fallen and fractured my spine while on holiday in Austria and simply could not move. Even breathing was excruciatingly painful. I passed out and awoke to find members of an ambulance crew had arrived and they had administered oxygen. When I thought about it afterwards, I concluded that the interfacing activities in these early parts of the process were efficient, quick and routine – just what one might have hoped for and expected. Someone had seen my fall and had kindly called the ambulance. It had arrived within minutes. The next set of interfacing activities were equally efficiently executed. The paramedics asked a number of questions, made an assessment of my condition, and radioed for a second ambulance with specialist equipment to recover a patient with serious spinal injury.

On admission to the nearest hospital, my wife ran into some interfacing activities which could have caused real delays while payment was sorted out but presenting a credit card ensured that formalities were kept to the minimum of collecting my details and signing a payment slip. I was examined by the A&E doctor who ordered a morphine drip and arranged for me to be transferred to the neurological wing for observation. My wife called the emergency number and found she had a direct link to the friendly staff in the outsourced emergency response team in Australia. Details were exchanged and she was advised to arrange treatment, pay the bills and make a claim when we got home. So far, so good.

The next morning a spinal surgeon examined me, recommended immediate surgery and told me it would be two or three months before I could be repatriated. Shocked, I persuaded him to speak to my daughter, a Melbourne-based general surgeon. The result was that some excruciatingly painful tests were immediately and successfully carried out and I was encased in plaster from my neck to my groin. Now wrapped and labelled, just like 'stuff' previously referred to, I was ready for shipment back to Australia high on barbiturates to manage the pain. Lots of interfacing had been accomplished in a short space of time including by three surgeons who were half a world apart, X-ray staff, porters, 'plasterers' and the hospital in Melbourne. Time was of the essence as any delay in treatment could render me a paraplegic. The insurance company supported the proposed course of action as it materially reduced its exposure. The company just had to repatriate me, a job it would have undertaken hundreds of times before.

First thing on Monday morning things started well. The always friendly person on duty in the Australian insurance office telephoned to say that the insurance company needed my doctor to complete a standard form which would be faxed over. This marked the beginning of the unmanaged interfacing activity nightmare. The first issue was that the faxed form was printed in a typesize so small that it was impossible to read. I telephoned the repatriation team who quickly enlarged it and re-faxed. This was unmanaged interfacing activity that would have surely occurred before I thought.

The next problem was that my unit doctor was a Guatemalan. His native tongue was Spanish and German was his second language. I called the insurance company to get staff there to send a copy of the form in German or Spanish. It was only available in English. The clock was ticking, a day had elapsed and still no completed form. I had to get out of Europe – the surgeon had stopped by and said that for my safety he really should operate tomorrow.

We arranged for someone fluent in Spanish to come in and translate for the doctor and the form was completed and faxed to Australia. My nurse thoughtfully gave me the fax transmission confirmation. We had only lost half a day. Impatiently I waited an hour before phoning Australia. They had not received it. Could I fax it again? My kind German speaking nurse understood the urgency and could see my obvious distress so she re-faxed it as soon as the administration office opened the following morning. Another half day had gone.

On Tuesday morning I telephoned Australia again and the insurance company confirmed that it had the form. Two hours later an angry Guatemalan doctor stormed in to see me. He had received a memo from Australia which he didn't fully understand but it clearly requested some of the same information he had already prepared for them. He refused to respond unless he had clearer instructions. I phoned Australia and the team member explained, 'There is some difficulty with our system and we can't find the previously faxed document, but we must have your doctor's answers urgently.' I decided to dictate a really simple questionnaire for the Australian team to send to my doctor so he could tick the boxes and sign it. A miracle occurred, my doctor responded immediately. I was on my way at last.

The next step, the Australian staff now told me, was to complete an airline form. Unbelievably, it was almost identical to their original form but much better laid out, with larger typesize and available in multiple languages. The translator was called in just in case, took the form to the doctor and charmed him into completing it and then stood by the fax machine to ensure that the completed document was successfully sent.

I phoned Australia again. They had not received the form and asked me to re-fax it. In frustration, I asked the team member if she could see the fax machine – she could she said, but she added that she was not supposed to leave her station. I begged her to go and check the machine. After a few minutes she confirmed that the fax was there and passed it over for action. The following morning I again phoned Australia to find that things were moving fast. They had booked me on a flight from Frankfurt leaving in six hours and they were on the phone to the ambulance service to take me to the airport at that very moment. I hesitantly asked whether she was aware that Frankfurt was nearly 600 kilometres from the hospital. "Is there time to get us there?', I asked. This was followed by a long silence. 'Oh... we didn't know that... we don't have any maps... no... I don't think we can do it.' So my escape was cancelled and the game of interface snakes and ladders started all over again.

On Wednesday morning the insurance team called me to say they had arranged flights on 6 October, now three days hence, being the next available flight with the essential flat bed accommodation. Now, actions to date had not filled me with confidence so I phoned my travel agent in Mornington, Australia and the airline. Both confirmed that the insurance company's travel agent had made a mistake. The airline did not operate with flat beds out of Europe. Oh dear. What would have happened if I had travelled the 600 kilometres to Frankfurt, gone through the airport to the aircraft door and then had to return? I shuddered, thinking about the wrong-side surgery example (case study 1.1 on page 25).

I phoned Australia again. The team member confirmed the receipt of both the travel agent's and the airline's e-mails. 'Our travel agent sends his sincere apologies for the oversight.' More disturbingly she told me, 'There are no suitable flat beds available now for at least another 10 days.' The outcome, the operation tomorrow. Abject panic overwhelms logical thought in my 'concrete' straight jacket and I hyperventilate. I am given oxygen and an injection. I am unconscious for the next half day.

When I awoke I phoned my travel agent Kathryn and explained my problem. Kathryn calls back within an hour – 'I have two flat-bed seats booked for you on 7 October with Cathay Pacific and with the right paperwork they can probably take you airside in the ambulance to load you.' Two more phone calls and the insurance company's travel agent agreed to take over the booking.

Midday on Friday, I phoned Australia to chase up our awaited itinerary and receive appalling news. 'Yes, we have made all the arrangements but we are just about to cancel your flights.' Time stands still for me and my throat goes dry. 'Why?' I just managed to croak. 'Your admitting hospital has a policy not to admit on Sunday evening, the day you will arrive in Australia, and you simply can't go home to wait.' Now I knew that they were wrong, my daughter was the admitting surgeon. If I still needed evidence that the interfacing activities were out of control, this was it. I begged them not to cancel the arrangements and I promised to get the surgeon to reconfirm the Sunday night admission. I then called the insurance company to confirm that they have received the instructions from the surgeon. Their response was revealing. 'You'll be pleased to know that we've found the original admissions authorization document. It was in our system all along, we just couldn't find it.'

On Saturday morning I was picked up at 5 am by an ambulance and I was transferred on a stretcher to Frankfurt Airport at an average speed of about 100 kilometres per hour. Ground handling in Frankfurt and Hong Kong were exemplary even to the extent of having a bed ready for me in the airport's sick bay. No more interfacing activities to negotiate, I remember thinking at the time, but how wrong can one be? When the Boeing 747's wheels touched the runway in Melbourne I shed a tear and breathed a premature sigh of relief.

Then there was a broadcast over the aircraft's PA system. 'We apologize ladies and gentlemen, there will be significant delays in disembarkation for all passengers today because of a quarantine embargo on the aircraft. We have a passenger travelling with a contagious disease.' That was me. No doubt the 300 passengers on board were relieved to find I had only broken my back.

A summary of negatives and positive from case study 3.1 is given below.

Positives for the insurance company	Negatives – best-practice principle failures
Available 24/7	Not disciplined
Well coached in friendliness and sympathy	Not customer focused
Contacts with service organizations set up	No evidence of integration (for example hand-offs to the service suppliers – or internally – were not managed)
Knew the functional activities that needed to be done	Critical interfaces not managed

Further examples and explanations of interfacing activity, and interfacing activity noise, are included in the appendix to this chapter. The objective in including this appendix is to provide the reader with some guidance on how to recognize and discuss noise in everyday business.

Mapping reality – the paradox

We think that by now we have provided sufficient examples that interfacing activities need to be mapped and managed, and there is a lot more support for this notion in later chapters. We want here to explore how to gather this data so that we can use it to explore activities and business processes further and maintain your interest.

The most common approach to mapping processes (or developing procedures or job descriptions) is the interview-based approach, where the interviewer sets the agenda. Further, the tendency is to concentrate on interviews with middle managers because it is believed that these managers are in the unique position of having sufficient knowledge of what is done combined with a business perspective that will help the mapper to navigate through

FIGURE 3.1 The relationship between process knowledge and authority

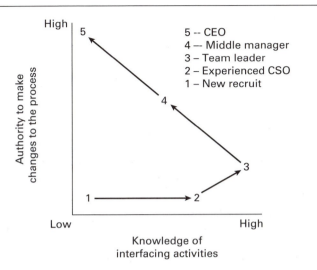

the business processes. This presents a paradox illustrated in Figure 3.1. The paradox is that the staff who have the detailed knowledge of what really happens, including the interfacing activities, have little or no authority to make changes and are rarely consulted. Those with the authority to institute change know little about the real activities which are routinely carried out and yet are inevitably the focal point for mapping exercises.

Figure 3.1 shows that when a new recruit joins, say as a trainee teller in a bank, he or she knows almost nothing about how to do the job. The new person is thus not given any authority to change the way things are done. New employees will typically attend a standard training programme at which the new recruit will learn what they should do. Back on the job and over the next few months the trainees will gain experience with the standard transactions and with handling the problems the customers bring to them. More often than not they will have to be briefed by more experienced tellers or the team leader on how to deal with each 'new' problem as it occurs, to allow them to use the standard transactional procedure they learned on their training programme. They will thus be receiving training from a more experienced person on the undocumented interfacing activities in use in their branch.

As a bank customer you will have seen your teller (or in other industries, your CSO, planning assistant, sales assistant, for example) go to another for advice and guidance. If you listen in on the conversation you will hear that the discussion is about things such as: 'How to I deal with this customer who does not have the needed information with him?'; 'How do I deal with this elderly person who can't or won't operate the ATM?'; 'How do I deal with this customer's query on her statement which she can't understand?,' etc.

These conversations are on the job training in interfacing activities learning about the fettled process steps.

So when the now experienced employee has learned how to do all these interfacing activities and is seen to be helping other newcomers to do the job, then he or she is ready to be considered for promotion. We contend that it is demonstrated knowledge of how to conduct the interfacing activities that leads to promotion – a thorough knowledge of what should be done as documented in the procedures is simply not good enough. Having demonstrated this knowledge the teller gets promoted to team leader (position 3 on Figure 3.1).

The newly promoted team leader will know everything there is to know about the processes carried out by tellers in that particular branch. He or she will have been trained, assessed and accredited in what should happen in the company programmes. In addition, he or she will have demonstrated real ability to deal with customers' issues by knowing intimately, and using, the real system that delivers the customer service via the interfacing activities relevant to that particular branch. Hence the team leader plots on the extreme right of the diagram.

We find that in spite of their day-to-day knowledge of the interfacing activities, team leaders rarely have the opportunity to participate in organizational change. They are most likely to be regarded as being too junior, or as having too narrow a perspective of how business processes function to be involved in a change team. In reality, they are more likely to have too many uncomfortable truths for the (ignorant) change agent to handle. In short, they will have little or no authority to make changes to the formal system even though they have often, of necessity, had to invent large parts of the interfacing activity to get their team through the day.

Change, perversely, therefore is usually conducted by people who have little or no knowledge of the interfacing activities. Further, and as we will demonstrate, these same team leaders and their staff will have invented, largely without oversight, the very interfacing activities that have a greater impact on the customer service and productivity outcomes than those proposed by the change specialists.

What becomes more interesting is what happens when a team leader is promoted to his or her first management position, the next level in the hierarchy. These employees would have attained their team leadership position because of their intimate knowledge of, and their ability to invent and manage, interfacing activities to keep everything working smoothly. Their next step will broaden their span of control so that they take over responsibility for other jobs where they will have little or no knowledge of the tasks to be done or the interfacing activities required. This obviously explains why the Peter Principle is alive and well in every organization. (The Peter Principle is a theory that employees will advance to their highest level of competence within an organization and then be promoted to and remain at a level at which they are incompetent.)

Of course, reading the job descriptions and procedures will hardly help these newly appointed managers as the critical interfacing activities will not have been documented. So at the same time that their authority to make changes has increased dramatically (and in position 5 on Figure 3.1 has become absolute) the knowledge of how the processes actually operate inexorably moves towards nil. Even more telling is that in many organizations the CEO is recruited from outside, even from another industry, so he or she can never get a real understanding of how things really work, even though in the position of CEO he or she has the authority to change anything. Obviously, a process for change, including gathering interfacing activity data, is needed to fill this knowledge void unless the management team is content to base its changes on judgement, experience and blind faith.

This paradox, the chasm between authority to change and knowledge of the critical interfacing and functional activities, must obviously be solved if an organization is to build strategic capabilities. We hold as true that, just as GPS systems use detailed maps of the interfaces between different roads to plan and manage an optimal route to a desired destination, managers and those driving change should have access to detailed interface maps of the activities that link different functional activities together to deliver the desired outcomes of the organization. We argue that organizational 'genomics' should be based on a full knowledge of both interfacing and functional activities.

Searching for an approach to mapping interfacing activity

So how does an organization acquire this detailed data? Our experience in the downstream oil business project was to prove to be just the first step on the long road to understanding the factors that allowed us to develop and patent a methodology that would reliably capture exactly what really happens in organizations. Inevitably, many blind alleys were to be explored in this quest before we recognized, and valued, the change in staff's attitude brought about in the oil terminal by their participation.

In the late 1980s we began in earnest to concentrate on tool and methodology development. At that point, some of our team were reluctant to accept that the staff actually doing the work could possibly be trusted to document honestly all the activities they were routinely doing. Members of our team therefore insisted on revisiting techniques related to work study organization and methods, which had fallen into disuse by the late 1970s. They argued these techniques would get the required detail by objective, independent observation.

Work study approaches require each of the activities carried out by staff to be broken down by observation into elemental parts. Each elemental part is then measured by standing by the person doing the task with a stop watch or obtained from data from prior industry observations. The techniques had not fallen by the wayside by neglect. The approach possessed three huge disadvantages. The first was that it took forever. It took a lot of time to prepare for the measurement, that is, to describe each elemental task. This was because we found that the longer we observed teams, the more different (interfacing) activities we saw. It would have been much easier just to focus on the functional tasks, such as pick an item, rather than all the different interfacing activities that occurred when something was late, incorrect or misplaced or when inexperienced staff did the job or even when it rained. It thus proved to be incredibly difficult to judge when to stop observing because we realized that the circumstances that triggered different sets of interfacing activities were subject to change. In some instances, for example in accounting, payroll and despatch teams, which interfacing activities were carried out depended on the day of the week or month. In other examples, such as in a warehouse or a call centre, they depended on where we chose to take our observations, as well as the day of the week. We realized that the observation schedule would need to include several days scattered throughout a month. Further, external factors, such as weather and process changes made by customers or suppliers, could trigger a whole set of previously unobserved interfacing activities – some of which were no doubt being invented in front of our eyes, but how were we to know unless the person doing the job told us?

The more we observed, the more we realized that the task we had set for ourselves was impossible. No wonder the staff always told us that their procedures and job descriptions never covered even half of the work they did. We found that a relatively simple main activity (selected from perhaps 20–40 main activities undertaken routinely by a work team) would take several days to document. It was simply impractical to document the 20–40 main activities in the 35–70 teams found in an organization of 500 employees. It would take years and then we would still have to measure each of these activities. Deployment of strategic change in our fast-moving world requires change deployment tools such as mapping to be responsive – fast and easy to use.

This led us reluctantly into the second huge disadvantage, which was to prove to be a game stopper. Documenting activities took forever but measuring, that is 'stop watching', activities was more than intrusive, it was obviously very threatening to almost every person whose activities were to be measured. It reinforced the very barriers we were trying to break down. This reaction by staff ruled out an observation-based approach and it was only when we accepted this conclusion that we began to realize that there was a third even bigger 'elephant in the room'.

The very presence of an observer was causing people to change what they were doing and thus rendered the outcomes unusable. Take, for example, the need to measure activities in a machine cell in an automotive parts manufacturer. In an attempt to speed up the development of the activities list, we used a workshop approach (which took people out of their working environment) to document meticulously the activities undertaken in the cell.

These activities were then broken down into their elemental parts and agreed in further meetings with the staff. Next the union and operations management teams were approached and their agreement was obtained to time the elemental activities. An experienced person then went into the factory to the cell to take the measurements. As the cell was approached it was noticed that one member of the cell team was standing on a chair at the back of the honing machine. He was making an adjustment and the machine was visibly slowing down. A debate then ensued, the gist of which was conveyed by one of the cell members who said, 'Yes, we have slowed down the machine, and yes you can wait until we speed it up again before you take your measurements, but mate, you will be standing around for a very, very long time.' So the effort to document the various activities over the previous weeks were to go to waste. Clearly, the openness and enthusiasm with the team in the oil terminal, which had gone largely unnoticed by me, would never be achieved by the direct measurement approach. Now we began to understand the real reason why we needed to engage the teams properly in interface mapping.

The approaches of work study and study of organization and methods were abandoned but we had learned a lot. Our observations had at least demonstrated that undocumented routine activities were endemic in every workplace we visited. Further, the number of undocumented interfacing activities always exceeded by far those documented in the procedures, job descriptions or process maps.

We then began to encounter a number of strong challenges. There were other successful ways in use to collect information on what was happening in organizations. It was argued that interfacing activities were to a greater or lesser amount always being documented. Workshops were being run to map out in detail the activities routinely undertaken.

We were fortunate to be able to observe many such workshops and we readily acknowledge that interfacing and functional activities were indeed being recorded (and sometimes quantified) in most of them. However, without exception the work we observed had narrow focus. To tackle resource alignment strategically, by definition it would be necessary to assemble the 'genomics' of the whole organization, or even more challengingly, for the whole organization and its suppliers and partners, not just the small part of the operation typically measured for a project. It would be rather like mapping the traffic lights in the 1 kilometre long High Street in Yass when the job was to reduce the time spent on the 1,000 kilometre drive from Melbourne to Sydney. How would we even know that Yass was an important issue? And, in any case, what about the bypass? The detailed interface mapping of the whole enterprise using a detailed process mapping approach would literally take years.

We concluded that the approaches that were commonly recommended had two key weaknesses:

- First, the documentation was triggered by a particular issue because someone had identified and reported a problem. We, on the other hand, were looking for something which would make all of the 'issues' obvious so that we could use the data to identify all gaps and weaknesses and non-compliance with the best-practice management principles and establish priorities strategically. We were also aware that there was no guarantee that particular problems, or even any problem at all, would be reported. We were aware, for instance, that in certain workplace environments, managers actually discourage problem reporting and these are often the environments with greater than average payback. Further, in some countries, for example Malaysia, we find that reporting problems is counter-cultural and simply does not happen.

- Second, the documentation being developed was issue-centric; that is, the upstream and downstream effects of the problem were never properly explored because such an investigation would not necessarily be welcomed in all parts of the organization, including where perhaps the problem originated. Further, the viral impact can only be assessed by accumulating the resource impact of what are often multiple small resource impacts scattered throughout the entire business process, and where each individual impact would be regarded as too small to worry about. So at best only a third of the benefit would be known about (see Chapter 5 and Table 5.6).

We saw that we needed something capable of mapping the activities in the business as a whole quickly. To illustrate this, take the case of a manufacturing company internationally noted for its cost focus. Here, we were invited by management to 'demonstrate' our interface mapping approach at the New South Wales site recognized as best practice in the group. The site, a plastics packaging plant, employed about 100 staff operating on two shifts, producing a particular type of packaging material for use in the adjacent customer's food-processing plant.

Each of the work teams simultaneously interface mapped everything they did, part time in less than three weeks. We also obtained benchmark comparisons from the process plant supplier showing that the output per production line hour was the best in the southern hemisphere so we knew we had a real challenge on our hands. The first thing the analysis of the interface mapping data showed was that in-team process failure was unusually low – it had been targeted by each team and eliminated. There was little or no wasted activity within each team because each team saw internal waste elimination as its objective – not overall plant performance (teams were not adhering to the integration of effort principle described in the last chapter). There were lots of opportunities which jumped out from an analysis of the end-to-end manufacturing process. For example, the accounting function, which controlled the consumables and spare parts store, decided that the store should be kept locked and the computer terminal password protected to eliminate something they were held responsible for: it would eliminate misreporting of use of spare parts and what they saw as the unnecessary weekly checking of stock levels of spares and consumables. The consequence was that when the high-speed line failed, the maintenance technician had to contact a member of staff in accounts and get that person to open the store. Even if the accounts person attended immediately (which rarely happened as it was not an accounts priority) this meant about 7–12 minutes' delay. This delay, it was argued, was not important in the overall scheme of things and it was argued that the cost of the technician's time lost was much less than issues arising from discrepancies in the store's inventory.

Unfortunately, the problem often occurred a number of times each shift and up to 49 people were then idle until the problem was addressed. This meant 7–12 minutes per incident involving 49 staff. This amounted to 9 paid work hours per breakdown or over US $140,000 per annum. Without being boring, there were many such instances (fork lift trucks, stacking routines, pallet strapper, cleaning equipment availability, tool availability, etc) where what one team did, or failed to do, significantly affected other teams and thus dragged down the overall plant performance while each team was seen to be meeting its goals exactly.

What had happened was that the changes made to rid each team of its waste had introduced wasteful, but apparently inevitable, interfacing activity in other teams, including customers' teams. The end-to-end interface mapping made all the different interfacing activities stand out so that priorities could be set for the whole business. The plant had focused on the principle of being time-based at the cost of ignoring the principles of ensuring integration of effort, creating customer value and being disciplined. The result of an increased focus on the management of interfacing activities was the creation of additional capacity enabling business volumes to be increased by 30 percent at zero cost and material wastage was also reduced.

So, when we look back, much of the interface mapping tool that has been developed and refined in 400 applications can be traced back to the application of the lessons learned from the chance events with the staff in the oil terminal in the early 1980s. Those experiences pointed to key elements of a methodology and supporting software to assist individual work teams very quickly and thoroughly to document and quantify everything they routinely do, including the interfacing activities, and then to analyse the resulting data set by business process.

Documenting what really happens

To explore interface mapping in some depth we have based it around a relatively recent case, undertaken in 2010, changing some of the details to preserve confidentiality. We were approached by a financial services organization which we will call Pensions. Pensions' business strategy called for step improvements in customer service levels and increased productivity in order to free up resources to fund the growth the business was enjoying.

A year before managers at Pensions looked at interface mapping, they had released five people from their normal duties within their organization, had trained them in traditional process mapping and analysis, and required them to map all their business processes. The managers selected a widely available process mapping tool and engaged an external expert to guide the five-person team through the work.

The process mapping work was completed on schedule in just over nine months. The team delivered a complete set of 15 process maps which they had prepared, supported by catalogued examples of screen formats and printed outputs. A map similar to those delivered is shown in Figure 3.2. Managers were disappointed with the output. They felt that they had committed some US $300,000 in salary and other costs to undertake the exercise and the process maps delivered did not pinpoint any significant opportunities required to streamline the business processes. There were no quantified benefits to show from the considerable effort, cost and disruption over the nine months. The best they could hope for was that an experienced change facilitator would be able to use the process maps to guide further investigation and workshops. The hope was that this would find opportunities in areas such as why applications were returned to members and whether the decision process could be streamlined.

The managers decided to look for other techniques. They became interested in the speed and detail offered by interface mapping to help to drive their Lean project.

After a two-day training exercise the company's team set about the three-week documentation exercise. The first step was to brief each of the business teams on what they were required to do, why it was critical to the business and how it was designed to make their life easier. Many staff voiced their concerns as the effort they had devoted to the ill-fated project of process mapping was very much fresh in the mind. They had willingly given their time to the exercise and had shared the disappointment that little had emerged from nine months of effort. From their point of view, they were still having to stay late to deal with work, and the many frustrations that had been discussed in the interviews had neither been acknowledged in the maps nor addressed. They were persuaded to at least begin the exercise.

The next step therefore was to list the activities captured in the process maps and develop a more comprehensive view. There were some 16 activities in this material (simply listed in Figure 3.3 in the tint box). In a workshop format, representatives of each work team were asked a series of rather obvious questions for each of the activities. Examples of the questions used for each activity were: Do you always receive everything complete? If not what do you have to do? Is the information you receive always on time? If not, what do you do? What steps do you do to get authorizations?

Immediately these questions were asked, the hostility began to melt away. One particularly aggrieved team leader commented, 'This is the first time I can remember in 20 years where the management have expressed any interest at all in what we really do here…'.

FIGURE 3.2 A typical process map prepared to support a strategic change initiative

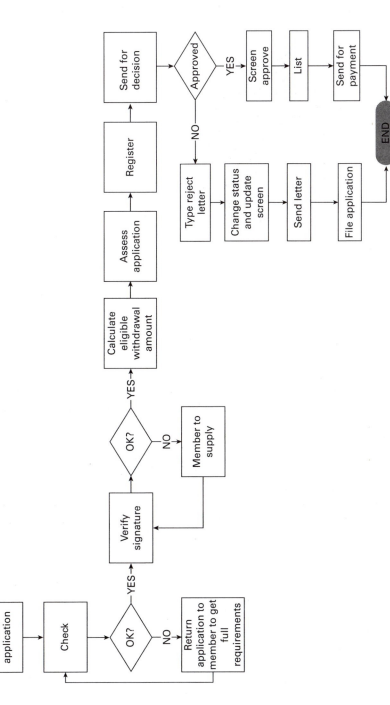

FIGURE 3.3   Undocumented interfacing activities

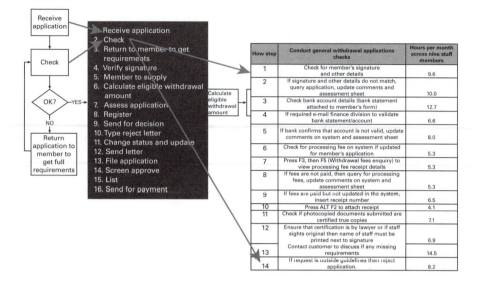

As is always the case, the results were startling. Figure 3.3 shows how just one activity, activity 2 (Check), increased by an order of magnitude to 14 detailed activities. Over all, the 15 process maps prepared by the original five-person team in nine months had documented 879 activities. In three weeks, interface mapping yielded 2,608 activities – a threefold increase. All 1,729 of these hidden activities were 'represented' in the original process maps as the connecting arrows.

This approach to interface mapping by engaging each of the work teams has now been used over 400 times. It has been used in a wide range of organizations. The smallest is a one-person operation, an accounting professionals' institute, and one of the larger businesses is a bank where some 6,000 people were included in the analysis from the head office and central functions, the regional offices and a sample of different branches. Some of the analyses have covered entire business units while others have been targeted on particular end-to-end business processes.

We developed a database of recent interface mapping projects to inform this book. The 117 organizations in it include one with 813 staff to the smallest which has just two staff. The average size is 119 staff. Table 3.1 shows the ratio between the functional activity count of 554 which is typically documented by organizations using the normal process mapping approach and the 3,374 real activity descriptions that result from including the interface activities. It shows that most organizations typically document less than a quarter of the activities routinely undertaken by the staff and managers before attempting a programme of strategic change.

TABLE 3.1 Ratio between documented and undocumented activities

	Number of staff in scope	Number of activities from process mapping	Number of activities recorded by staff using interface mapping
Average	119	554	3,374
Larger	813	1,418	13,382
Smallest	2	38	292

Sample size: 117

So the key question which we now must consider is whether a fourfold increase in the activities recorded are of value strategically and operationally to companies or whether they are just a mindless padding of the numbers and nice to know.

Importance of missing interfacing activities

Figure 3.4 is a repeat of Figure 3.3 with some of the activities highlighted with a cross. Even to the casual observer, reading these highlighted activities reveals the nature of the issues that may need to be addressed if the business objectives of improving customer service and improving productivity are to be met. At the micro level, activity 2 in the list, which the data shows absorbs 10 staff hours per month and therefore costs some US $7,000 per annum, indicates that there is an opportunity to improve the editing for web-submitted applications to save this time and cost and eliminate the delay to customers that errors would cause. To labour a point, this is a saving US $7,000 per annum from addressing just one of the 1,729 interfacing activities revealed for the first time by the interface mapping.

A full analysis of the data for this process reveals that addressing the top 15 drivers analysed from the data would release almost US $921,000 per annum out of the total salary bill of around US $2.303 million for this process. This was the information managers had been seeking from the work.

We contend that the missing data, largely the interfacing activities, is of vital importance to organizations contemplating organizational change and

FIGURE 3.4   Expanded activity 2 from the original process map

1. Receive application
2. Check
3. Return to member to get requirements
4. Verify signature
5. Member to supply
6. Calculate eligible withdrawal amount
7. Assess application
8. Register
9. Send for decision
10. Type reject letter
11. Change status and update
12. Send letter
13. File application
14. Screen approve
15. List
16. Send for payment

How step	Conduct general withdrawal applications checks	Hours per month across nine staff members	
1	Check for member's signature and other details	9.6	
2	If signature and other details do not match, query application, update comments and assessment sheet	10.0	X
3	Check bank account details (bank statement attached to member's form)	12.7	
4	If required e-mail finance division to validate bank statement/account	6.6	X
5	If bank confirms that account is not valid, update comments on system and assessment sheet	8.0	X
6	Check for processing fee on system if updated for member's application	5.3	
7	Press F3, then F5 (Withdrawal fees enquiry) to view processing fee receipt details	5.3	X
8	If fees are not paid, then query for processing fees, update comments on system and assessment sheet	5.3	X
9	If fees are paid but not updated in the system, insert receipt number	6.5	X
10	Press ALT F2 to attach receipt	4.1	
11	Check if photocopied documents submitted are certified true copies	7.1	
12	Ensure that certification is by lawyer or if staff sights original then name of staff must be printed next to signature	6.9	X
13	Contact customer to discuss if any missing requirements	14.5	X
14	If request is outside guidelines then reject application.	8.2	X

that conventional process mapping (Figure 3.5) which represents interfacing activities as connecting lines is not fit for the purpose of providing the basis for strategically oriented organizational change.

Confidence from interfacing activity data

In the next chapter we will present new frameworks for analysing these larger activity databases. However, it might be instructive to visit some instances where just the raw interface-mapped data guided organizations to very profitable change.

First, though, let's summarize the characteristics of data from interface mapping:

- It includes interfacing and functional activities.
- It is always signed off as correct by the staff and team leaders who do the work; that is, those who plot in positions 1, 2 and 3 in Figure 3.1 (see page 59).
- It takes an elapsed time of less than three weeks because the data is developed by each work team.
- Documentation starts with the higher-level (functional) activities done by each team that can be checked against existing process maps or procedures.

FIGURE 3.5 Conventional representation of interfacing activities

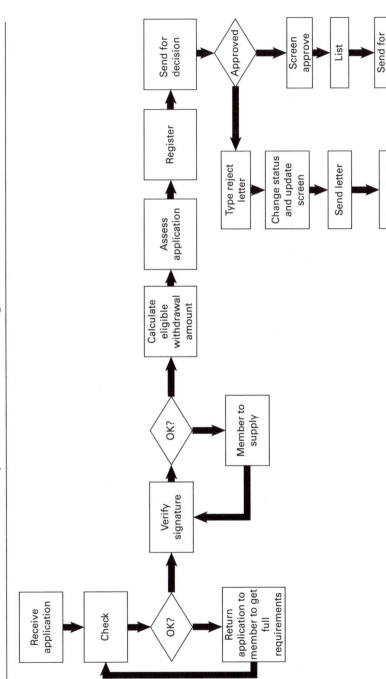

- Often, during the process the team leaders admit to being unaware of sets of activities being done so it is both a documentation and a discovery process.
- Each activity is quantified.

There have been many instances in our direct experience where top teams have been convinced that certain key activities are being carried out when in reality this was not the case. Take, for example, the business of one of the world's major international shipping companies. Interface mapping was used there to understand the drivers of the company's profitability. The top team were only too aware that they were incurring large costs unnecessarily because they were contracting space on vessels that they were subsequently unable to use. They did not understand why this was happening. They knew that they were not in a position to reduce the contracted space until late in the cycle because they had to service the variation in volume from one of their company's largest accounts. Sufficient space was contracted ahead to ensure that the critical customer's need could always be serviced. The managers also knew that their staff received updated shipping information weekly from this client to allow these staff to sell the surplus space at carefully managed discounts. The top management were confident that their business processes had been deployed well in order to manage their classical 'airline seat' problem.

After completing the interface mapping, a workshop was conducted with the top team to work out the activities their staff would need to undertake to manage the surplus contracted space. There was an immediate issue. The top team tended to think in terms of objectives rather than activities, so they were much happier stating, 'Fill the spare capacity,' rather than detailing the steps to do it, such as collect the schedule, calculate unused space, send data to sales force. The workshop delivered its first valuable output – the activities necessary to deliver the strategy were defined by those who owned the strategy – the top team. They defined activities and attributes including: ensuring that they had the data from their key client on time; that it was in the right format; that they used it to calculate the shortfall in booked space utilization, and that this information was formatted for immediate use by the sales force; that the sales force knew which customers to approach to sell the spot capacity; that sales were made quickly; that information about the available, unsold space was kept up to date; etc.

We then issued the interface map of the process to these top managers – the information put together by their staff. After 10 minutes of combing through the data and marking up various activities a deep silence fell on the group. Each functional director realized that the activities they so confidently had said their staff were doing were being done but they had all discovered the problem that was damaging profitability. There was a significant amount of interfacing activity they were unaware of, such as chasing information (caused by late receipt from the key client, late circulation of available space to the sales force, sales not notified by the sales force, etc) and transposing information into usable forms (which delayed circulation). They had all realized that their (unmanaged) and previously undocumented interfacing activities were making it impossible to have the time needed for effective spot sales. The interfacing activities they recognized as being critical to the achievement of the company's objectives were not being managed. We are pleased to report that particular interfacing activities were soon being very closely managed to eliminate the interfacing activity delays.

Interface mapping thus allows organizations to audit compliance to policies in a way that process mapping cannot. Not only can it document what is actually being done because the mapping is carried out and certified by the staff doing the work, it provides the platform for staff to be able to relate the activities each person is doing to the performance of the business. As we explore in Chapter 8, interface mapping is the mechanism to implant the best-practice management principle of relating the micro to the macro in a business.

The management challenge quantified

It is hardly surprising that managers are not confident that activities that must be done are being done if the organization primarily relies on process mapping to inform its change plans. Nor can they be confident that their staff are doing only the activities that have been defined. Interface mapping is thus perhaps the next important step to take, followed by setting up an ongoing process to direct and manage change. The process is needed because we do not know how one person can 'control' the activities of any reasonably sized organization. Figure 3.1 is repeated below as Figure 3.6 to demonstrate the difficulty in planning and deploying change. In an 800-person organization in our database the CEO, who has the authority to make any change needed, presides over the 18,725 activities routinely conducted in the business. However, this CEO and the management team were unaware of the existence of 15,419 of these, the critical but undocumented interfacing activities.

In contrast, the team leaders in position 3 who lack the authority and perspective to make strategic changes have the best grasp of the 924 detailed activities undertaken in their team even though 734 would probably not have been documented in the procedures, job descriptions or process maps.

Summary

This chapter has explored the nature and importance of the interfacing activities that are found in every organization and, with the example of the international shipping company, we have hinted at the way that interfacing activity data surrenders vital management information forensically.

FIGURE 3.6   The real management challenge

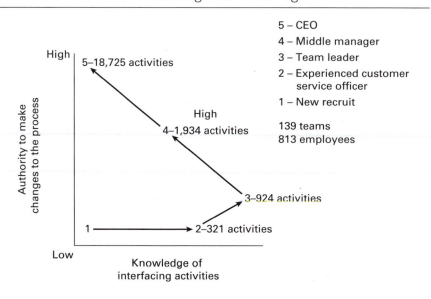

We have explained why the achievement of top-down, strategically focused change is particularly difficult in organizations where an interfacing activity knowledge gap exists. On one hand there is little awareness of the actual activities being done (we have proved that organizations are likely to document properly at best only one in four of the activities their staff routinely undertake). We have also begun to demonstrate the value that is embedded in this largely missing information.

It should therefore be of concern that change management is being undertaken without understanding interface activities.

What should be the logical role of a manager engaged in change or an external consultant? First, help those in the firm to develop the interface activity data. Then assist them to analyse it, so that the firm can strategically align its key processes by managing them consistent with the best-practice principles.

Appendix

Better understanding interfacing activity noise

All organizations suffer from high levels of interfacing activity noise, that is, interfacing activity that must be undertaken to correct errors, omissions or delays in material or information that is presented to a step in a business process.

Interfacing activity noise additionally includes the rework that occurs downstream as a direct result of the noise being allowed to enter the business process. We have referred to this downstream impact as the viral consequences. As already illustrated in Chapter 1, case study 1.1, unrecorded interfacing activity left unmanaged can kill. Our analysis of 117 organizations in Chapter 5 reveals that 33.6 per cent of employees' time (or $1\frac{2}{3}$ days per week for every 5 days worked) is wasted in interfacing activity noise. This interfacing activity noise lies buried out of sight because it is never properly recorded and therefore it cannot properly be managed.

An exercise

Case study 3.1 included many examples of interfacing activity noise which had not been managed. The case study was written in a way so that the causal factors, ie the interfacing activity noise drivers, are generally straightforward to deduce. For instance, the first document faxed through for completion by the Guatemalan doctor was unreadable so interfacing activity noise was required in order to have it refaxed in a larger typeface. The causal factor was that the typeface was too small to meet the business need. Each of these noise drivers can be related to one of the six management principles described in Chapter 2 which were:

a. wishing to be out front;

b. integration of effort;

c. Being disciplined to document what should be done and then adhering to it;

d. Focused on the customer value;

e. Being time based, eliminate time wasting activities;

f. Creation of strategic capabilities.

The reader might like to first review the case study to identify the various incidences of noise and note the causal factor or noise driver. Then it would be useful to relate them to the best practice management principles using a simple scale (0 – no relationship, 1 – some relationship and, 2 – significant relationship). Some examples have been inserted in the spread sheet on the next page.

Having completed the table it might now be instructive for the reader to consider the consequences of each of the incidences of noise. The consequences or risks arising in this case would provide a strategic assessment of priorities for change.

Uncovering **noise** in your own organization

Where should you start to look to find interfacing activity noise in your organization and how can you begin to understand it? As we have already said, interfacing activity and noise is to be found everywhere. Perhaps you have a call centre dealing with account enquiries or on a smaller scale a switchboard or a receptionist? As you walk into the call centre you will observe teams of

TABLE A3.2 Exercise to identify interface activity noise and causal factors and relate to best practice management principles.

Interface activity noise	Driver or causal factor	Out front	Integration of effort	Discipline	Customer Value	Time based	Capability creation
Faxed document not readable	Print too small	2	2	2	2	2	2
Fax not understandable	Only available in English	2	2	2	2	2	2
Ins company & airline form very similar	Should have been combined	2	2	2	1	2	2
Need to cancel the flight as there was not sufficient time to transfer patient to Frankfurt	Access to key information – a map of Europe with driving times	2	0	2	2	2	2
Chasing 'missing' information	No awareness of what had been received on unattended fax machine	2	2	2	2	2	2

people on the phone talking to customers, busy doing their work. Don't just observe, strike up a conversation with an operator. Ask him or her if there was any information they needed in the last few minutes which was not readily accessible. Ask whether having that information available would have saved time and perhaps enhanced the customer experience. Then ask what he or she had to do to get that information. You are now discussing interfacing activity. Interface activity noise would include the steps needed to get access to any elusive information. Next ask the operator whether there is any needed information the customer has difficulty providing. Ask how they help the customer to find the information, perhaps suggesting where to look for their account number on a statement. Ask them how they do it. This is all interfacing activity that could be avoided if, for example, the number was made more prominent on the document, web page or e-mail or always appeared in a particular position. Ask the operators if they ever have to deal with a customer who complains about something, for example having to wait or having been passed on from a first contact. Ask them what they say or do to deal with the situation. They will describe yet more interfacing activity noise steps to you. If they cannot answer the customer and have to call back, ask them about how they record this need and what they have to do before they can call back. Ask them who they have to seek authorization from, etc. These are some of the downstream or viral noise consequences.

What will quickly become obvious to you is that in many instances the interfacing activity noise could easily be eliminated. As we have tried to draw out in the exercise based on case study 3.1 above, you will find that understanding the interfacing activity noise will often uncover an obvious, low cost solution. 'Why would such obvious solutions not have been addressed?' you will find yourself asking. Perhaps the transparency provided by interface mapping alone justifies the effort involved. However the key is to be able to justify doing something about it – understanding the cost of the various noise drivers is critical to getting action (or discarding the many inconsequential noise occurrences). If this is the case then the feature to accumulate interfacing activity by causal factor across the whole end to end business process will allow you to discard or justify the needed action. Perhaps your discussion of obvious solutions will uncover the barriers to effecting the change. Often these barriers will be related to the lack of authority of the person suffering the noise to make the changes needed. This will be especially so if the noise emanates from another part of the business or from outside the organization. Interface mapping with an across the business tool will allow the major incidences to be justified and the justification will, if properly managed, engage those with the authority to effect the change.

Seeing noise everywhere

Now think yourself into a position in another industry, perhaps retail and a departmental store. You have just purchased some items that you need to pick up from the back of the store.

You arrive at the unattended counter and press the bell for service...

Or, imagine you are making a claim from your private health insurer and you download the forms from their website. You are a little confused and decide to call the help line where you have to enter your policy number which you have difficulty finding. You are then placed in a queue...

Maybe it is simply that your new washing machine has broken down and you can't remember where you put the receipt...

Interfacing activities, business strategy and business process innovation

04

Objectives

In this chapter we will first demonstrate the inadequacies of the widely used activity categorization of value adding and non-value. We then reveal the Core Support Discretionary Noise (CSDN) framework used in the XeP3 interface mapping tool, which has proved to be very powerful in over 400 organizational applications consistently to drive strategic alignment of resources, and productivity and process innovations.

While the interfacing and functional activity data described in Chapter 3 provides extremely fertile ground for finding process improvement opportunities, the relatively large size of interfacing and functional activity databases is likely to deter all but the most determined business process enthusiast from exploiting their richness strategically. Further, and with justification, it could be argued that the use of the data without a new and more relevant analytical framework would merely allow interface mapping to be used to put existing Six Sigma or Lean programmes on steroids. We argue in this chapter that something new is required to improve the efficiency of the data mining and analysis of process steps. We therefore develop the foundations for the mechanism to generate robust and relevant linkages to strategy so that strategic capability, not just efficient business process, results.

The need for strategic activity categorization

We begin with a historical example. Business strategy has always been firmly founded on military endeavour and therefore, drawing on Bungay (2000), we have chosen to visit one of the more recent and well-researched battles, the Battle of Britain. We will use this to illustrate the need for new thinking on the nature of activity categorization to be used for forensic analysis of strategic business processes.

World War 2 broke out in 1939, having been triggered by the invasion of Poland by the Germans. The largely obsolete 600 aircraft Polish airforce was eliminated from the conflict almost immediately with many of its aircraft being destroyed on the ground. The bombers that made the attacks were protected by the German Bf 109E single-seat fighters that swarmed overhead and made repeated low-flying attacks with cannon fire when the opportunity presented. This fighter cover allowed virtually unopposed attacks on specific targets, including the terror bombing of the city of Warsaw as well as key military targets. This aerial assault allowed the German infantry, supported by powerful armoured divisions, to sweep through the country. Poland capitulated within days.

The same Blitzkrieg strategy was employed in May 1940 when the German armies drove through the Ardennes forest to overrun Belgium, Holland and France in just weeks. The Germans employed the same powerful capability, terror bombing of key population centres such as Rotterdam, following the early elimination of the 1,800 aircraft French air force. Again, many aircraft were caught where they were at their most vulnerable, neatly lined up on the ground. The victory was achieved so rapidly that a high proportion of the French aircraft never even left their storage locations.

The RAF with its modern fighter squadrons proved to be impotent in the face of the German onslaught. The RAF was able only marginally to slow the German advance. The RAF therefore lost aircraft and precious pilots for little gain. The result, in the dying days of May and the first few days of June, was a disastrous rout and the almost miraculous evacuation from Dunkirk of 364,628 men, the bulk of the defeated British Expeditionary Force (BEF) together with a large contingent of the French army. The BEF left behind more than their reputation as a fighting force, and their morale on the beaches of Northern France. They left most of their war material with the result that just three anti-tank guns were able to be deployed to defend the beaches around Dover. The Dover beaches formed the stretch of coast that had been identified as the preferred landing zone for the German invasion force, code named Operation Sea Lion. Britain was on her knees.

When the Dunkirk evacuation began Churchill had been Prime Minister for three weeks. Just four weeks later the Battle of Britain began. The date battle commenced was 10 July 1940. The RAF faced the fight of its life against a nightmare scenario no one could have countenanced just two months earlier. The opposing forces would be just 30 miles away arrayed along the Channel coast. The opposing forces included 1,107 Bf 109E single-seat fighters and the 1,808 bombers, all of which had been quickly moved up to the captured French, Belgian and Dutch airfields.

At the start of the battle therefore the cards were stacked very much in favour of the Luftwaffe. The German Bf 109E fighter squadrons outnumbered the RAF's Spitfire and Hurricane force of 754 by 3:2. This same RAF, just weeks previously with three times as many aircraft when working with the 1,800 aircraft French air force, had been quite impotent against the Luftwaffe. The Germans could well have been forgiven for their expectation that, within weeks, they would have destroyed the RAF by easily exceeding the 5:1 kill ratio (the German target set by Osterkamp – he calculated that he could sustain a 20 per cent loss ratio to leave the Luftwaffe with 900 fighters to support the invasion needed to dominate the skies over the invasion beaches). The 3,000 invasion barges to carry up to 500,000 men, which were being assembled in the Channel ports, would then be directed to head for Dover.

The German advance then stopped dead. Why? The initiative had been with the Germans just as it had been in their wildly successful Polish, Belgian, Dutch, French and Norwegian campaigns. Popular myth at the time attributed the victory to the technical superiority of the Spitfire. Bungay however demonstrates convincingly that this was not the case. He presents three well-researched arguments. First, the Spitfire was not the predominant RAF single-seat fighter; in fact 70 per cent of the RAF's single-seat fighter force was made up of Hawker Hurricanes, which were lower performing and cheaper to build. Secondly the Spitfire did not outclass the Bf 109E; indeed the two aircraft had very similar performance characteristics (see Table 4.1)

TABLE 4.1   Comparison of Spitfire and Bf 109E

	Spitfire I	Bf 109E
Fuel capacity	85 gallons	88 gallons
Fuel consumption:		
all-out level	89 gal/hr at 17,000 ft	69 gal/hr at 14,763 ft
climbing	81 gal/hr at 12,000 ft	66 gal/hr at 16,404 ft
Dive speed limitations	450 mph	466 mph
Service ceiling	34,700 ft	33,792 ft

and arguably the German aircraft marginally outperformed the Spitfire with its superior fire power and fuel injection system that overcame the Spitfire's tendency to lose power in tight manoeuvres. Thirdly, the Luftwaffe fighter force far outnumbered the RAF. How could the Germans have lost?

The information in Table 4.1 shows that the Spitfire (and the Bf 109E) had a limited endurance of about an hour, of which 10 to 15 minutes would be spent gaining height. The RAF fighters therefore did not have the endurance to patrol the skies to wait for the enemy to appear. Had they adopted this tactic they would have been unlikely to have found the enemy and would have been vulnerable to being caught on the ground refuelling and re-arming as had been the case all too often with the doomed Polish and the French airforces. The only way the relatively small RAF numbers could provide an effective response was to achieve, in business terms, a very high utilization of their equipment, that is, the RAF fighters had to spend a high proportion of their in-air time sharing the enemy's air space. They had therefore to be efficiently positioned in the right place at the right height with full tanks to intercept the many incoming German bomber raids at the right time.

This positioning had, in modern parlance, to be achieved just in time. This meant that activities had to be performed that would drive a successful outcome – in this instance: detect the size, distance and height of an emerging German attack using radar; track the path and height of the incoming threat through the Royal Observer Corps; plot the resulting information in the control centres. This had to be done in such a way as to enable the various squadrons to be deployed at the right time, just in time; and then vector in each squadron to the German forces through direct communication – pilot-to-control radio communication. This was the Dowding system, which had been put in place by early 1940.

Revisiting Chapter 2 and calibrating our international research, consider this question. Did the RAF, under the direction of Air Chief Marshal Hugh Caswell Tremenheere Dowding, 1st Baron Dowding GCB, GCVO, CMG, operate a best-practice business process?

The six management principles associated with focusing business processes on strategic intent are listed below. In Chapter 2 we showed that all six of them needed to be in place. They are:

- having the desire to be out front;
- ensuring integration of effort;
- being disciplined;
- creating customer value;
- being time-based;
- creating strategic capabilities.

Without doubt, the RAF was required by the British Government to be out front. It literally had to lead the pack and win against the German onslaught simply to ensure that Britain and the free world survived. It faced the most powerful military machine ever assembled. The RAF set out under the Dowding system to strive actively to enhance creation of customer value. It positioned the pilots in their fighters in the sun above the immediate path of the incoming bombers to give them the ability to use their time effectively and to be advantageously positioned, that is unseen and above, for attack.

The Dowding system was time-based. In positioning the fighter squadrons, advantageously and just in time, over the incoming bombers and their escorts, the RAF was practically never caught on the ground before or after action and wasted no precious fuel stooging around looking for the enemy. The system was integrated. Large, widely dispersed organizations such as the radar stations, the Royal Observer Corp, the plotting centres, the ground crews and the fighter pilots all had to perform activities in an integrated way to achieve the desired outcome. The system was disciplined. There is overwhelming evidence that the business processes had been well thought through and documented before the war began and they were invariably adhered to even at the height of the battle. Finally, strategic capabilities were clearly created and used.

The RAF, judged by its performance against what was then the most powerful of military forces, must by definition have been a leading organization. It does also satisfy the six management principles test.

Relating value-added activities to a strategic framework

The need for core and support activities

While the RAF's just-in-time positioning activities described above are undoubtedly value adding, some of them, the performance drivers (for example the communication from the radar detection and observation and tracking, the immediate updating of the nature and location of the threat in the plotting centres and the just-in-time deployment of the aircraft) need to be described differently because they made the difference between success and failure – according to Bungay they actually determined the outcome of the battle. Without these core value-driving activities the RAF would have suffered the same fate as the Polish and French forces before them – they would have flown around looking for the enemy, been in the wrong place when needed and would have been caught napping on the ground.

It is instructive to note that when these core activities were not carried out then the strategic objectives of knocking out the enemy were not achieved either. For instance, Dowding's system was not understood or supported by everyone. Some argued strongly against using the Dowding system in favour of the 'Big Wing' where squadrons were scrambled early to then expend time and precious fuel meeting up with other squadrons to form up. There is little evidence that the Big Wings ever successfully engaged the enemy. They were not compliant to four of the management principles focusing on strategic intent – creating customer value, ensuring integration of effort, being time-based and being disciplined.

Further evidence of the effect of this flawed approach arose in the defence of Malta. Malta was a vital link in the chain of supply needed to win in North Africa in 1942 and was almost overrun when Air Vice-Marshall Keith Park, who had been in day-to-day command in the Battle of Britain, arrived. The Big Wing approach was again in use. By the time the defenders found their attackers, the bombs had been released and they were fast approaching their own territory. On 25 July 1942 Park issued his Fighter Interception Plan, which required his controllers to place a squadron in the sun above the incoming bomber force, a squadron to engage the bomber escorts and a squadron to focus on a head-on attack on the heavily laden bombers. In the first half of July 34 allied aircraft had been destroyed on the ground. In the latter half of July just four were destroyed. The bombing was virtually halted in three weeks, again, with 1,819 German sorties in July reducing to 391 in September.

We argue therefore that these value-driving core activities are something very special. They are the 'DNA' of high-performing processes and therefore, high-performing organizations, and must be singled out. Further, these core activities are the process embodiment of the six principles focused on delivering strategic outcomes.

We can only speculate that Dowding must have had these six management principles firmly in his mind when he was planning his successful Battle of Britain system. However, in Chapter 2 we gave an example of a retail pharmaceutical company that wanted to improve its sales performance significantly. We described the dilemma the sales managers faced. They had two 'rogue' sales people who would not carry out specific orders given to them to go out and get orders when the month's sales targets were obviously unlikely to be met. The sales managers were wishing to dismiss them but were hesitating because the two 'rogues' were by far their best business getters. This was a real case study where the data actually confirmed that the rogue sales people had fully adopted the six principles against all odds – and their 'system' was ultimately adopted by the company resulting in huge performance gains.

It is instructive to look at extracts of the different sets of activities, all of which can be classified as value adding, which the rogue and run-of-the-mill sales people reported by interfacing mapping their activities (see Table 4.2).

The data confirmed first that the whole sales force was doing what was asked of them. All ensured that existing stock was counted. All recommended product order levels to the pharmacy manager and all presented new products to their customers. What differed was how they achieved what was required of them – the differences lying in the interfacing activities they conducted.

The rogue sales people persuaded the pharmacy managers to get the stock levels counted and justified it to them by saying that they could then add

TABLE 4.2 Comparison of sales force activity

Main activity	Rogue sales people	General practice
Shelf stock management	Get pharmacy staff to count stock and e-mail day before visit	Count stock at beginning of visit
	Review stock to identify opportunities for additional lines or variation in levels	Complete order document for pharmacy manager to sign
		Send order document to supplier
	Recommend ordering needs to pharmacy manager	
		While checking stock, out sort items with out-of-date-codes
		Generate credit note request
Handle returns		Package out-of-date stock and return to company
		Present all new lines to pharmacy manager
Introduce new products	Recommend relevant new lines and order quantity changes	
	Prepare training packages on features of new lines	
	Train all sales staff on features and benefits of new and underperforming lines so staff can recommend to retail customer	

value by spending their time thinking through what products and levels to go for in the quiet of their homes rather than being hassled to try to do the job on the run in the middle of a busy retail store. In contrast, the run-of-the-mill sales people spent most of their time in store counting the stock and writing out an order without necessarily checking what should be sold in that neighbourhood or being able to think properly about volumes. The result was the run-of-the- mill sales people had then to deal with the consequences of their previous actions – manage the return of out-of-date products, which occupied another chunk of their time.

All the sales people managed to present new products to the pharmacy manager. However, the rogue sales people went on to spend most of their in-store time training the store's staff on how and when to recommend these new products and grow the sales of the existing range.

The core activities are boxed in the table. The relationship between conducting these core activities and impressive, profitable, business growth was confirmed by statistical correlation. When these new processes were first implemented across the country, the sales volumes quickly grew by 30 per cent and returns became history.

As with the RAF, an examination of how the rogues implemented the six management principles shows that they had created high-performance strategically aligned processes that they followed. The rogues were determined to be out front and even defied their management to achieve this. They were focused on creating customer value – they focused their effort on ensuring that the stores got the right product mix on their shelves and added further client value by training the store's staff in when and how to recommend the company's products, thus benefiting their firm and the store. They were time-based, they got the stock counts e-mailed to them just in time so that their order recommendations would be up to date and they got the count efficiently by engaging the store's staff in the process. They clearly integrated their efforts with those of the customer (if not with their management!). Undoubtedly, they were disciplined and had created, judged by the results, strategic capability. They had created a high-performing process according to the six management principles, which they had implemented through the highlighted core activities.

Support and core activities

We began to divide value-adding activities routinely into core and support 20 years ago. Support activities are in the majority and are the many activities that need to be performed routinely to provide a service, in effect the functional activities that the run-of-the-mill sales force was doing. In the RAF example, these support activities would include refuelling and re-arming aircraft, transmitting orders to scramble and maintaining radar installations on line. More generally in business, support activities would include entering an order, printing a production schedule, setting up a file for a claim, preparing board meeting minutes, producing salary slips, etc. A business cannot exist without doing support activities but spending more time doing them will not increase the bottom line or improve performance.

Core activities, in contrast, can be statistically correlated with driving success. Examples would include, for the RAF, determining exactly when to scramble aircraft and, for the pharmaceutical company, training the retail outlet sales staff on when and how to offer products. More generally, core activities are likely to be upselling a customer on a larger order, defining a production schedule to increase machine loading, assessing an insurance claim and assessing staff performance against specific criteria. In contrast to support activities, the more core activity that is done, the greater is the resulting increase in performance or profit.

Relationship between core activity and noise

There is another important insight buried in the arguments about core activity developed above. Bear in mind the management principle of creating customer value and consider just-in-time. Now revisit the system advocated by the Dowding doubters. It is easy to classify some of the activity, actually interfacing activity, time spent to interface with the enemy, as non value adding. The resource time wasted forming up the Big Wing and all of the resource time the Big Wing then went on to waste wandering around the sky trying to find the invading German aircraft is interfacing (with enemy engagement) activity and must clearly be non value adding. Further, this wastage of time is a direct consequence of not heeding or using the core activities involving the radar, the Observer Corps and the plotting centres to define when and where to deploy the resources of pilots and aircraft. What a waste. They committed the time of dozens of precious aircraft and scarce pilots to stooging around the skies just in case they could find some Germans. One can speculate that had the Dowding doubters prevailed, the outcome of the war might have been very different.

From a strategic perspective we argue that there is a need to classify this type of wasted time separately as interfacing activity noise. Process noise is non value adding time that is a consequence of not doing the strategically correct core activity earlier in the process.

Let's revisit the pharmaceutical company's run-of-the-mill sales people's activities. The sorting out, documenting and authorizing of credit for out-of-date stock was only being done because of prior process failure, the overstocking caused by not doing the right core activity of setting the right stock levels on previous visits. It was therefore interfacing activity noise. There were three potential reasons for this failure. First, it might have been because of the impracticality of expecting the sales staff to work out sensible order levels while subjected to the hurly burly of the store (a failure in the management principle of being disciplined). Or, second, it might perhaps have been because the sales people thought their job was to merchandize the stock and therefore concentrate on appearance and orderliness (either a failure in the management principles of ensuring integration of effort or of being disciplined). Third, and the main cause, that in company terms was much more serious, was that the sales people were directed by their management to deliberately overstock to ensure that the sales managers' personal goal of meeting their sales target was met (a failure in the principle of ensuring integration of effort – the sales managers had actually lost sight of the company goal, that was to maximize sales profitability and not maximize returns). So the whole of the effort associated with returned, out-of-date stock was coded as noise. This noise extended way beyond the orbit of the sales force. All the time spent recording, transporting and destroying the returned stock elsewhere in the business was also coded as noise as was all the time the finance function spent accounting for it and issuing credit notes. The boundaries even extended to the purchasing, manufacturing and logistics time spent producing and distributing the wasted product.

Interfacing activity noise is always measured in resource hours. It is the time staff and managers devote to carrying out activities that only need to be done because of prior failure; that is, failure to do the necessary core activity called for in the strategy of the organization. Interfacing activity noise levels in organizations are often high and it is not unusual to find 50 per cent of staff and managers' time absorbed entirely in noise activity. The primary cause of this noise activity is failure to manage interfacing activity.

Interfacing activity noise drives process innovation

Interfacing activity noise, as described above, is the downstream wasted activity carried out by staff and managers as a consequence of an organization's failure to carry out core activity earlier in the process that would have driven the required strategic outcomes. We have examined in some depth above the strategically aligned business process, or strategic capability, which was developed by the RAF under Dowding's stewardship and enabled the Battle of Britain to be won so decisively. Further, we have shown how the departure from elements of this strategically aligned process by the doubter generated a great deal of waste; that is, interfacing activity noise. Further, in the pharmaceutical company we described how the failure to establish sensible product stock levels for retail pharmacies generated interfacing activity noise that permeated the business.

We came to the conclusion that noise is an incredibly powerful tool to drive process innovation. The innovation process is:

- identify the interfacing activity noise;
- accumulate it by causal factor;
- prioritize according to strategic intent for the most significant noise drivers;
- design and deploy the required change;
- measure achievement;
- achieve gains while increasing compliance to the management principles focusing on strategic intent and, thereby, advance to world's best practice.

To illustrate this, let's turn the RAF's and pharmaceutical company's situations around and look at the detailed content of their business processes forensically through an interfacing activity noise lens. In the case of the RAF if the time spent forming up the Big Wing and stooging around looking for the enemy had been captured (it is interfacing activity), and then coded as interfacing activity noise (it is clearly non value adding) then this would prompt some key questions: How do we eliminate the time wasted in forming up Big Wings? How do we eliminate the need to stooge around looking for the enemy and potentially running out of fuel? How do we ensure that we are engaging the enemy and not be caught on the ground while refuelling?

Answers to the questions would quickly lead to the identification of the need to manage the interfacing activity by scrambling the aircraft just in time, positioning the aircraft in the sun above the incoming raiders, etc. We contend that this would lead to the development of a system like Dowding's. Further, if the aircraft subsequently landed to be refuelled without enemy contact (as was likely with the Big Wing) then this landing, provisioning and take off (interfacing) activity would be coded as noise activity and would prompt more questions that would add weight to the resource benefits obtained from a system like Dowding's.

Of course, we don't know how Dowding came up with the idea for his system or even whether he thought of forming up time and stooging around as interfacing activity noise, although it obviously is. He must, however, have gone through this type of disciplined thinking. In contrast, the collection and analysis of the functional and interfacing activity data for the pharmaceutical company's sales force really did happen. The data was developed and used to generate the insights. Early analysis in week 4 revealed the high levels of noise, for example the noise activity caused by the return of product that was out of date. This wastage of resource prompted some very hard questions. The questions centred on why the mechanism for setting stock levels in retail pharmacies did not work and why the two highest-performing sales people never had returns. The interfacing data allowed comparison of the activity footprints of the two high-performing sales people, the rogues, with the others. This led directly to the identification and confirmation of the nature of the core activity needed to address both the returns and the performance issues. Discreet discussions with sales managers resulted in the two rogue sales people being reclassified as role models. Sales managers implemented variations on the rogue processes to drive sales. This analysis of interfacing activity noise drove the business process innovation that delivered sales penetration increases of 30 per cent over a six-month period and dramatic margin growth as return handling became the exception.

There are many, many examples in every industry of where forensic analysis of what is causing noise has immediately led to innovative and often low-cost solutions being found. An unlikely example was encountered from the interface mapping that was used to prepare an airport to handle double peak-volume traffic for an international event. Here, managers had set an objective to improve equipment serviceability to 99.9 per cent. They recognized that the then relatively low availability on aerobridges, escalators, moving walkways and even toilet cleanliness was a major barrier to them meeting their peak throughput objectives. They commissioned an interface mapping analysis of the functional and interfacing activities in their maintenance processes. When coded the data revealed many things. Among them were the high levels of noise associated with travelling to get parts and travelling to fix faults. Taking the first noise driver, the fitters were being despatched to fix a problem without full information of the nature of the fault. The fitter might then have to travel up to 1.5 kilometers from his or her workshop to find out what parts were needed, then do the whole journey again to go back to stores for the needed items, perhaps something as mundane as a light bulb. The size of the noise opportunity prompted the obvious questions and it was quickly ascertained that the maintenance system had features that were not being used. It had been designed to record the nature of faults and the characteristics of the equipment at each location but had never been used because recording had not been seen as a value-adding activity. The features were quickly switched on and recording the nature of the fault at the time a fault was reported became a core activity to enable fitters to make the journey just once. Time and cost was saved, effective capacity was increased and equipment uptime and utilization met managers' targets as a result of the process innovation generated by interface activity noise.

In the second example involving the airport it was found that there was no urgency attached to entering reported faults in the system because the system was being used primarily for costing. As a consequence, the fitters' data showed that they would frequently attend minor issues, such as a leaking tap, only to find on return to the workshop that they were immediately despatched to the next washroom to deal with a similar problem. The fitters took pains to ensure that this frustrating activity was coded as interfacing activity noise. The person responsible for inputting the data into the maintenance system was the first to realize, rather gleefully we thought at the time, that entering this data should be a core activity and should be done immediately a fault was reported. At the end of a three-month period, availability of aerobridges and moving walkways was raised to the 99.9 per cent target needed. Maintenance costs fell and the vendor of the maintenance software began to use the airport installation as its showcase site.

There are thousands of examples of process innovation generated by interfacing activity noise in our files, each yielding high returns in industries ranging from banking; insurance; funds management; distribution; retail; automotive parts; automotive service; food manufacturing; road, rail and air transport; regulatory bodies; utility companies; call centres; hospitals; etc.

Noise as an indicator of potential

Most people, and especially those holding positions where they are dependent on others to receive their work input (most of us), are quick to grasp that noise is a potential provider of huge benefit. Then the questions they most often ask include:

- How much noise do we have in our business?
- How do we compare with other organizations?
- What proportion of our time could we redeploy to driving performance without incurring any capital costs?
- How soon can we get the results?

Answers to these questions and more will be found in the next two chapters but as a rule of thumb organizations can expect to free up about 50 per cent of the interfacing activity noise by implementing business process innovations involving low or zero investment in about six months. The average levels of interfacing activity noise for the last 117 applications of interface mapping absorbed 33.6 per cent of total staff time – $1\frac{2}{3}$ days in every five-day week worked so there is a surfeit of opportunity.

Summary

In this chapter we have described an activity categorization tool that enables the massive amounts of data generated by interfacing mapping to be coded strategically. We have exposed the need to distinguish between the value-adding elements that drive strategic outcomes and those that merely support the day-to-day operation of a business or business process. We have also illustrated the use of this strategic categorization against military and business examples and further related the categories to the best-practice management principles described in Chapter 2.

We have advanced the case for a new framework to be used for the examination of the activities carried out routinely in all businesses. We have argued that the rather simplistic categories of value and non value adding are a 'cop out'. They distract people from drawing the vital direct links between an organization's strategy and the core activities that drive the strategic outcomes required. We have argued that the use of these new categories enables proper analysis of business processes to displace the widespread use of judgement and experience in planning change. In particular we have proposed that value-adding activities should be broken into two categories – core and support activities – where core activities by definition drive strategic outcomes. Finally in this chapter, we have fully exposed the power of interface activity noise, first as a predictor of the potential to improve performance and productivity and second as the mechanism to drive process innovation and manage an organization's critical interface activities.

Interface
activity noise
The foundation
of strategic
change capability

05

Objective

This chapter focuses on the analysis of functional and interfacing activity data in the database of 117 organizations. The objective is to demonstrate the value of more comprehensive analysis categories introduced in the last chapter.

The data

As described in Chapter 3, we have taken part in over 400 projects to interface map and analyse the functional and interfacing activity variously for parts of organizations, entire organizations and multiple organizations that make up industries' value chains. We have hands-on experience of interface mapping in various languages and cultures including: New Zealand, Fiji, the United States, Canada, the UK, France, Spain, Italy, Argentina, Mexico, Hong Kong, Malaysia, Mongolia and Japan. In every case, the activity mapping has been undertaken by the staff in each of the organizations to obviate the common complaint that maps and procedures typically address only a fraction of the activities routinely carried out. In order to obtain the data, the staff were always trained and supported to document and quantify everything they routinely did. The data is collected by team and held in organizational databases.

TABLE 5.1   Database parameters

Number of staff who documented their work	13,657
Number of activities documented	395,832
Total hours per month	1,775,377
Annual salary bill	US $1.45 billion

When we initially began interface mapping we used spreadsheets but it soon became clear that purpose-built tools were needed to analyse data by function and business process, accumulate interfacing activity noise by driver, model alternative scenarios, plan and manage change initiatives, monitor achievement and keep procedures up to date. Team-based interface mapping avoids the potentially threatening focus on the individual. Further, it takes advantage of the knowledge of the whole team both to validate and certify the data before proceeding with analysis. In addition, staff retain possession of their data and this provides them with a foundation they fully understand on which change initiatives can be built – the usefulness of which will be explored in later chapters.

The most recent 117 interface mapping databases were assembled for the analysis undertaken to support this book. The composite database therefore includes domestic and international organizations in a wide range of industries including manufacturing, professional services, banking and finance, regulatory bodies, transport and distribution, energy, call centres, pharmaceuticals, health, education, defence and not-for-profits. The largest organization in this sample is a high-achieving electricity distributor that employed 813 staff. The staff there documented that they routinely undertook 13,382 different functional and interfacing activities in order to carry out their work. Other examples in the database include a food manufacturing plant with 523 staff who reported that they routinely undertook 13,283 activities, and the head office of a retail management company that employed 237 staff who routinely undertook 6,642 activities. Table 5.1 shows the database parameters.

The data reveals that 196 activities are undertaken by the average organizational team of 5.6 staff (see Table 5.2) and 163 of these are interfacing activities.

A huge opportunity

Waste of the staff resource – 33.6 per cent

Analysis of the database provides an insight into the opportunities that exist in the average organization. The most significant finding from interface

TABLE 5.2 The average work team has 5.6 staff and routinely conducts 196 discrete activities

	Average
Number of staff	119
Number of teams who collected data	21
Average team size (staff)	5.6
Total – functional and interfacing activities recorded and quantified	3,374
Average number of functional and interfacing activities per team	196

mapping and categorizing the 395,832 activities is that one-third of the staff and manager's time (33.6 per cent, see Figure 5.1) is routinely absorbed in interfacing activity noise. Being rather harsh, this is the resource that organizations commit every day to upsetting their customers and employees, raising their staffing costs per transaction by 50 per cent and distracting the organization from its performance drivers.

Interfacing activity noise consists of those interfacing activities, including checking, correcting and chasing, which are necessary to enable 'stuff' to enter the business and be passed from one business process step to the next. As already established, it includes both the work that needs to be done to enable difficulties at entry to be resolved and the downstream effort required to compensate for not managing prior interface activities properly. Noise interfacing activities are therefore often mistakenly classified as essential. This is because if they are not performed to compensate for the problem associated with a particular transaction at that step in the business process, the 'stuff' cannot be processed. Clearly, in a best-practice organization upstream interfaces would have been properly managed by designing and deploying core activities that prevent the viral interfacing activity noise from entering the business process in the first place. It would thus prevent the further disruption downstream from occurring.

To work with 33.6 per cent noise, 1⅔ days out of every five days worked by each person is clearly a costly waste of resources and a powerful indicator that previous improvement programmes have largely failed because they have left too much money on the table and too much disruption in the business processes. We do, however, find that in these organizations there is little wrong with the change approach they have used. The problem invariably lies in poor definition of the change needs, as the role of interfacing activity noise in highlighting non-compliance with the six management principles focusing on strategic intent is neither recognized nor understood.

FIGURE 5.1 Failure to manage interfacing activity absorbs 33.6 per cent of everyone's time

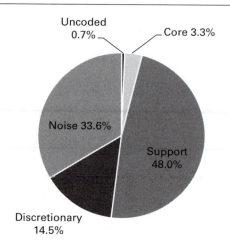

All sectors suffer from noise

Table 5.3 lists in industry sequence some 41 organizations that have undertaken interface mapping. These organizations have been selected randomly from the 117 organizations in the database and are presented here to illustrate the ubiquitous nature of noise. The database itself, as we have stated before, contains two organizations that can be found in Australia's top 10 listed companies and a number of most highly respected international organizations. Where the database contains several different organizations operating in the same sector, a number of entries have been included to emphasize the general point we are making on the ubiquitous nature of waste from interfacing activity noise.

You will see that two of the entries in Table 5.3 are marked with an asterisk*. The asterisk indicates that the strategic activity coding (CSDN) framework was adjusted to meet the specific management requests in these organizations. The hospital's managers required all activities covered by the formal training of a medical practitioner or a nurse (all aspects of a medical procedure, applying and changing dressings, etc) to be coded as support activities. This meant that rework caused by technical errors, for example the task of re-application by a more experienced nurse when a trainee nurse made a mistake in applying a dressing, was coded as support. This had the effect of materially reducing the noise percentage and increasing support. The interface mapping thus highlighted the cost of failure to manage the interfacing activities in the administrative tasks.

A similar issue was encountered with the pharmaceutical sales and marketing team where all of the time spent on face-to-face contact with

TABLE 5.3 Noise affects every type of organization

	Core %	Support %	Discretionary %	Noise %
Airline operations	0.1	48.0	19.1	32.8
Airport ground operations	0.1	43.9	21.4	34.7
Retail bank	3.7	30.5	24.3	41.4
Retail bank	6.3	42.4	19.2	32.1
Call centre	1.0	51.5	9.5	37.6
Computer maintenance	0.9	55.3	12.1	27.3
Finance company	3.8	45.6	19.1	31.3
Finance company	2.4	44.1	18.3	34.7
Finance processing centre	0.1	55.2	5.8	36.4
Finance processing centre	0.4	63.7	11.4	24.5
Financial services business	0.2	51.7	15.1	32.9
Government regulator	0.3	63.5	11.3	24.9
Government supply business	1.8	49.8	12.2	36.1
Hospital*	4.6	73.8	5.6	13.4
Insurance	0.8	35.1	19.1	45.0
Insurance	2.7	46.1	20.0	31.2
Insurance	0.5	33.0	15.6	50.5
Leisure	0.2	38.3	11.9	49.6
Manufacturing – food	1.7	44.4	18.0	35.8
Manufacturing – food	0.9	62.3	5.3	31.5
Manufacturing – home wares	2.1	41.4	5.5	51.0
Manufacturing – home wares	6.7	49.6	13.1	30.6

(*Continued*)

TABLE 5.3   Noise affects every type of organization (*Continued*)

	Core %	Support %	Discretionary %	Noise %
Manufacturing – packaging/paper	0.2	56.0	7.6	36.2
Manufacturing – packaging/paper	5.4	50.5	10.2	28.3
Mortgage broker	5.9	56.8	2.8	34.5
Mortgage broker	9.7	53.2	15.6	21.5
Not for profit	1.5	28.2	42.9	27.4
Office supplies	0.1	33.5	18.6	45.6
Pharmaceuticals – sales and marketing*	21.9	41.4	7.6	28.6
Primary industry body	0.5	41.1	20.0	38.4
Professional institute	0.5	49.4	19.4	30.1
Recycling business	10.8	49.0	6.7	28.2
Shopping centre operator	7.6	41.5	17.1	33.8
Telecommunications supplier	10.5	27.6	15.4	46.5
Transport/logistics	0.1	53.0	4.7	42.2
Transport/logistics	1.6	43.4	20.0	34.9
University	3.4	64.3	9.5	22.7
Utility distributor	1.5	65.7	4.8	22.4
Utility distributor	0.4	39.0	31.4	29.2
Warehouse	1.9	61.9	5.0	29.1
Warehouse	0.0	56.7	11.7	31.6

NOTE: Discretionary activity will be discussed later in the book.

customers was coded to core. This had the effect of lowering the recorded discretionary and noise activities when compared with the other organizations using the tools. The insistence by this organization's management illustrates the difficulty in some organizations of getting management to think strategically about their business processes.

Table 5.3 is quite representative of the whole database of 117 organizations. The average of the core activity is 3.4 per cent, which mirrors the whole database average of 3.3 per cent. The minimum recorded in the table is 0.1 per cent core and the maximum is 21.9 per cent, which is the sales force with the strategically incorrectly applied categorization. The next largest core percentage is 10.8 per cent in a recycling business.

The average for interfacing activity noise for the businesses in Table 5.3 is 33.2 per cent, which again closely mirrors the 33.6 per cent noise level in the full database. The minimum level of noise is 13.4 per cent, which was recorded by the hospital, but here the management decided to exclude surgical and technical errors and omissions.

High levels of noise

Every sector can suffer from high levels of interfacing activity noise. What might be expected, in view of their early adoption of continuous improvement programmes, is that the manufacturing and distribution sectors might on average have done a better job of managing their interfaces. An argument could be made that their earlier adoption of these techniques should have led to lower incidences of interfacing activity noise in their business processes. The data shows that this is not the case. However, this is hardly surprising as there is no evidence that interfacing activity has been properly documented in manufacturing or for that matter any industries. Further analysis of the database demonstrates that high levels of interface activity noise are not confined to particular industries.

Organizations with a higher incidence of interfacing activity noise, that is where noise consumes more than 40 per cent of the organization's people resources, were found in manufacturing, energy, transport, education, supply, regulatory bodies, banking and finance, insurance and retail. There were a number of examples of finance and manufacturing businesses in the database. The full database contains nine manufacturing organizations (food, automotive, paper and packaging) and nine financial services organizations (retail banking, insurance, finance). Noise ranges in these two industries are reported in Table 5.4. There is a remarkable consistency in the data between organizations in these two very different industries. The consistency can be seen in the average as well as the upper and lower bounds. The upper bound, close to 50 per cent, indicates that, in each case, half of the organization's staff are engaged full time in this wasteful interfacing activity noise.

The highest level of noise ever recorded by an organization's staff using interface mapping is 73.1 per cent; that is, 3½ days per week, every week, of everyone's time was spent handling the effect of failure to manage the internal interface issues and those with their customers and their advisers. The organization is a major international player in the life insurance industry. A staggering 7 out of every 10 employees thus on average spend all of

TABLE 5.4 Interfacing activity noise in manufacturing and in banking and finance

	Average noise	Upper boundary	Lower boundary
Manufacturing	35.4%	47%	31%
Banking and finance	36.9%	51%	31%

their time correcting errors and omissions, chasing up missing information, duplicating tasks already undertaken or handling the viral consequences – and, to repeat, this is from data prepared and coded by the staff themselves.

Every team suffers from noise

Noise is to be found everywhere where people work, that is in every team in every organization. Table 5.5 supports this point. It contains 10 commonly found functional teams. These examples of different teams have been taken from a range of organizations and industries. They are particular teams, not averages, and should not therefore be used as benchmarks. Every team suffers from interfacing activity noise. The lowest level of noise in Table 5.5

TABLE 5.5 Noise is found in every team

	Core %	Support %	Discretionary %	Noise %
Insurance claims team	1.8	30.2	11.3	54.8
IT department	0.7	26.8	25.5	47.0
Purchasing team	1.2	41.6	11.1	46.0
Production planning team	5.6	47.6	7.6	39.2
Sales team	6.8	40.3	15.2	37.7
Payroll team	0.1	46.8	17.7	35.5
HR department	0.6	44.0	20.1	35.3
Hospital outpatients	0.8	57.5	8.7	33.0
Finance team	4.7	22.1	43.2	29.9
Hospital operating theatre	1.9	68.8	2.3	26.9

FIGURE 5.2　Noise wastes US $25,000 per annum per employee

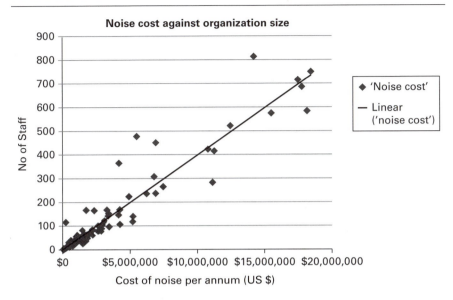

is 26.9 per cent where noise absorbs approximately 1¼ days per week of each staff member's time. The highest level in this table is 54.8 per cent noise, which absorbs nearly three days per week of each team member's time. Many organizations contain teams with very high levels of noise, some being 100 per cent noise. High levels of noise are usually found in call centres, accounts payable, policy units, help desks, claims, payroll, invoicing and credit, maintenance and customer complaints (rather obviously!). As about two-thirds of this noise will be 'given' to these teams by other teams in the business then interfacing activity noise elimination must require these other teams to be included in interface mapping.

Noise in large and small organizations

Large and small organizations incur similar levels of noise. Figure 5.2 plots the size of organizations against the cost of interfacing activity noise, assuming an average salary cost of US $75,000 per person employed. The graph demonstrates that interfacing activity noise levels appear to be little influenced by organizational size. In other words, a small organization is just as likely to have the same level of interfacing activity noise that would be found in a much larger, more complex organization.

On average, Figure 5.2 shows that an organization employing 800 staff will devote some US $20 million per annum of its human resources, or US $25,000 per head, to interfacing activity noise. These figures take no account of the cost of lost opportunities or the wastage of materials and equipment.

So, albeit unintentionally, organizations that do not manage their interfacing activities spend about US $25,000 per employee per annum upsetting their customers, at the same time as driving down employee satisfaction and destroying business value.

If just half of the interfacing activity noise could be saved, then the impact on the profitability, performance and productivity is enormous. For example, an 800-person service company with a turnover of US $100 million would be losing US $10 million per annum from its profit.

Outcome achievement

Noise is accretive

Interfacing activity noise has many causes. It can take the form of checking, chasing and correcting errors and omissions on information provided by customers or suppliers, and dealing with the downstream viral impact. This is externally generated noise. Equally, the correction and chasing can be caused by errors and omissions committed in other parts of the same organization or even within each team, and by dealing with the downstream viral impact in each team.

An example illustrates the vast range of drivers of noise that are likely to occur. Consider a straightforward purchasing process, one that exists in virtually every organization. Perhaps a call centre wishes to acquire a new PC for a new employee. The process requires IT department staff to define the specification before passing the requisition on to the purchasing department staff who will place an order with an approved supplier. The new PC is then delivered to goods inwards and the receiving team accepts the order and signs to confirm receipt. The IT installation team is then notified that the PC has arrived, arranges for it to be picked up and delivered to operations and then installs it in the call centre. An invoice is sent by the supplier to the purchasing department who placed the order to be approved and forwarded to the accounts payable group for payment. Finally, the transaction is logged into the general ledger against the cost code in the budget for the requesting department. The process is quite straightforward, if somewhat tedious. What could possibly go wrong?

The call centre's team leader completes the requisition and passes it to the approving manager who is absent on sick leave. It sits in that person's in-tray for a month and the new employee joins. There is a frantic search to find where the PC is, all of which is interfacing activity noise. Calls are made to purchasing department staff and take up time (noise). Purchasing staff make enquiries on their files only to find that they have never received the order. The attention then switches to IT department staff who similarly search their records and conclude that they have never seen the document. The search goes on and someone finds the document safely awaiting authorization in the in-box of the call centre manager's PC.

But this is hardly the end of the interfacing activity noise. Nothing has yet been resolved and the new employee still needs a PC. An emergency requisition is raised (noise), signed off by the divisional manager who has to be tracked down on a training course (more noise), it is hand-delivered to IT department staff (noise) who process it quickly and take the trouble to check with the supplier to ensure that the correct PC is available (noise) only to find that the approved supplier is out of stock as a model change is underway. So the IT person begins to call other suppliers to find a suitable PC (noise) and is, fortunately, successful after making 16 telephone calls (noise). However, the price differs from what was budgeted and the supplier is not accredited so the purchasing department has to raise a manual payment authorization (more noise) to enable the equipment to be purchased from a non-approved supplier. A special audit notification has also to be raised to cover the situation (more noise), and because of the high cost of the PC, this has to be signed off by an associate director. It is hand-carried to the director (noise) who questions whether it is strictly necessary and thus sparks off an investigation (noise). The new employee is still waiting for a PC and is therefore ineffective (noise).

The PC is finally delivered and at this point it is found that it has been delivered with a non-standard operating system. The IT department staff have to rectify the situation (noise) and decide additional software has to be purchased so another emergency requisition is completed (noise) but because it is a non-standard situation it requires the signature of... etc, etc.

These paper chases can occur anywhere. It may be an urgent enquiry about leave entitlements to the HR department but the person who has access to the data only works mornings so someone else has to record the needs, contact details, etc, and ensure that the person who can deal with it has the information. More likely it will just be a simple note: 'Julie called – extn 1234'. The entitlements person will now have to call Julie (noise), find she is not there so has to leave a message (noise) and make a note to call back (noise) and when they do finally catch up it is realized that the information was accessible by Julie's boss all the time (all noise)! It is almost surprising that the level of noise in interfacing activity is only 33.6 per cent of total resources or US $25,000 per annum per person in the average organization.

There is, however, some good news in this dismal tale of tedium. There is one particular attribute of noise that, like a virus entering the human body, makes it hard to detect but potentially provides huge payback when properly diagnosed. As illustrated in the all too common situations described above, noise is accretive. It propagates and creates more interfacing activity noise downstream. The longer the errors and omissions go on uncorrected, the greater will be the resource commitment. The example below (Figure 5.3) is taken from a call centre. It graphically demonstrates accretion by showing

FIGURE 5.3 Eliminating interface activity noise upstream provides huge benefits

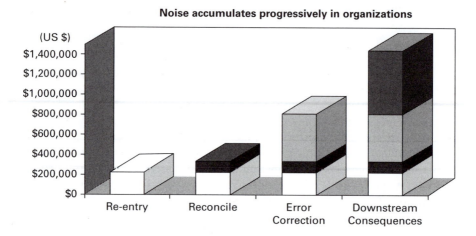

Noise accumulates progressively in organizations

the impact of poorly integrated accounting systems. The business management, at first sight apparently correctly, argued that the cost of the duplication in entry of information into multiple systems and spreadsheets was insufficient to justify an upgrade of their systems. The cost of the duplicated data entry was a fraction under US $200,000 per annum and absorbed the energies of some three staff.

Interface mapping revealed the real extent of their opportunity. This proved to be seven times the benefit that had previously been derived from a functional activity analysis the business had carried out. While the functional analysis was mathematically correct in that just under three staff were engaged in the duplication of data entry (all duplicated entry was coded as interfacing activity noise by definition), this entry led to additional interfacing activity in accounts who had to check (discretionary activity) that the entry was correct. This led to additional interfacing activity noise to correct the errors made in entry and additional interfacing work (all interfacing activity noise) to investigate the errors, chase the correct information, re-run the systems with the corrected data, collect back erroneous information already sent out, etc. Most of this additional work took place in other parts of the business and had been ignored by these other teams as it was seen as just 'part of their normal routine work'.

We argue, therefore, that it is critical to accrue all of the downstream impact of noise from the time that a particular interfacing activity noise element enters the organization. Accumulation is critical because there are always hundreds of different noise 'viruses' in any business, most of which probably should be ignored because their cumulative impact is so small. The application of the Pareto principle to the drivers will highlight the areas for intervention to exercise the 'viral' impact.

TABLE 5.6 Externally generated interfacing activity noise is dominant

	Finance	Corporate services	Operations	Top management	IT	Average
Total noise	46%	25%	33%	35%	53%	38%
Internal	23%	**12%**	**11%**	**5%**	**19%**	**14%**
External	23%	**13%**	**22%**	**30%**	**34%**	**24%**

A whole-organization approach

There is a need to interface map the whole organization. The overall noise level in the call centre business featured in Figure 5.3 was 38 per cent. It is instructive to collate the noise activities generated within each division and, separately, those driven by factors outside the division's control – those viral elements of noise 'given' to them by other divisions or their customers.

Table 5.6 breaks down the source of noise across the call centre. Overall, 24 per cent of the people's time is absorbed by interfacing activity noise generated from activities undertaken outside that division. Only 14 per cent of the interfacing activity noise is generated within a division. In the operations division for example, which is made up of a number of large call centres and is where most of the staff are to be found, two-thirds of the interfacing activity noise is generated externally. Therefore the managers of the operations division do not have the authority to address two-thirds of the interfacing activity noise. Any internal analysis they do will under-report the potential benefit of a change by 200 per cent and this will often mean that no action is taken. This organizational undervaluing of opportunities is typical.

This emphasizes the need for change priorities to be set for the business by analysing end-to-end business processes in accordance with the best-practice principles described in Chapter 2. Without interface mapping to quantify the activities and enable causes to be associated with accumulated effect, it is hard to imagine how best-practice business process management can be planned and agreed and this is why we believe that powerful improvement tools often disappoint.

The need to accumulate all of the many incidents of noise is further supported by Figure 5.4, which shows that the vast majority of the activities collected in interface mapping take less than three hours per month. Unless the noise activity is accumulated by cause, there would be every reason for managers to say it is too small to worry about it and so justify ignoring it. Taking this together with the way that interfacing activity noise is spread

FIGURE 5.4   The need to accumulate interfacing activity noise by cause

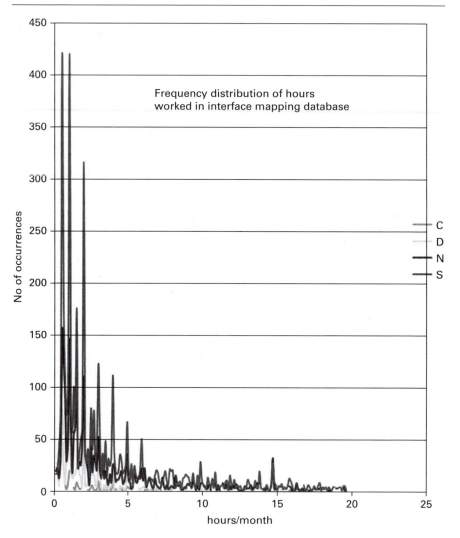

throughout the organization is why so many process failures are never properly recognized and therefore never rectified.

Implications for systems and process design

The viral analogy related to interfacing activity noise has a particular significance for systems engineers engaged in the installation of new systems. There is a widely held view that when undertaking new systems installations, it is best if systems engineers do not try to change the software, rather install the 'vanilla' system and change the activities of the staff involved in the process during the installation training phase. Without doubt this is sound advice.

However, all the major system platforms have parameters to enable the screens, print outs or interfaces to be tailored to individual business needs. It would, of course, be ridiculous to attempt to use the parameters to adapt to every single one of the hundreds of drivers of interfacing activity noise in any business. But imagine a scenario where the drivers have been prioritized to address strategic needs including customer service, employee satisfaction, productivity and performance. The precise parameter adjustments can be defined for the key interfaces that need to be managed and controlled. Interface mapping provides the information to achieve this. In contrast, conventional process mapping represents interfacing activity rather unhelpfully as connecting lines, which fails to meet this need.

Transferring noise to core

Figure 5.4 also reveals that a very small proportion of time is devoted to the activities that drive business value – just 3.3 per cent of the time is committed to core activity. This amounts to just 10 per cent of the time spent on the unproductive interfacing activity noise. Revisiting the examples in the previous chapter of the Battle of Britain and the pharmaceutical company's sales force, there has to be a huge latent opportunity to reduce noise activity and transfer some or all of the released time to driving value. Our rule of thumb is that transferring time from interfacing activity noise to core activity increases the payback on simply achieving cost saving by a factor of three. This benefit appears variously as increased volumes, margins, plant utilization, etc and is much preferable to cost cutting and downsizing.

Benefits are quickly realized

Our experience has been that at least half of an organization's interfacing activity noise can be eliminated for little or no capital cost and this outcome is comfortably achievable within six months. The result from these quick wins is always a dramatic improvement in staff and customer satisfaction. In addition, they release on average about 15 per cent of the staff and management resource to more effective use, net of the upstream investment, in core activity to prevent the noise from entering. As an example, Figure 5.5 shows the response time and variability for a regulatory body. One of the organization's key tasks was to issue licences. The average noise level in the organization when the interface mapping was undertaken was 45 per cent to a large extent because more than 300 customer complaints were being received each month. Figure 5.5 shows that the average response time was

FIGURE 5.5   Rapid results from interface mapping

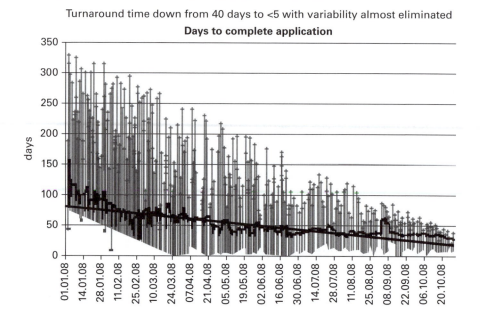

Turnaround time down from 40 days to <5 with variability almost eliminated

reduced from over 40 to under 5 days, and complaints were eliminated as variability in response time plummeted from 330 days at the start of the work.

Setting priorities strategically

So far we have looked at the relatively high level of resources absorbed by interfacing activity noise (US $25,000 per person employed) and shown that it is found in all organizations. We have looked at some of its characteristics. Here is a summary:

- It is accretive. It behaves like a virus once it enters a business and keeps interfering requiring more and more interfacing activity noise to keep the 'stuff' flowing across the interfaces.
- It needs to be accumulated by causal factor because individual elements of noise are generally too small to be of interest.
- Externally caused noise drivers dominate – and are more difficult to eradicate because of the need to manage for the whole business or the whole supply chain. A case needs to be developed to justify why other divisions must invest time and effort for the benefit to appear elsewhere.

FIGURE 5.6   Large number of causes of interfacing activity noise

XeP3 — Activity (noise) drivers

Key	description	Key	description
1	Incorrect or incomplete information returned by employee	38	Manual processing
2	Choose candidate that did not want position	39	Lack of staff understanding of e-time
3	Rework in hire process (rejects, change dates)	40	Project code problem
4	Spend time waiting for busy staff member	41	Timesheet approval problem
5	Correct/complete paperwork not received from HR	42	IT fault
6	Standard reports/access to staff details is inadequate	43	Manual keying of timesheet adjustments by payroll
7	Activation of SAP import into e-time is not automated	44	SAP and e-time not integrated online
8	Staff number has not been downloaded onto system	45	Payroll error in processing/data entry
9	Employee information incorrect	46	No automated check of leave balance at approval stage
10	Mail has been incorrectly addressed/sent to Payroll	47	Lack of up to date OH&S list in Payroll
11	Application for leave/special leave is incorrectly filled out or incomplete	48	Payroll adjust salary
12	E-form unavailable to staff member	49	System unable to automatically apply allowances to leave as appropriate
13	Change of staff details/status information unclear/ incomplete or not provided	50	Leave issue
14	Duplicate activity/activity performed in wrong team	51	Leave balance not calculated automatically from leave taken
15	Manual calculation/duplicate entry required	52	Lack of suspension report requires complicated checks
16	Appropriate level of approval not gained	53	SAP not integrated online
17	Recent changes to system have made title changes and BU changes difficult	54	System does not automatically calculate pay in advance
18	No solid process in place for updating system for package changes	55	Report format inadequate
19	Information received regarding system package changes is incorrect	56	System limitation
20	Issues arise when testing system for daily package changes	57	Data problem with paygroup
21	Miss a payroll run due to late approval of Annual Incentive	58	Overpayment
22	Untimely information received regarding employee relocation/termination	59	No notification from other sections
23	Insufficient or untimely approval received	60	Data Integrity issue
24	Standard information insufficient or not available	61	Hardcopy report transferred
25	Leasing company slow in supplying information for vehicle leases	62	Payroll should process confidential EFT/cheque payments
26	Staff fail to purchase laptop in six-week period given from approval	63	Not all vendors on EFT
27	Insufficient standard reports create need for ad hoc reporting or manual calc	64	No access to payment summary archive for staff
28	Functionality/training issues	65	Perform non-payroll work
29	Insufficient knowledge/training	66	Global staff details and e-time not integrated
30	Changes made to shift rotation/roster	67	Lack of HR/payroll agreement or understanding on e-form content
31	Employee allowances do not match the award	68	Termination explanation unclear
32	Need to check leave accruals in arrears manually		
33	Do not receive shift allowance payment authorization on time		
34	Missing timesheet report inaccurate		
35	Out-of-date e-mail addresses on missing timesheet report		
36	Timesheet is missing/not submitted		
37	Staff make error adjusting timesheet		

These three factors alone suggest why most organizations are invariably disappointed. The final issue is that there are always many different drivers of noise within any organization. Figure 5.6 lists the 68 drivers of noise that were encountered just in a payroll process. This high number has two implications. First, there is an obvious need to apply Pareto and focus on the major causes, otherwise there are simply far too many drivers to tackle. Interface mapping quantification allows this. Second, is to beware of relying on 'judgement' and 'experience'. Without doubt people will have encountered many, even all, of the drivers in any particular business process – but are unlikely to know which ones really matter in your business. Without interface mapping the risk is that minor issues will be tackled because there is no mechanism for prioritization.

The strategic need is to decide which drivers of interfacing activity noise to address. Managers obviously need to understand with some precision both the quantum and nature of the drivers of each element of interfacing activity noise. Only then can they set priorities to address them and thereby eliminate the associated waste, delays and frustration in a manageable sequence, as well as target the strategic imperatives.

Situational dependency

So let's get the data and then decide where to focus. There are two reasons for this. First, we have already made the point that noise is accretive, so thinking of Figure 5.4 (on page 106) and Figure 5.6, it must be sensible to measure the cost and service impact of a particular driver of interfacing activity noise throughout the length of the entire business process. This will allow managers to appreciate cost and strategic impact properly and thus enable priorities to be correctly established. This step alone would eliminate the ever-present risk of underestimating impact, as illustrated in the call centre (Figure 5.3 on page 104) where only 3 of the 20 full-time staff equivalents had been allocated to the duplication in entry of the drivers of interfacing activity noise.

Second, interfacing activity noise is situational. If an organization has multiple branches or offices, multiple teams of, say, sales people or several factories or warehouses, management may optimistically assume that the activities carried out in each are largely the same and focus on just one of them. Such an assumption is wrong. Only the functional activities will be the same. The interfacing activities, and therefore the drivers of interfacing activity noise will be significantly different. This is because customers' behaviour (and staff's and managers' behaviour) will differ from branch to branch. Physical layouts may also differ – there may be different equipment, roles tailored to suit larger and smaller operations, different access mechanisms, etc. In the extreme, we encountered one manufacturing business that had raised situational differences to an entirely new high. One of their production plants was separated from the warehouse by a divided highway. Imagine the additional interfacing activities this incurred and how these differed from other facilities. Organizations therefore need to develop a list of drivers such as those listed in Figure 5.6 and prioritize the list for each location.

So, at this point in our discussion, interface mapping enables an organization to capture and quantify everything that is done in the business. Activity categorization then allows the large database of activities to be coded strategically. The next need is to be able to accumulate the noise in each business process by causal factor so that priorities can be set strategically (that is, for the business as a whole). The mechanism for this is described in Chapter 7. Before that we need to demonstrate how to transfer into productive activity some of the wasted US $25,000 per person employed that is absorbed by noise. This is addressed in Chapter 6.

Discretionary activity

It would not be appropriate to move on from this chapter without briefly visiting the last of the four activity categories, discretionary activities. Discretionary activities on average absorb 14.5 per cent of resources (see Table 5.3 on page 98). Noise and discretionary interfacing activities taken together absorb half of an organization's resources (48.1 per cent).

The classification of activities as discretionary often leads to a great deal of valuable debate. The discretionary category enables managers to determine, deploy and monitor a practical and effective risk-management policy and this is discussed further in the next chapter.

Summary

In this chapter we have focused on the strategic nature of an activity categorization framework and the conclusions drawn from applying the framework to the data from the 117 organizations in the database of case material. The following points emerged:

- The routine (functional) activities that are required in an enterprise for it to achieve its strategic objectives absorb just under half (48 per cent) of the total staff resource. This time is classified as support activity.
- The functional activities are linked together by interfacing activities that, as shown in the previous chapter, are rarely if ever properly documented. With no visibility it is impossible to manage interfacing activity.
- The failure to manage the interfaces effectively both within an organization and with the outside world wastes one-third (33.6 per cent) of the average enterprise's staff resource. Activities such as rework, chasing and unnecessary duplication and activities associated with the downstream impact are classified as interfacing activity noise. This level of organizational waste is found in all sectors of endeavour and all sizes of organization.
- Interfacing activity noise exists in roughly equal measure in all teams, departments and organizations.
- It costs organizations about US $25,000 per annum per person employed.

- Interfacing activity noise is accretive. Once noise enters an organization it acts like a virus and continues to disrupt processes until it is eliminated. However, the benefit of this characteristic is that elimination at the point of entry of the major causes of noise will deliver enormous benefits.
- Organizations devote about an hour per week per employee to activities that potentially will drive (deliver) performance increases.
- There is a huge opportunity to take advantage of prioritized interfacing activity noise in tailoring new systems installations to address strategy imperatives.

Increasing performance

Objective

The last chapter made use of the process analysis framework developed in Chapter 4 to analyse the database of 117 organizations to understand fully the nature of interfacing activities. This chapter focuses on how organizations have made use of interface activity mapping to achieve a step increase in performance.

The chapter's primary objective is to show how organizations have analysed and prioritized their data so as to reap the dividends strategically and avoid the inherent distractions and commonly encountered barriers to change. These distractions include chasing the myriad of business process problems, errors and delays that have little impact on business performance but hold change and improvement teams hostage, dancing to the tune of 'he who shouts loudest'.

Continuous improvement or strategic process alignment?

In the last chapter we described the latent opportunity that exists in all organizations to make a step increase in performance through eliminating interfacing activity noise by increasing core activity. Many first-time users of our interface mapping tool, XeP3, have argued that focusing on interfacing activity noise essentially provides just a tactical, inward-looking productivity approach. They have said to us that using interface mapping to quantify and make noise visible merely enables organizations to put their continuous improvement programmes on steroids. We can only agree that interface mapping will enable existing organizational improvement teams to scale new heights and achieve levels of performance that they have only dreamed of. Interface mapping is, however, capable of doing much more than merely providing a mechanism to help the change specialists to do their job better.

Other users of the interface mapping approach and tools express the opposite point of view. They maintain that eliminating noise, by definition, results in the delivery of positive external benefits such as increased customer service, a strategic outcome. Further, that understanding interfacing activity noise drives business process innovation. Certainly, interfacing activity noise elimination has delivered benefits to stakeholders far beyond efficiency gains. It always raises levels of employee satisfaction and improves work–life balance. Improved maintenance regimes have led to reduced spillage and this has achieved strategic environmental outcomes. In other organizations the removal of rework and unnecessary chasing and checking has eliminated bottlenecks and this has removed chokes on throughput that have been acting as a brake on the efficient use of resources. These are all strategic outcomes – but the question still remains of how to target the changes needed to address the strategic imperatives.

Interface activity noise, by its nature, demands attention when it occurs: for example, when there is a jam on a production line, a breakdown of an ultrasound machine, an angry customer returning a product with a fault, customers demanding that the bank gives them back their savings now or an unhappy shareholder tipping manure onto the front steps of head office, management and staff have to drop everything to pitch in and deal with the problem there and then – a complete distraction, a waste of time and a heightening of risk in the business. So the real question is how to manage out interfacing activity noise so that productivity improves at the same time that carefully targeted strategic outcomes are delivered. In these circumstances replacing noise with core is an extremely attractive way of achieving strategic outcomes – the organization achieves its strategic goals and does it at the same time that costs fall.

The objective then in converting interfacing activity noise to core should not just be seen as a cost or productivity exercise except when that is the only strategic goal. Priority should be given to selecting important, cost-justified productivity initiatives that, while they will inevitably free resource, are also carefully selected and engineered to achieve specific strategic goals such as customer service, employee satisfaction, capacity utilization, volume growth, safety improvements and lowered environmental impact, as envisaged by Wernerfelt(1984). The benefits he envisaged included superior utilization of equipment, more effective customer relationships, or more effective production.

When specifically targeted change is delivered through managing the strategic alignment of business processes, then the business is truly building strategic capabilities and the initiatives selected and deployed will be totally consistent with the management principles focusing on strategic intent, described in detail in Chapter 2.

Value revealed by interface mapping

At the beginning of the last chapter, in Table 5.1 (on page 94), we presented the overall analysis of the 117 organizations in the database using the analysis framework developed in Chapter 4.

Interface activity noise

Let's go back to some of the main points from Chapter 5. The database revealed that, on average, a company's staff and managers devote a massive 33.6 per cent of their time to interfacing activity noise and this costs almost US $25,000 per annum per person employed. On average 1⅔ days out of every person's five-day week are devoted to upsetting the customers and making life a misery for his or her fellow workers, customers and suppliers. In devoting this time to interfacing activity noise, staff are distracting themselves and their co-workers from doing the real job they are paid to do and thereby progressively destroying value in the business.

There is therefore an overwhelming case supporting the need to understand interfacing activity noise by interface mapping of business processes. Once understood, quantified and prioritized the causal factors will be understood and can be addressed and the benefits and savings harvested.

Discretionary activity

Organizations devote 14.5 per cent of their time to discretionary activity; that is, 3/4 of a day out of everyone's five-day week or around US $11,250 per annum per person employed. Discretionary activity provides the mechanism to deploy risk management steps into every business process. It includes the checking and assessment steps in each process to ensure business integrity is maintained relating to:

- fraud prevention;
- compliance with legislation;
- achievement of company goals in:
  - occupational health and safety
  - environmental issues
  - work-place relations;
- achievement of required business outcomes.

In case study 1.1 (on page 25) we identified where specific elements of the discretionary activity should have been mandated in the medical field. Aircraft-style pre-flight check lists may well have been the vehicle to do this, as aircrews meticulously adhere to a checking procedure for every single flight on penalty of instant dismissal. However, in case study 1.1 there was no evidence that the critical elements of discretionary activity, or for that matter any of them, were documented, understood or being managed and the outcome of this lack of management was a patient's death. We have encountered similar situations in the petrochemicals industry and in transport.

In case study 3.1 (on pages 55–58) we saw the process through the eyes of the patient, the victim of unmanaged interfacing activity. Those responsible for patient transfer at Melbourne Airport were ignorant of the very specific handling instructions given for repatriation to avoid the risk of inducing paraplegia, instead the communication was interpreted as dealing with a communicable disease. There was again an overwhelming case for ensuring that these critical instructions reached those responsible for patient transfer well before the aircraft landed. There would then be no costly risk of the plane and passengers being embargoed in quarantine and potential harm to the patient would have been rendered impossible. Instead, the result of unmanaged interface activity was erroneous communication and huge risk taking.

We argue therefore that there is a need to define and enforce the use of specific discretionary activities. Interface mapping ensures that existing practices are precisely understood as the first necessary stage in enabling steps in a business process is to assess the degree to which they meet prudent and regulatory requirements.

Support activity

Staff and management devote 48 per cent of their time, that is, two and a half days per week or around US $37,000 per annum per person employed, to conducting the functional activities to sustain the business. These support activities include changing the dressings on a patient in a hospital, assessing an insurance claim, driving to an address to deliver a washing machine, delivering a module on a training programme, collecting a pharmaceuticals order, etc. These support activities are always well documented. They are the functional activities that are carried out to deploy the strategy.

It is rare to find a business in which the staff and managers do the wrong functional activities. These activities have generally been studied to death. However, support activities provide a rich area to gain step improvements in outcomes when quantified in the course of an interface mapping exercise.

The quantification of effort for each incidence of support activity enables new strategic insights to be gained. For instance, consider a sales person who, equipped with a vehicle, is a relatively high-cost employee. Sales people are needed if there is to be a high impact on the success of a business because they get new business and manage critical customer relationships. One would not raise an eyebrow on being told that sales people had to undertake administrative tasks in the normal course of duty, indeed one would be surprised if they were not devoting some time to administration. However, now add the quantification provided by an interface mapping exercise into the equation. The revealing data invariably challenges the assumptions about the nature of the job of sales people and the level of administrative burden they carry.

Take an example from interface mapping work in a paper business. It revealed after three weeks that the average sales person spent just one day per week in new customer contact tasks. Of this under half a day, just 3.6 hours per week, was actually spent with potential new customers. This information was shocking enough, but the data also showed that the average sales person spent over a full day driving around, travelling between locations, and almost three full days on administrative and head office tasks. Clearly, you are thinking, the data in this case revealed a sales force that was out of control. Yet the company was highly regarded and these ratios are far from unusual in our experience now of over 50 examples of mapping the interfaces of sales forces.

The data exposed that the managers of this company were not operating the business in accordance with the five management principles focusing on strategic intent that are found in the leading companies. These principles, with some suggestions of how this organization failed to adhere to them, are listed below:

- Ensuring integration of effort. The sales people were doing a lot of work which others, such as administrative staff, could do. Administrative staff do not carry the overhead of a car, have a lower salary cost and are usually better placed and equipped to handle many of the administrative tasks that over time inevitably migrate to the sales force.

- Being disciplined and creating strategic capabilities. There was no awareness of how the sales resource was actually being used and it is rare to find measures in place that keep the sales force focused on business growth and margin.

- Creating customer value. It is quite usual to find, paradoxically, that interfacing activity noise is transferred to the sales force. They are required to deal with errors and omissions in services and products often emanating from head office. It is very difficult to sell in new services after spending time focused on rectifying customer service issues.

- Being time-based. The sales force spent too much time on administration and noise.

The understanding of how resource is being used would obviously be invaluable, for example, to an IT analyst preparing a business case for a new computer system. We again argue therefore that there is a need to employ interface mapping to document support activities so that the nature of each detailed activity and the associated time it absorbs is understood. An interface mapping database thus becomes an invaluable tool to understand where resource deployment is out of line with strategic intent and management expectations; and to quantify with precision, and model, the impact and benefit from various automation and technology proposals.

Core activity

On average just 3.3 per cent of time, that is, about one hour per week per person, or just US $2,500 per person employed, is committed to driving value by undertaking core activity. Core activity by definition improves key business elements such as customer service, raw materials cost and equipment uptime. There is therefore a huge potential opportunity to free up time from interfacing activity noise and misdirected discretionary activity and transfer it to core. Freeing up just one hour per week per person and transferring it to core activity would double the effort to perform value-driving activities in the 117 businesses in the database.

Again, we argue that there is a prima facie case for using interface mapping, in this case to pinpoint both core activity and the differences in practice.

Difficulties in addressing noise

The accretion attribute of interfacing activity noise described in the last chapter means that the longer noise is allowed to continue unchecked through an organization and on to the customers, the more disruption it causes and the more resource it wastes. In extreme cases the huge consequences are well documented. Take, for example, the recent problems with accelerator pedal design or usage Toyota had to contend with and the catastrophic equipment or procedural failure BP experienced in the Gulf of Mexico. The downstream effects just keep expanding until, and in the BP case, the rectification (noise) activity ultimately spread to thousands of people as well as wildlife and hundreds of square kilometres of their habitation.

We are therefore often asked where in organizations to find this noise and how to go about it. People just want to know how to find the noise so that they can stamp it out. Many want to realize the benefit, get the recognition from so doing and get on with the job of creating value for the organization and its stakeholders. Others just want to be free from the frustration, time wasting and customer issues that the noise is causing them.

Individuals will often have taken a good look at what their organization or team is doing before they ask the question of where to find interfacing activity noise. They are likely therefore to be somewhat frustrated. They will not have been able to find the noise in large enough chunks to justify committing time and resource to address each occurrence. They therefore conclude that mounting an initiative to address noise or even save the time lost would be a waste of effort because it could not be justified. In short, they come up against barriers to change. Three of the more intractable of these are: expectations of service culture, the need to differentiate between role definitions and value driving, and the need for a mechanism to overcome organizational inertia. Interface mapping provides the mechanism to overcome these.

Overcoming organizational inertia

Obviously the easiest interfacing activity noise to eradicate would be the interfacing activity noise generated within an organizational unit. This is because a unit's manager has the power to require any internal change to be made in much the same way that a team leader has the implicit authority to 'invent' new interfacing activity workarounds within his or her span of control to accept transactions that are not clean. In contrast, noise given to a unit from outside, perhaps by the customer or another (think, more influential) division is much more difficult to address because those upstream would gain no benefit from investing time fixing the issue.

Eradication would require changes to customers' behaviours and/or standards and/or the company's policies and these are notoriously difficult to achieve when requested from deep down within a hierarchy. Indeed, inter-division and inter-business changes often require resource redeployment between the divisions involved to make the core investment of time upstream in one division to eliminate the interfacing activity noise downstream in other divisions. This resource investment in one place in a business to gain large benefits in other divisions is something divisional managers will usually resist unless a watertight, unarguable case is presented to them.

A strong business case is clearly required to put to higher management. Interface mapping will provide overwhelming evidence of the need and top teams can then enthusiastically support change. Interface mapping of the whole territory provides the data needed to construct a business case to overcome this organizational inertia.

All too common barriers of role definition

Users of interface mapping often initially argue that far too little resource is coded to core activity. They see a low core level as an affront to their professionalism and this becomes a potentially large barrier to recognizing interface activity noise.

The average core value-driving activity in Figure 5.1 (on page 96) is 3.3 per cent or about an hour per person employed per week or around US $2,500 per employee per annum. We have already put forward an argument in Chapter 5 that small injections of core activity to control major interfacing activity noise drivers have huge leverage on the business by preventing noise from entering. A small investment of activity is an essential part of the ability to eliminate swathes of interfacing activity noise downstream.

The argument we most frequently encounter occurs because people tend not to differentiate between role definitions and creating strategic value.

Most professionals simply have never thought about it. For example when coding the detailed functional and interfacing activities in a finance team, an accountant will often argue, 'I am employed as an accountant so accounting work done must be core,' or an engineer may argue, 'I am employed as an engineer so all the design activities must be a core activity.' Similarly, a sales person will argue that all sales activity must be core to the business because without sales activity there would be no business. The issue that needs to be understood is that there is a huge difference between doing functional work for which qualified people are employed and doing core activities that deliver strategically critical outcomes to a business.

Clearly, accounting work in the real world includes interfacing activity noise such as chasing information that is late, checking and correcting errors in information received and copying information from one system to another. These activities are interfacing noise activities that deflect accountants from doing the job they are paid to do. Further, levels of interfacing activity noise in some accounting areas such as payables and payroll often exceed 60 per cent. After all, the accounting function is a service to the business and should help the other departments to fix up their errors, shouldn't it? Well no. Accounting staff should do core activity to train their users to get it right first time (the principle of creating customer value) and then they should reject any data with errors (the principle of being disciplined).

The first concession from the accountant is usually that noise should be properly coded but 'all the rest must be core'. Similarly, taking design (which is a functional activity for the engineer), finding and correcting the specification, chasing up the test results, correcting errors made by a junior, looking for missing standards data, etc, are all noise activities and design departments usually suffer from relatively high noise levels absorbing as much as 30–45 per cent of their resource. Sales staff are no different. As already discussed in the context of the pharmaceutical sales force, dealing with returns is downstream interfacing activity noise. In addition, sales people often go to great lengths to satisfy customers so they can get an order. We have encountered several sales forces who insist that delivering samples or prototypes to the customer is core activity. This is core activity, to quote, because 'the samples are so often wrong that we need to be there to apologise/correct/massage/offer discounts to the customer when they inspect the work'. In this instance, the sales person is engaged in interfacing noise activity because of errors made elsewhere in the business, or, in too many cases, because the same sales person has not got the work instructions or specification right and complete in the first instance.

The question, we argue, should therefore be, yes, accountants, engineers, sales people, etc are essential to a particular business but everyone needs to know, unequivocally, which of the many activities that they undertake actually drive the required, improved overall business outcomes. Once this thinking framework is understood then the organization will have instilled the best-practice management principle of relating the micro to the macro, which is discussed more fully in Chapter 8. The staff, especially professional staff, need to think through and prove which activities drive performance and can thus be coded as core activities.

So, in summary, and as we realized many years ago, core activities and noise activities cannot be identified and coded at a team, department or functional level. Categorizing activities at the team, department or functional level will prevent an organization from complying with the principle of ensuring integration of effort described in Chapter 2 because the interpretation will be applied functionally. Core activities are, like support activities, value adding but to classify an activity as core requires the link to business improvement to be clearly established.

Expectations of service culture

There is a further point to be made on role definition. There are a number of teams in organizations where high percentages of noise are always to be found. They are teams in departments where most of the consequences of the omissions and errors of other departments eventually end up – payroll, purchase ledger, sales administration, credit control, etc. They therefore appear to be excellent places to start as high levels of interfacing activity noise are guaranteed to be found. The problem is that eliminating the noise will require two sophisticated changes in thinking to be made. The first is concerned with how the service team members think about service. They need to think differently about their job. The job is not to demonstrate helpfulness by repeatedly fixing up problems every time they occur. It is to train their internal customers 'to get their transactions right first time'. The second is the corollary of this. It is to get the often more powerful users of the service to accept this new role. This is a hard concept to sell in an organization used to being mollycoddled by its service teams. So, if you must start here, then ensure that the user departments are included with the service teams in the interface mapping so that cause and effect are made obvious.

Analysing noise drivers to achieve strategic outcomes

There are many causes of interfacing activity noise in organizations and the number will usually run to over 100. This is because many of the causes of this noise will differ depending on the day of the month, the customers' expectations and differences from site to site, or branch to branch, in a geographically dispersed business, etc. Interfacing activities change because of differences in physical layouts; tools; levels of experience; training; cultural and language differences; time of the day, week or month; weather variations; changing customer needs, customer staff and systems; product and packaging, legislative and technology changes; etc. Priorities need to be established based on the benefits that would be delivered in each area.

The need therefore is to accumulate by cause all the incidences and effects of interfacing activity noise across the business or the end-to-end industry delivery process. Priorities can then be set by applying Pareto's principle – 80 per cent of the benefit will arise from the top 20 per cent of the noise drivers.

The remainder of this chapter examines how two organizations have used interface mapping to understand their business and then used the information to reallocate their people resources to achieve their target outcomes for strategic intent and business performance.

Our first example comes from the financial services industry. The company, we will call it FinCo, is part of global financial services business that provides its services to 22 of the top banks in the world. In Australia FinCo provides mortgage processing to major players in the mortgage lending industry. In 2006, the company had growing concerns that while it was able to satisfy its contractual turnaround time of four days, its customer service complaints made it acutely aware that some applications were taking up to 15 days to complete. Further, the business was suffering from escalating costs and worryingly, costs were increasing and almost exactly matching revenue growth. Profit growth was not being delivered in line with revenue increases.

The company mounted an initiative in one of their businesses led by an experienced manager, actually an experienced Six Sigma practitioner. The company set out to improve customer service and profitability by breaking the nexus between cost and revenue. It engaged 40 of its staff in conducting an interface mapping exercise across eight teams. The teams used an interface mapping tool and documented that they routinely carried out 1,341 functional and interfacing activities in their business processes. This was an average of 167 activities per team compared to the database average of 196. The analysis of the data showed that the business was incurring 30.78 per cent interfacing activity noise in its processes. Noise therefore absorbed the working time of some 12 of its 40 staff. The need was then to convert a significant proportion of this interface activity noise to effective use – support activity for revenue earning processing and some core activity to eliminate noise from the business process.

The causes of the interfacing activity noise were identified and prioritized. Various options were considered and modelled to satisfy the initial objective of obtaining a reduction of 10 percentage points in noise from implementing zero and low-cost changes. The staff were then re-engaged to implement the changes in their workplace.

The results are shown in Figure 6.1. Volume throughput increased by 11.3 per cent and a further 8 percentage points were predicted. After just six months the change process had reached an enviable position. Ideas from staff about how to reduce interfacing activity noise were being generated and implemented at a rate that resulted in the natural business growth being absorbed without increasing staffing levels. Strategically this meant that

FIGURE 6.1 Programme to reduce interfacing noise levels

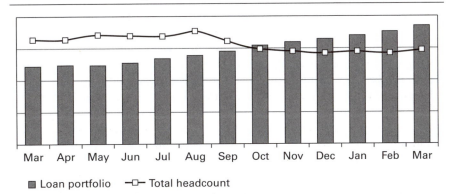

■ Loan portfolio   ─□─ Total headcount

nearly all of the newly-won fee income fell straight to the bottom line. At the same time the customer service imperative was addressed. Cycle time improved between 15 per cent and 42 per cent depending on the service line.

What had happened was that the use of interface mapping had enabled the company quickly and participatively to pinpoint and quantify a large number of opportunities that were then exorcised. The company had thus developed the capability routinely to convert interfacing activity noise across into the required small core investments to deliver the change, and to convert the rest into fee-earning support activity.

So what had the company, led by its management and change team, actually achieved judged against the best-practice management principles? (For a reminder of the best-practice management principles see Table 2.2 on page 33).

First, the managers had the desire to be out front. They had been determined to realign their business processes to improve customer service and decouple cost growth from revenue increase. They therefore made significant investment in the tools and skills to conduct the programme.

Second, they were striving to enhance creation of customer value. At the start of the work they were exceeding their contractual customer service level agreements. Had they been complacent, they need not have done anything to improve customer service. However, they recognized that the complaints they were receiving affected both their business and that of their contractual customers, who gave them their transactional business.

Third, they were time-based. They were focused on progressively eliminating waste and delays by targeting their interfacing activity noise activities and redeploying the time to productive, revenue-earning use. With regard to the principle of ensuring integration of effort, the whole organization from the top management through to the staff doing the work all believed in the direction taken and acknowledged that the interface maps and the categorization of strategic activity provided their focus. They then got on with the job exhibiting all the characteristics of a disciplined organization – they documented what they were doing, used it to model the outcomes they desired and then tracked their performance on a web-based monitoring system to demonstrably create the operating capabilities their customers needed. Finally, they did it in such a way that they progressively built the change process in the business, a strategic capability, to deliver the ongoing improvement. They had used the approach to implant the best-practice management principles.

Our second example involves refocusing a sales force. We look at the sales force of a well-known financial services company and track its interface mapping journey through from inception to delivering results.

The average organization in our database devotes just over one hour per week per person to core activity that creates value for the business. This gave rise to two issues: how to free up a significant portion of the 33.6 per cent of staff time absorbed by interfacing activity noise; how to make use of some of this time to increase the time commitment of 3.3 per cent core activity.

The financial company in this example offers investment and life and general insurance products through agents and advisers, its intermediaries, to its customers. The sales force therefore sells to and supports intermediaries who in turn offer the company's products to their customers. The business strategy called for significant growth in volume and margins from an historically low-growth position. The objective was therefore to examine the interfacing activities and look for opportunities to transfer any time absorbed by interfacing activity noise to the revenue-driving core activity.

There was a general feeling in the business that the continued business growth underperformance was due to poor management and staff quality in the sales area so the interface mapping, against our advice, was confined to the sales area. This meant that barriers to change described earlier in this chapter, if encountered, would be difficult to break through.

The first step was to understand what the sales people were actually doing and how they were using their time. The sales people were therefore invited to participate in a short interface mapping exercise. A first analysis provided a broad allocation of time. This is shown in Figure 6.2. Just 9 per cent of the sales people's time was spent on face-to-face (given as 'F2F' in Figure 6.2) selling time – less than half a day per sales person per week. The directly associated preparation and post-visit activity for these visits, including follow-up of opportunities, planning action to take, measuring outcomes and adjusting tactics, absorbed a further 11 per cent.

Obviously a key reason for the low sales growth was now clear. Only one day per week was being spent by each sales person on business development tasks. The sales people were spending just a day per week driving growth through customer interaction. Face-to-face customer contact time ranked equal fourth behind travel, solving customer problems largely emanating from other teams in the business and solving internal issues. The same

FIGURE 6.2   Allocation of sales people's time

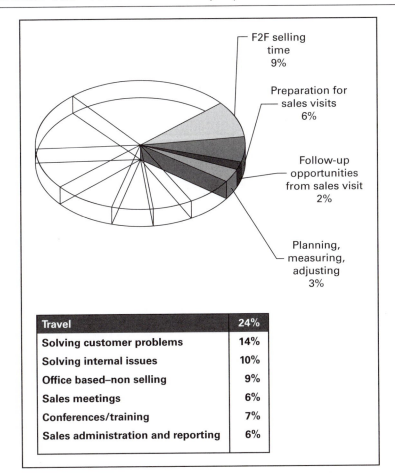

F2F selling
time
9%

Preparation for
sales visits
6%

Follow-up
opportunities
from sales visit
2%

Planning,
measuring,
adjusting
3%

Travel	24%
Solving customer problems	14%
Solving internal issues	10%
Office based–non selling	9%
Sales meetings	6%
Conferences/training	7%
Sales administration and reporting	6%

amount of time was devoted to various, non-specific office-based activity as was spent on face-to-face business development meetings.

The interface activity noise analysis cast further light onto the situation. Numerically, interfacing activity noise (Figure 6.3) absorbed 22.1 per cent of the sales people's time. This was about 2½ times the amount of time devoted to the value-driving core activity. In other words, releasing the sales force from just half of the noise burden and transferring the time to value driving would potentially double their effectiveness.

So what were the major drivers of this interfacing activity noise burden in this company? They are shown in Figure 6.4. These make it obvious that sales support, marketing and operations were not adhering to the management principle of being disciplined nor were they complying with the principle of ensuring integration of effort. So by this early stage in the analysis we

FIGURE 6.3 Opportunity presented by analysis of interfacing activity

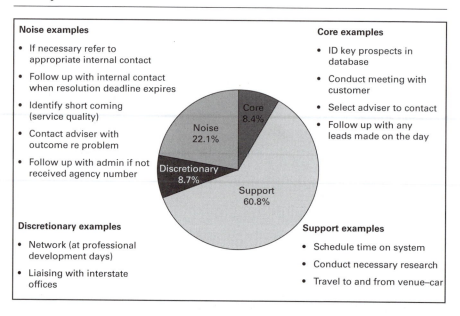

Noise examples

- If necessary refer to appropriate internal contact
- Follow up with internal contact when resolution deadline expires
- Identify short coming (service quality)
- Contact adviser with outcome re problem
- Follow up with admin if not received agency number

Core examples

- ID key prospects in database
- Conduct meeting with customer
- Select adviser to contact
- Follow up with any leads made on the day

Discretionary examples

- Network (at professional development days)
- Liaising with interstate offices

Support examples

- Schedule time on system
- Conduct necessary research
- Travel to and from venue–car

Core 8.4%
Noise 22.1%
Discretionary 8.7%
Support 60.8%

knew that the barriers described earlier in this chapter were likely to emerge because the likely source of most of the noise had not been interface mapped.

Having isolated the drivers of the noise and discussed the opportunities to restructure, the way forward was clear. First the main noise drivers had to be eliminated and some of the work transferred out of the sales area into support. This required the support areas, particularly sales support and marketing staff, to lift their game – follow through in a timely way and eliminate their errors and mistakes highlighted by the top six drivers of noise and support activity (see Figure 6.4). These drivers absorbed 12 percentage points of the noise and 11 percentage points of the sales force's support time.

The change took an inordinate amount of time because there was little commitment or understanding of the need for process change outside the sales area. After all, sales support and marketing staff were convinced that the problem existed in the sales area and rejected suggestions that the problems to a large extent arose because of the way they were undertaking their work. Organizational inertia and cultural barriers were in play.

Eventually senior managers, having seen the analysis, intervened. The other areas were interface mapped and the solutions and monitoring measures were agreed and introduced. The upstream teams who interfaced with the sales staff should have been mapped at the beginning at the same time as the sales force. A joint discovery process through interface mapping would

FIGURE 6.4   Pareto analysis of drivers of interfacing noise activity and support activity for the sales force

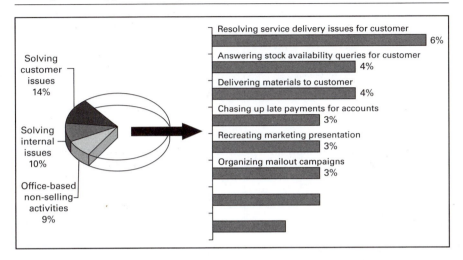

have avoided the unpleasantness and delays inherent to the blame game that had begun before management intervened. The result was that the interfacing activity noise levels were quickly halved. Further, the new understanding resulting from everyone participating in interface mapping had also enabled task restructuring of some of the support activities from sales to the office-based teams. For example, 3 per cent of the sales people's time was eliminated without effort by the agreement to share a library of marketing presentations. This also eliminated duplication and the risk of using out-of-date material.

As a consequence, customer service levels improved, complaints dropped and intermediaries commented that they were passing through more business because of the improvement. The company thus benefited from customers being more inclined to pass business to the company and the sales people had more time to focus on business development.

Figure 6.5 shows schematically the measures used to confirm that the agreed changes were having the desired effects. They show over a period of six months the progress made, although for obvious reasons the scales have been removed. The number of sales force visits made to solve customer issues decreased by two-thirds. The number of phone calls needed to address missing and incorrect information similarly declined. Account targeting improved as evidenced by the number of follow-up calls booked and then subsequently followed through. The number of business reviews with customers tripled.

Figure 6.6 confirms the impact on the business with actual sales gains made with superimposed trend lines.

FIGURE 6.5   Measured effect

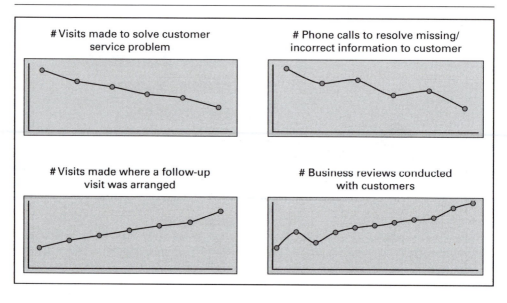

FIGURE 6.6   Outcome

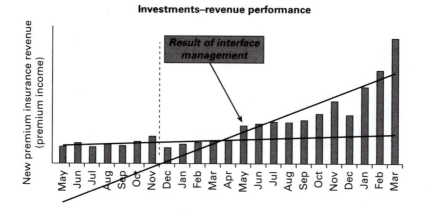

Summary

This chapter set out to establish the link between interfacing activities, the framework for categorizing strategic activity and business outcomes. In summary:

- Interface mapping will always raise the delivery performance of continuous improvement, Lean and Six Sigma programmes by dramatically reducing the effort needed to define the problem to be tackled and by enabling the full potential to be defined and thus targeted.

- An understanding of the impact of interfacing activity noise can only be obtained by interface mapping all relevant parts of the business so that the accumulated total impact of each causal factor on the business can be used to set change priorities.

- The participation of staff and managers inherent to interface mapping enables some of the most frequently encountered change resistance to be easily managed or avoided altogether.

- Transferring noise to core to achieve strategic alignment of business processes is achieved through a process that implants the management principles focusing on strategic intent we identified in our international research.

Organizational 'genomics'
Strategic process analysis focused on implementation

07

Objectives

The case for interface mapping as a mechanism to understand business processes has been made in previous chapters. The resulting potentially large database needs to be structured to enable it to be updated and analysed by business process and for its complexity to be managed, and especially so in large organizations. The requirement is therefore for a comprehensive and systematic framework, and approach, to identifying, prioritizing and implementing the process changes that deliver the maximum 'bang for the buck' of business benefit to effort.

There is also a latent need to combine databases from a number of organizations in order to analyse the end-to-end business process for today's multi-organization value chains. This chapter explores this requirement and describes the practical and easy-to-use mechanism that has evolved to meet the need.

Introduction

Chapter 3 explained how most contemporary business process change is undertaken with scant knowledge of the critical interfacing activities that determine cost and service outcomes. Instead, managers are more likely to place their faith in experts who will rely on their own judgement informed by high-level process maps, which cover only a quarter of the steps undertaken by the staff. Chapters 4 and 5 contained an extensive analysis of the interfacing activities that had been documented using an interface mapping tool with the full participation of the staff, that is, those staff actually doing the work in each of the organizations. The analysis demonstrated that activity data, particularly interfacing activity data, has the potential to enable process changes to be precisely and explicitly defined.

A tool that unambiguously links the staff's 'micro' activities to the 'macro' strategic framework was also unveiled. This is the framework for categorizing strategic activity. It is made up of four categories: core, support, discretionary and noise. Chapter 6 reviewed examples of two companies that demonstrated how they had released themselves from their enslavement to dysfunctional interface activity noise activities and successfully transferred much of this wasted activity to value-driving core activity and revenue-earning support activity. One of the companies had achieved this by setting up a new business process, a process to build strategic capabilities, continuously to define and deploy strategically focused changes to their business processes. This new business process then continued to be used to release resource engaged in interface activity noise, and use it to fund performance-driving core activity and revenue-generating support activities as business volumes increased. This capability continually to realign business processes strategically had been achieved by deploying the management principles focusing on strategic intent described in Chapter 2, the management principles needed to align business processes to build competitive advantage.

In Chapter 6 we raised a frequently encountered issue, the frustration generated when staff tried to identify the noise in their interface activities then tried to develop a cost-justified case to address it. Most people found that this was impossible to do. On one hand, the existing process mapping tools are all but blind to the critical interfacing activities, and on the other, even if some interface mapping had been undertaken, the sheer size of the database provided an almost impenetrable barrier to unstructured analysis. Further, even if it had been possible to accumulate the interfacing activity noise by causal factor and prioritize the change needs then the cultural and other barriers described would render multi-division change all but impossible.

The key question this chapter addresses is how to manage and use the mass of data generated by interface mapping to enable the priority strategic change needs to be analysed, and solutions unambiguously defined quickly, efficiently and with the full engagement of the affected staff. The chapter describes the framework needed for this, which replaces and *integrates* the required two views of an organization, the vertical view of its structure and the horizontal view of its business processes.

The largest organization where we have used interface mapping included over 7,000 staff. Combing through this vast quantity of data, in this case well over 100,000 activities, to draw out the opportunities is a daunting undertaking. In the early days the work was carried out using spreadsheets that we navigated through using conventional (ie mainly functional activity) process maps. This led to the realization that there had to be an opportunity to use this real data derived from interface mapping to construct an organizational 'genome' that could be used much as cartographic databases are used by GPS software to define routes to destinations and then navigate to them. This realization ultimately set the goal for the development of the XeP3 tool that allows precise description of how businesses operate. It allows managers and change professionals to abandon the use of 'models' and 'representations' that require the application of huge quantities of experience and judgement to 'envision' solutions. This is replaced by engaging operational staff in the documentation and then in developing the practical solutions they themselves can largely apply, using the interface maps to plan and implement these solutions efficiently. Engaging staff in generating solutions has two huge advantages – a vastly reduced need for capital expenditure to align business processes and resistance to change becoming yesterday's problem.

We present more on the obsolescence of 'models' in a later chapter. For the present let's dive deeper into the functional and interfacing activity data itself and the use and value of the new analytical framework for activity analysis.

Need for a new 'genomic' framework – summary

If the interfacing activities in a business process remain undocumented and unknown then it is impossible to describe with certainty all the activities needed to achieve a different outcome. Ignoring the interfacing activities and pressing on with change is hardly a wise option, as demonstrated by the high levels of waste endemic in most organizations however much they have invested to date in improvement initiatives.

Organizations cannot simply assume that interface activities will be unaffected by the deployment of (functional) change. They will change because interfacing activities are always materially affected when elements of any business process change: interfacing activities 'glue' the functional activities together, so a need to 're-glue' is almost inevitable. So if an organization ignores interfacing activities it does so at its peril because the unknowns in its change programme will simply increase in ways not anticipated and play havoc with the outcome by creating a new raft of 'viral' noise. In Chapter 8 there is an example of what then happens when interfacing activity is ignored. We ask you a key question: how can organizations justify ignoring interfacing activities when liberating noise would fund their change programme and, at the same time, virtuously deliver useful benefits as a by-product?

Sadly, a lack of knowledge of interfacing activities has never deterred anyone from promoting change. At the same time prudent managers, many of whom will have experienced disappointments in change actually delivered, have learned to insist that something must be measured so that they can have confidence that commissioned change actually takes place. A whole industry has thus grown up to paper over this rather glaring gap in planning and executing change. So how does it usually work? Solutions protagonists passionately believe will deliver the desired business outcomes are postulated using the 'judgement' and 'experience' of those engaged. The plans to implement these educated guesses are then reviewed and accepted by senior managers and specific budgets and delivery dates are agreed. Hey presto, with the sleight of hand of a practised conjuror, we now have proposed action steps, a budget and a date, all of which can easily be monitored and progress measured. The only casualty in this masterfully executed deception is the objective of the change itself, the business outcome required!

The project then progresses, staged payments are authorized and paid and the change is delivered on budget and on time. Then, to everyone's feigned surprise after so much careful planning, the change does not deliver the required business outcomes. The providers will be quick to point out that every one of the planned steps was carried out, the project was on time and it came in under budget. Oops! The only option left for management is to authorize rectification work and 'bug' fixing at additional cost, and try yet another judgement-based change. Meanwhile, customer service and the business will continue to be disrupted and staff will be struggling with the redesign and investing new interfacing activities to work around the effects of another change initiative that didn't quite deliver. The driver of all this noise is the failure to manage interfacing activities.

Success is therefore rarely couched in business outcome terms. How often do we hear management talking of success, or writing about them in annual reports, with terms such as: 'SAP is a great system, it only took us a year to get it going'; 'The new HR system went in on time and ahead of budget'; 'The new sales force structure has been fully implemented'; 'Everyone is now using the latest operating system on their desk tops'; 'We had the usual problems with outsourcing our call centre but the transfer was finished well ahead of schedule'. But what about business outcomes? What is not talked about is the business benefit, and the degree of compliance to the desired strategic outcome. That got lost in the sleight of hand when the transposition from outcome to cost and budget took place.

The real issue with interface mapping

So how can an organization set itself up to achieve strategic alignment of business processes that is focused on outcome, and avoid taking the wrong steps? The answer to achieving the required strategic outcomes must lie in first understanding what really happens. Interface mapping delivers this knowledge quickly and easily by documenting what really is going on so as to inform the change planning.

When interface mapping is proposed it is not unusual to hear comments like: 'Will the staff cooperate – bound to be tricky isn't it?'; 'How do we know all that data will be right, who is going to check it?'; 'Getting that level of detail will take forever, after all we put two people on to process map the whole business two years ago without getting to that level of detail and we still haven't finished!'; 'Every time we try to use process mapping it interrupts our staff's work so much they always complain and we have only tried to get functional activities'; 'Have you thought about how many activities would need to be analysed? It was 18,725 in an 800-person organization, and we are bigger than that.'

Surely, if getting this data to do a job with outcomes that can be properly modelled means managing a lot of data, these objections are not important. Navman, TomTom, Google search engines and Google Earth and Street View have built huge businesses by providing a small device or software system that contains a reasonably complex bit of software and a huge database. A GPS device clips onto the dashboard and manages a large database of road interfacing data, in order to advise the driver of when and how to change his or her route. These devices have demonstrated that they contain every street and alleyway in the United States, Australia, Europe, Japan and elsewhere.

We have all heard complaints about GPS systems, but never ones that suggest simplifying the database by leaving out potentially vital links. Perhaps if this were the case the GPS cartographers would only map major roads and drop out small villages, leaving the driver to use his or her judgement. In fact the really serious complaints about GPS systems occur when their cartographers have not been detailed enough. Heavy goods vehicles have got stuck on narrow farm tracks (one had to be lifted out by crane) or been directed onto roads that have not been made yet. The truck drivers in these unfortunate situations are left to sort out the mess, much as the hapless junior employee has to work out how to cope with the ill-defined implementation of change originating from poor business organizational 'genomics' and the triumph of hope over experience. What is the difference in principle between developing the cartography of a road network for defining a route, and using the functional and interfacing activity 'genome' in a business, a linkage network, to define change, other than organizational interface mapping is much, much easier?

First, let's look at the facts to expose the real problem with interface mapping, a problem we struggled hard to solve for a number of years. We actually rolled out the solution for the first time in 1996 in a project under-taken in partnership with HP to address their demanding work–life balance goals. The project was undertaken under the stewardship of Roy Armour to whom we accord a great deal of thanks. But back to the facts in order to dispel the myths that surround both process and interface mapping.

Conventional process mapping is usually carried out by an expert who will start at the beginning of a process and follow it through to the end, in effect pretending to be a transaction passing from activity to activity until the need it represents is satisfied. It is perhaps somewhat like a patient enter-ing hospital with a need and then being passed from activity to activity to first diagnose the problem and then render the cure. The mapper's objective is to develop a map of where the transaction goes on its journey through the business. We used to try to do mapping by following the process through to get the detail and, additionally to get the buy-in of the staff. We never got the details we felt were really needed, nor did we ever get the buy-in of the staff. When data showing process failure was revealed to staff they always denied that it was their data. Also, it was never possible to present the data in such a way that they could easily read and understand it and would be willing to use it. We found it impossible to get to the detail level to capture all the functional and interfacing activities for a number of reasons:

- Someone had to determine what makes up a process before the work starts to set up the interviews. It is common practice for the interviewer to do this. The first challenge then is how the interviewer can do this with little knowledge of the business and access usually only to the managers who do not know the detail anyway (see Figure 3.1 on page 59). Remember, from Chapter 1, the 4,000-person US business where only 14 per cent of the activities routinely carried out were mapped as a prerequisite to the redesign of their process for a worldwide roll out? The most frightening thing was not the number of routine steps that were left out (86 per cent of them) but that the managers did not know that these steps were being done every day by their staff. No wonder their initial benchmarking comparisons showed they were grossly overstaffed. Chapter 8 describes a case with the same benchmarking trap.

- There are often specializations and variations in how non-mainstream transactions are handled. It does not seem really feasible to spend a couple of hours with everyone in the business to pick these variations up. If there were 800 people in the organization, two hours spent with each, for example, would amount to a year of effort. Then there would be the need to quantify it and check that it was correct.

- Then there is the problem of fitting all of the data into a process map format and connecting all the activities together. The result, with at least four times as much data (see Table 3.1 on page 69) if it were possible, would make Hampton Court maze look as simple as the blinking of an eye. We know, we should have been awarded a medal for persistence as we tried and tried for years.

- Usually, only the expert mapper really understands the process map he or she produces; it is, like all works of art, the mapper's interpretation of reality.

- Then there is the problem of variations. Think of the patients in a hospital. Some enter through emergency and are triaged, others are admitted directly. Some need an x-ray, others need an x-ray, an ultrasound and a CAT scan. Some are allergic to penicillin. And so on. All these side processes need to be mapped (easy) and fitted, with interaction consequences into the main flow (hard). It is hard enough to connect everything together at high functional level, without trying to fit in all the thousands of connections, to map the noise arising from essential contact with others.

- Finally, and this is the killer, now that you understand the value of interface mapping, how do you get the elemental times for each activity? How long would it take with a stop watch to time all 18,725 activities in Figure 3.6 on page 74? Of course compromises would be made, only the major activities would be measured and three in four of the activities, the interfacing activities, would be ignored again.

A tool is needed to cope efficiently and effectively with the volume and complexity of the data, just as a GPS device gives users a tremendous 'live' map with sufficient detail to guide decision making.

Interface mapping only suffers from one of the above problems, and that in a minor way. The big difference with interface mapping is that it is carried out by those doing the job. So those doing the mapping know intimately everything they do (and if they do not then there is no one else to turn to). Second, when mapping say 70 teams, 70 or more 'cartographers' are engaged in doing it, all following a standard documentation approach. However, even after staff have attended training and received a thorough explanation they often view even the interface mapping process with initial suspicion. They just do not believe that what really happens will be properly recorded. As soon as they get into documenting their interfacing activities, however, all lingering scepticism and reluctance turns to enthusiasm and commitment. The danger in managing staff in this part of the process is that they will get so caught up in it that they will spend too much time getting it all just right or start to make significant organizational change on their own.

The facts for interface mapping are:

- It takes three elapsed weeks in virtually any size of organization because all the teams develop their data in parallel. The largest organization we have been involved with mapped 22,000 staff in this time frame and the smallest, one person.

- Specializations and variations are included because they will be documented by the people who do them, and those people always insist that this happens.

- No time is wasted trying to fit the activities into a 'picture' or map. The staff use familiar listing formats to record their activities in a structured way within their team. Software is used to drag and drop chunks of process to assemble the end-to-end process activity maps needed for strategic analysis.

- Nothing can be left out by oversight, or deliberately because it could not be fitted in. The staff ensure that everything they do is captured. When the process maps are constructed using interface mapped data every activity has to be allocated to a process with accounting-like discipline. Those involved are prompted to address any activities left out. A process home has to be found for them.

- Quantification of resource is carried out by members of each team allocating their time at the same time as validating that everything that is done is present and correct. Then they are usually invited to code the strategic activities that link the micro (the detailed activities they do) to the macro (the business strategy in the database and in their minds). This is both a short, sharp education session and a mechanism to agree the interfacing activity noise activities and therefore highlight the opportunity to move noise to core.

A summary comparison of the features of interface mapping and process mapping is shown in Table 7.1.

So in a typical case, at the end of the three-week period the data comprised 18,725 activities, the collective output of the 70 teams in an 800-person organization in our database of 117 interface mapping users. The organization's staff had worked enthusiastically, very much part time, to document, strategically code and certify the data. These same staff had all retained copies of their data to ponder over, and they were largely confident that all the interfacing activity noise, the rubbish (staff in all organizations all over the world usually use the same, rather different word to describe interfacing activity noise) messing them around every day, had been documented to the best of their ability and they were proud of their effort.

The problem was then how to analyse strategically and rigorously the 18,275 activities conducted in the 800-person organization, with the data being held in 70 'buckets', one for each organizational team.

Organizational 'genomics'

The data is held in the database separately for each of the 70 work teams. These teams are actually the component parts of the organization, the members of which deliver the services to the customer or to other teams

TABLE 7.1   Comparison of features of interface mapping with conventional process mapping

Conventional process mapping	Interface mapping
It takes three months to over a year	It takes two to three weeks
It looks at functional activities only	It looks at functional activities and interfacing activities
	Every activity is quantified
	Rework and duplication are highlighted
	The process is signed off by staff doing the work
Experts are required to interpret the results	Staff interpret the results and recommend practical changes for managers to prioritize
Experts understand the changes needed	Staff understand and subscribe to the changes needed
If extension is required, there is usually a need to start again	The database can easily be combined to include other enterprises, eg customers and outsourced suppliers

to achieve the objectives of the organization. The organization's structure shows the functional location of each team and the reporting lines. An analyst could therefore access and analyse the data through the organization's structure and model different structural scenarios. Accessing the database by strategic business process would, however, be very difficult. The need is to be able to access and analyse the data strategically. This means accessing the data for analysis by each of the strategic delivery mechanisms, the organization's business processes.

It is now common practice, refreshingly, in operations management texts to represent a business in a way that shows both the structure and its processes on the same chart (Slack *et al*, 2006: Figure 1.8, 17). This form of representation indicates that functions have in reality two sets of objectives, their own functional objectives and those associated with the part they play in the end-to-end business processes. The functional, or structural, dimension of the business is usually represented on the vertical axis and the process dimension on the horizontal axis. Across the top of the chart can be placed the organizational units, the divisions or departments charged with delivering their functional skills in a coordinated way through each of the business processes in which they participate. Arrows, representing each business process and pointing from left to right, then represent the portfolio of processes being used to deliver outcomes in accordance with the strategy of the organization. There would perhaps be a process for processing claims; operating on a patient; dealing with a legal matter; order to delivery; or for new product design and introduction, or market development.

The picture can then be completed by entering on the extreme left-hand end of each process its defined process objectives such as customer or stakeholder needs and business goals. Similarly, on the extreme right-hand end of each process arrow can be placed the ongoing measures of the performance of the process in meeting each of its goals. These measures are the KPIs for that process derived from the Balanced Scorecard for the business.

The challenge is to bring Slack *et al*'s (2006) logical schematic to life. Practical change cannot be determined from theoretical representations, however good they are. So an organization needs to populate the picture with real data, structure, processes and measures and provide the mechanisms to keep it up to date with business performance and changes in resources and processes. If that were possible to achieve it would provide an organization with the organizational 'genomics' to form the platform to implement one of the management principles focused on strategy (described fully in Chapter 2) – being disciplined. It would achieve this by providing the living knowledge platform that could be used by managers and would relate the functional and interfacing activities both to the business process for strategic analysis and to the organizational structure for managers to enforce.

Further, organizational 'genomics' would enable the required analysis to be carried out to use time as a critical organizational dimension to manage the end-to-end business processes. It would thus enable managers to embed within their organization another management principle focusing on strategic intent – being time-based (also described fully in Chapter 2). Table 7.2 relates how such organizational 'genomics', if it existed, would allow managers to embed within their organization, and manage by, all five management principles focusing on strategic intent (see Chapter 2) that our international research found were present in leading organizations.

How interface mapping meets the need

The interface mapping database already described exactly meets the needs of one dimension, the vertical structural dimension. The teams can be located along the top of the 'picture' arranged next to each other in a convenient sequence for each department or division.

TABLE 7.2   Enabling principle-based management to focus on strategic goals

Strategic focusing management principle	Characteristics of principle (see Chapter 2)	Enabling role to be provided by new organizational genomics
Ensuring integration of effort	The organization is focused on value creation and process management, not functional needs and hierarchies	It enables cross-business process analysis to reveal how all functions interact in delivering the outcome. Interfacing activity noise is a primary indicator of dysfunctional lack of alignment
Being disciplined	The organization invests in policies, procedures and standards and applies a strong system perspective in everything it does	It allows up-to-date knowledge management of functional and interfacing activities, business processes, procedures and policies. It enables a systems perspective to be applied to all change initiatives
Creating customer value	All employees understand the set of order winners and actively strive to enhance creation of customer value	All business processes can be analysed to identify compliance with customer needs. Core activity can be implemented to drive creation of organizational value and customer value
Being time-based	Time is developed as a critical organizational value. The business practises the principles of time-based competition	The data enables drivers of delays noise to be pinpointed to focus change initiatives on eliminating them. Elimination of interfacing activity noise will fund most strategic change initiatives
Creating strategic capabilities	Business and organizational capabilities are defined and prioritized and drive critical development and investment decisions	It provides the repository that describes the existing state of the organization's capabilities. it enables modelling of future states. It provides the mechanism, potentially, to manage change to keep the focus on gaining strategic alignment.

We then investigated various ways of efficiently and quickly cross-coding every detailed activity to enable it to be the base record to be accessed functionally and by process. We had to take some important and increasingly obvious decisions at this stage. The base record would be the individual detailed activity determined by the staff and there would be a hierarchy of activities that would connect the activities to the team and the team to the organizational structure. Further, every base record would be cross-coded to the position in the business process in which it played a part. This provided a mechanism for generating procedures with links to standing instructions and for providing process descriptions at whatever level of detail was needed. Further, the need to link change initiatives to the activities that would be affected was anticipated and this subsequently enabled web-based reporting of progress through measures that could be presented by structure or by process.

The software developed to meet this need was also set up to flag any activities not allocated to business processes. This ensured adjustments were made to maintain the integrity usually insisted on by engaged staff (see **www.xep3.com**).

This transformed what otherwise would merely be another way of theoretically representing a business into a complete description of the real business. The database can support scenario modelling; automatic update of company procedures; maintain an up-to-date record of process descriptions; link in and track the progress of all changes and planned changes to activities; track changes by process and by function, etc. A screen dump of the top-level two-dimensional organizational database is included as Figure 7.1 and the first page of the interfacing activity process map for business process 5 is included as Figure 7.2, a screen print from the tool.

Analysing and using interface mapped data

Having access to a database that links every individual activity (and therefore every group of activities) to a strategic business process gives an analyst a huge advantage. The sequenced process listing in Figure 7.2 (one page of 31) shows every functional and interfacing activity; which team does it; how much resource it absorbs; how it relates to the strategy through the activity coding; how it relates to all the other teams in the process, including those in other connected businesses such as customers, suppliers and outsourced support services; etc. The level of noise and core, for instance, can immediately be quantified and the upstream causes and downstream consequences of all noise are laid out for everyone to see.

This data thus becomes extremely valuable to the strategic process analyst. It allows the analyst, or any staff member, to code each and every interfacing activity noise occurrence in the process to its cause and thus to

FIGURE 7.1   Interface mapping relationship between structure and business processes

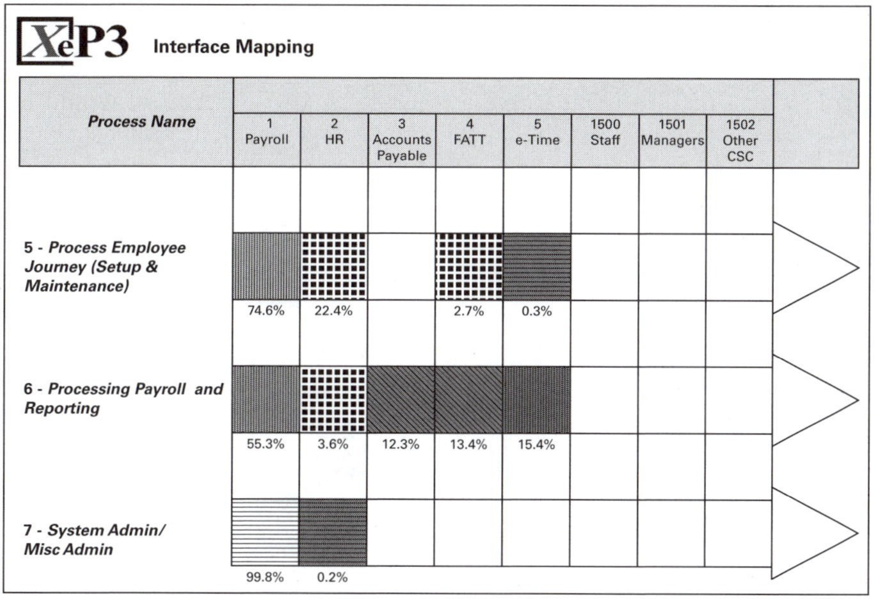

XeP3 Interface Mapping								
Process Name	1 Payroll	2 HR	3 Accounts Payable	4 FATT	5 e-Time	1500 Staff	1501 Managers	1502 Other CSC
5 - Process Employee Journey (Setup & Maintenance)	74.6%	22.4%		2.7%	0.3%			
6 - Processing Payroll and Reporting	55.3%	3.6%	12.3%	13.4%	15.4%			
7 - System Admin/ Misc Admin	99.8%	0.2%						

accumulate the resource level absorbed by each of the causes in order to generate a priority list. Further, the analyst and staff members can just by inspection see what is causing the noise and pinpoint the team where it enters the process. So even if the noise is 'given' to the organization by its customer, and cannot therefore immediately be addressed, the contagion can be prevented from entering the business (ie errors and omissions can be detected and rectified by the receiving team) and all the consequential downstream noise eliminated. The contagion is thus prevented, the disruption can be avoided, its cost can be harvested and redeployed and service levels improved. A small part of its cost can be reinvested either in internal core activity that eliminates internally caused noise, or in mandated discretionary checking to detect and contain the externally generated noise (from the customer, etc) until an initiative can be put in place to ensure that it is eliminated.

The same data, again with little more than a glance, shows which teams are suffering from the noise and by how much. This means that the people who know everything there is to be known about how the noise originates, and how it affects the business, can be named and invited to a meeting to agree how to resolve it. The most common solution therefore is not capital expenditure; it is low-cost training, changing instructions or injecting a small amount of core time to make sure the problem is eliminated and

FIGURE 7.2   Interfacing activity process map

XeP3					Process Chart Report					
Process 5 - Process Employee Journey (Setup & Maintenance)										
Step No	Step	Cat	Hours	Annual Cost per Step ($000s)	1 Payroll	2 HR	4 FATT	5 e-Time	1500 Staff	1501 Managers
1	INITIAL HIRE AND SETUP NEW STARTS									
2	Hire Perm Employee and Initiate Pre Start									
2.1	Make offer to candidate (ensure they have all documentation)	S	0.0	0.0		■			■	
2.3	If informaton not returned by candidate, chase up prior to start or ASAP	N	5.86	0.0		■			■	
2.5	Initiate Pre Start Induction (employee #, IT, Desk Security)	S	0.98	0.0		■				
2.6	Receive New employee advice by e form (New Appointment Form)	S	1.3	0.0	■					
2.7	Issue employee number	S	1.3	0.0	■					
2.8	Email to resource manager and HR recruitment team	S	1.3	0.0	■					
2.9	If in centre also email to Resource manager request	S	1.3	0.0	■					
2.10	If offer not accepted, reverse Pre Start	N	0.98	0.0		■				
2.11	(If start date change manager updates E form)	N	3.91	0.0		■				
2.12	(If manager does not notify start date potential payroll/system issue)	N	3.91	0.0		■				
3	Add Perm Employee to System and e Time									
3.1	Receive complete information from employee	S	1.3	0.0	■				■	
3.3	Check bank details are correct if new BSB	D	2.73	0.0	■					

mandating an even smaller amount of discretionary time to make sure it stays eliminated.

It all sounds rather simple and straightforward, and indeed it is. If the right data is available then priorities are easily established, the causes identified and usually low-cost solutions envisioned and deployed. As Jack Welch, the former head of GE comments, give the members of any management team the same, good data and they will come up with pretty much the same cost-effective solution. Without the information everything requires an injection of significant time and resource to do every step in effecting the change. A team will need to be selected. This team will only by chance involve anyone who understands the issue so its members will have to do a lot on investigation; they will need to think through how to go about it. When they start their investigation, they are unlikely to become aware of all of the ramifications in the business so at best only a third of the benefits it will be harvested. They are also likely to make assumptions and use their judgement, and far from getting staff on side, they are likely to become a cause for concern.

Strategically defining business process change

It is now time to revisit the issue of achieving strategic alignment of business processes. The process described immediately above is primarily focused on eliminating interfacing activity noise, leaving customer service, equipment utilization, risk reduction and staff satisfaction to emerge untargeted.

Once the interface mapping exercise has been completed and the business processes populated the scene is set for a strategic analysis. There are two ways of looking at business processes in order to achieve strategic alignment and thus effectively deploy the organization's strategy. The first is to understand the strategic goals of the key service delivery, risk management, environmental impact, product or policy development processes etc, and to analyse that business process to pinpoint non-compliance with the management principles focusing on strategic intent. The second is to analyse the business process to identify and prioritize the interface activity noise drivers, align them with the principles and seek out those that will provide the greatest benefit. Both are approached using the interface maps (Figure 7.2). Obviously, the more precisely the non-delivery of a strategic goal is understood, the quicker it is to find and address the elements of the business process that are not compliant because of the high level of interfacing activity noise induced. Ideally, you will know the strategic goals for each process, which of them need to be improved and by how much.

To illustrate how to move from productivity focused change to strategically focused change we should consider an example. Let's revisit the example given in Chapter 2, involving the transport industry. Here's a reminder of the details.

The strategic need arose for two quite separately managed organizations. One of them was a supply group reporting to the organization's headquarters. The other, which was the customer of the supply group, operated and monitored the crucial items of equipment. The strategic issue was that costs in the supply group were rising out of control while equipment serviceability was falling in the operations business raising the spectre of massive and unbudgeted investment.

The interface mapping data was collected over a three-week period and then the first strategically focused analytical step was taken. Priority was given to building the maintenance and parts replenishment process from the collected activity data for immediate analysis. This was because the cost of maintenance was rising at the same time that the KPIs showed that waiting for parts was the most common reason logged against unserviceable items. The analysis of the staff and management development process, the major equipment upgrade process and the long-term replacement process were not immediately addressed even though the highest noise levels were to be found in them. This was a strategic choice because the highest-priority strategic process issues are not always where the highest levels of interfacing activity noise occur. Indeed, in those critical business processes where there are few staff employed the interfacing activity noise will obviously be lower than that found in large processing centres or in large production facilities.

The situation was tense. The fitters said they were constantly chasing missing parts and consumables and were demanding that something should be done about the obvious 'failure to supply' by the contracted supply companies, virtually all of whom had significant order backlogs. The fitters were asking why supply staff couldn't devote more time to working with the suppliers to help them get on top of the backlog. The supply staff, however, were overstretched trying to cope with the situation but maintained it was not their job because most of the replenishment systems were run by the supply companies. There was strong, and growing, pressure to agree with the fitters' demands to get out there to the companies and work closely with them to improve their performance.

The list of noise drivers in the end-to-end business processes of maintenance and parts replenishment were quickly established. There were many different drivers, but the highest level of interfacing activity noise was associated with chasing suppliers for urgently needed consumables and major spares. The analyst worked with the supply staff to code each of the drivers to indicate the degree to which each influenced the volume and cost of spares (the principle of being time-based) and had an impact on reducing equipment serviceability (the principle of creating customer value). There were sub-noise drivers associated with fielding urgent enquiries from operations on availability of parts when an item went unserviceable; follow-up enquiries from the maintenance fitters on when parts could be expected; arranging immediate transport for urgent spares; authorizing penalty rates for urgent items; additional payments to suppliers for rescheduling refurbishment programmes; assistance to the fitters to deal with their backlog of administration tasks; serviceability assessment on refurbished units; and many others. A number of the coded drivers stood out. One was the amount of effort being devoted to assessing, reworking and transporting refurbished units that had been found to be unusable when required. A second was the unusual interfacing activity of helping and supporting the obviously hard-pressed maintenance fitters to keep their records up to date. Both of these had been coded to driving excessive costs and reducing serviceability.

The issues were crystal clear. Consumables and spares operated on a system where usage and lead time triggered replenishment by the supply companies. How could they operate if the usage records were six weeks or more out of date? And why were refurbished units not serviceable? They were being cannibalized or used way ahead of planned changeovers to compensate for shortages in spares. The solution was an injection of core activity to ensure the records were kept up to date and discretionary activity to ensure that it was being done. Maintaining up-to-date usage records by the fitters (the people shouting the loudest and suffering most from the shortages) were reclassified as one of their core activities (achieved therefore at zero cost as they had to do it at some time) and an audit procedure (discretionary activity) was mandated to monitor that the usage was indeed being kept up to date weekly.

This type of measure we refer to as a behavioural change indicator (BCI) for reasons that are obvious. Clearly, if the behaviour had changed and the records were kept up to date then the orders for the spares would be placed weekly according to the schedule and lead times provided by the suppliers. The BCI would show that the critical interface between the fitters, the supplies group and the suppliers was being managed. This BCI was of course applied at a particular place in the process on a particular team. It was therefore one of the key measures that drove a particular business process KPI outcome in the Balanced Scorecard. We tend to look on this operationalization of the Balanced Scorecard as establishing the 'DNA' of the business. If BCI s are established for all the core activities needed to prevent interfacing activity noise from entering the business process then compliance means that the interfacing activity 'glue' is properly tuned to the needs of the business. A weekly visit (discretionary activity) was thus mandated on the fitters' manager to ensure that this core activity was being done. Ten minutes per week invested in a mandated check was the key to improving equipment availability, saving all the time wasted on interfacing activity noise.

One could rightly argue that the solution would have been obvious to any experienced maintenance person. Of course, an experienced maintenance person's mental checklist would include records up to date; replenishment lead times correctly set; lead times being met; algorithm to calculate replenishment levels appropriate for today's circumstances; invoices being paid on time; correct spares being used; spares being fitted correctly; fraud; theft; correctly accredited staff in suppliers; adherence to quality assurance procedures; normal usage patterns for the equipment. How long would it have taken to get to the bottom of the problem if someone had started at the wrong end of the checklist? How many changes to any or all of these checklist items would have been discussed, planned, agreed and unnecessarily deployed, disturbing the fragile interfacing activity portfolio before the right one was addressed. Finally, because eventually the right solution would be deployed, how would the managers know that the new regime was being adhered to? Would it not simply be yet another good idea that did not work because of the cultural barriers to change?

Summary

The objectives set at the beginning of this chapter were to explain the need for and then the implementation of and a new but easy-to-use and efficient way to structure organizational data so that it can be analysed strategically (ie by process) and the changes enforced and benefits harvested at team level (ie by organizational structure). The mechanism described has been extensively used. It allows organizations to manage and analyse interfacing and functional data easily and thus navigate through the detailed 'organizational cartography' with ease. The aim of the analysis tool is to enable an organization efficiently to design initiatives that would achieve the strategic alignment of business processes, obtain full buy-in from the staff, deploy the changes and ensure that the benefits are fully harvested. In this way organizations will be able to build and continually maintain their strategic capabilities keeping pace with regulatory reforms and other changes. We have gone a step further down this road and introduced the concept of 'organizational DNA' and the very powerful BCI measures to ensure changes stay in place.

The term organizational 'genomics' was suggested by Suzy Goldsmith of the Department of Management at Melbourne University. She argued that new terminology is required to encourage managers to think differently. We are grateful for her advice. Whether this name will stick we don't know but the need for such a mechanism should now be clear.

The chapter has explored the differences between process and interface mapping. While you may still argue that an expert may have sufficient time allocated, and the wit and experience to be able to incorporate the critical interface activities into a conventional process map, the needed quantification is impracticably difficult. Further, conventional process mapping may alienate staff. It will certainly fail to build the understanding and enthusiasm in the staff and managers that is so vital to successful deployment of change. Change imposed is change opposed.

The chapter has also established the relationship between the organizational 'genomics' and the management principles focusing on strategic intent so characteristic of leading organizations. The organizational 'genomics' provides the platform to define what needs to be changed to achieve strategic alignment of business processes by establishing in an organization the management principles focusing on strategic intent and imparting the ability to catch up with the principles used by the best in the world.

Principles by which leading organizations drive change

08

Objectives

This chapter is focused on:

- Ensuring that the implementation of change occurs. All too often, even efficient organizations do a much better job formulating their forward strategy than implementing it. Strategy implementation is substantially about process and change management, which requires realistic and full knowledge of the existing process as the starting point.

- Embedding the capability to deploy change systematically in the organization. Instead of having external advisers come in like 'seagulls' and advise or impose change, then 'fly away' until next time, there is no better way to drive improvement than to involve staff closely from the start in the process. Strategic change needs to be based on possessing the process capability to make the changes.

- Effective management of the culture needed to support and drive change. Behaviour needs guidance and leadership in order to be effective and goal-directed. Performance management is important, which requires sound measurement as a base. This needs to be done in a way that allows for employee ownership, and trust in those measures.

This chapter provides a practical means for achieving these challenging capabilities.

Introduction

The leading organizations taken from our international survey and described in Chapter 2 are characterized by living and breathing four segments of management principles. The first of these is the determination to achieve leading status – the desire to be out front. These organizations strive to lead the pack in every aspect. They achieve their strategic focus from the adherence to the second segment of principles, those that determine how the leaders define their strategic capabilities and keep them up to date. These have been termed the five management principles focusing on strategic intent. By adhering to them the organizations continually redefine their business processes to maintain integration across the business using a disciplined approach to deliver customer value and eliminate waste. Chapters 3 to 7 explored the pivotal role that interfacing activities play in enabling leading organizations to embed within their organizations these management principles focusing on strategic intent.

However, prioritizing, defining and quantifying each element of the change needed to build these strategic capabilities can only deliver value when the changes are actually deployed. So this chapter explores the third segment of management principles, those employed by leading organizations to create the culture needed to deploy their strategic change. The management principles to create this culture for deployment from our survey are: relating the micro to the macro; establishing a learning culture; embracing change; supporting distributed leadership; measuring and reporting; being up front; and gaining alignment. Table 8.1 (an extract from Table 2.2 on page 36), is included below.

Need for the deployment culture management principles

We were asked recently and urgently, to help a well-known consumer goods company to strategically realign its business processes following a downsizing exercise imposed by its corporate office that had gone horribly wrong. The downsizing exercise, which had been mounted in the manufacturing plant, had failed primarily for two reasons. First, the top-tier consultants retained for the task paid scant attention to interfacing activities. They had defined and implemented dramatically reduced staffing levels using data from international benchmarks without understanding local market influences or how the company managers had achieved market dominance and high profitability. Second, a perfect storm had been created because the disenfranchised managers were not committed to the change nor did they work closely with the staff to make the change happen. They neither understood nor supported the management principles needed to establish a culture for

TABLE 8.1 The third set of management principles used to create a culture for deploying strategic change

Relating the micro to the macro	All employees know how their particular activities and individual efforts contribute to the 'big picture 'of business success
Establishing a learning culture	All employees demonstrate a willingness to develop skills and knowledge and are involved in a learning/development programme
Embracing change	All employees demonstrate a willingness to embrace and accept change as an essential part of doing business. The organization excels in implementing new ideas
Supporting distributed leadership	Individuals and work teams are assigned, and accept, responsibility for operational decision making and performance improvement
Measuring and reporting	The business measures and reports to all employees the financial and non-financial performance information needed to drive improvement
Being up front	All employees demonstrate integrity and openness in all areas of their work and dealings with others. Relationships are highly valued
Gaining alignment	There is good alignment of employee behaviour with stated company values and direction at all levels in the organization. Employees are involved

deployment of change found in leading organizations, which would have been needed to achieve such a massive productivity step change if customer service levels and market dominance were to be maintained. We presume that this hands-off approach was adopted because the managers were, perhaps understandably, trying to send a message back to their overseas headquarters to back off. We say perhaps this was understandable because the business had been one of the most profitable in the world before the change had been imposed. Desperate as the situation became, the case does provide an ideal platform to illustrate the nature of the management principles needed to establish a culture for the effective deployment of change.

The company, let's call it InterCo, is well known and always seen as extraordinarily successful. It distributes its products in over 100 countries. It has multiple manufacturing plants situated in every continent.

The operation's impressive array of high level KPIs revealed an organization where, in the last six months, customer service levels had dropped from over 98 per cent to around 85 per cent, wastage had spiralled out of control, overtime had skyrocketed and staff morale and turnover had become major issues. On our initial visit to the factory the director of manufacturing, who had recently been transferred from a similar-sized overseas plant in the group, showed us around. He had been charged with fixing the mess and was intent on doing it quickly to prove his capability and avoid further harm to the brand. He appeared to be somewhat isolated from the other senior managers.

The company's overseas parent had insisted that the company should use consultants who were flown in to benchmark the operation's production facilities and then lead a downsizing exercise they claimed would achieve international best-practice staffing levels and massively raise already exceptional profitability. The consultants had access to benchmark data from the firm's other plants as well as data pertaining to other major manufacturing operations. As a result of their work, some six months previously, 30 per cent of the staff had been made redundant.

Our initial brief was to use interface mapping to examine the business processes to pinpoint and quantify the major operational impediments to efficient factory and warehouse operation, in order to get performance back up to pre-downsizing levels. The manufacturing director was confident that managers in the manufacturing team would be able to manage the implementation themselves. All they wanted to use interface mapping to achieve was to document the needed actions.

Members of the manufacturing management team were therefore anxious to get things moving quickly and tabled the extensive process maps of the pre-downsized business processes – prepared as a prerequisite to benchmarking and downsizing. These maps were, as is sadly almost always the case, pitched at the functional level and revealed little of the interfacing activity and none of the interfacing activity noise. They were very similar in appearance to those prepared by the Pensions team in Chapter 3 (see Figure 3.2 on page 67) before managers refocused on interfacing activity using interface mapping. The maps suffered therefore from the usual limitation, and at that stage we could not know, that perhaps as many as three in every four of the activities actually being done routinely had not been documented (the explanation of why this occurs in virtually every organization is given in Chapter 3 and the analysis in Figure 3.4 on page 70).

Our immediate request to spend three weeks working helping the staff to document exactly what they were actually doing – their functional and interfacing activities – was at first rejected by the managers. Two reasons were given. The first was that the managers felt that the work, in the form of the tabled bound volumes of process maps, had only recently been done over a period of months. They did not wish to disturb the now hard-pressed staff again and, in any case, they were doubtful that we could achieve any more detail in only three weeks. The second was that the managers expected that the workforce, and particularly the plant's unions, would be antagonistic.

The managers were, however, quickly persuaded to support interface mapping. They recognized immediately the potential importance of interfacing activities when they studied some extracts of the much more comprehensive data that had been prepared by staff teams in another, non-competing, but similar manufacturing company. They also were quick to observe that the downsizing would certainly have forced many changes to the interfacing activities undertaken routinely by their staff so their maps would be out of date. In fact they commented that their problems were almost certainly buried in these little-recognized and as yet never documented interfacing activities.

The workforce and unions presented a greater challenge, but again the offer first to get a real understanding of what was happening eventually won through. A large meeting was called by the senior union representatives. All of the site union representatives were required to attend along with a full-time union official. Production managers were requested not to attend. Some 20 people attended what proved to be a very tense meeting. The meeting convenor welcomed everyone and thanked them for their time before outlining the recent history of the plant in which he acknowledged the deteriorating performance. He placed the deterioration in the context of a clear and present threat to everyone's job and said that the meeting had only taken place because it might result in a positive outcome from a break in the current deadlock. He also said that the staff as a whole was dead set against any further intervention by consultants. He then introduced us, as consultants, and walked away to sit down at the back of the room.

A personally painful period followed. We felt quite isolated standing in front of the group of shop stewards. Hostile challenges came from everywhere with questions such as: 'What can you possibly do to help?'; 'What do you know about factories?'; 'Did you know that until the last lot of consultants intervened we were among the best performing in the industry?' Then we somehow managed to say a key word without realizing it. The word was training. 'What training?' someone shouted and others began to join in and jeer. 'We haven't had any training here now for over a year.' Everyone seemed to be laughing at a joke we were not able to share. 'Training to write down what you really do, not what your procedures say you should do,' we answered, and to our astonishment the attendees sat forward in their chairs and started to listen. We explained about interfacing activities and interfacing activity noise. They nodded in agreement. We showed examples of how poorly planned downsizing had inevitably increased interfacing activity noise and therefore increased the loading on the remaining staff, perhaps the real victims of the change. 'That's us mate, are you sure you didn't get one of us to do that for you?' the meeting convenor said. They laughed again, this time all of them joined in because they recognized their own predicament in the data. We also explained that the victims we were referring to were the people left in the organization after the downsize, they had not had the benefit of the redundancy package and they had to manage the workload increase. The atmosphere had become electric. Finally, we were able to explain how and why most organizations simply never document or understand interfacing activity. One or two of them actually clapped when we showed them Figure 3.6 (see page 74) giving details for a similar organization to their own.

The whole tone of the meeting changed. The questions on many attendees' lips became much concerned with who was going to collect this real data. How were they going to know the interfacing activity data would be what really happened, warts and all? Who was then going to analyse this data? 'You', we said. The proposal from one of the shop stewards, a middle-aged lady who had launched some of the most barbed of questions, was immediately accepted. Her proposal was that a team consisting of employees who were largely union nominees should be trained to facilitate the data collection – 'so that all the issues that resulted from the downsizing can be properly written down'. The data collection started on the following Monday morning at 8.00 am with a company team, half of which was nominated by the unions and the other half by production management. The data was completed in record time in well under three weeks with an exceptional level of detail.

Sample inspection of the interfacing activity data revealed huge tracts of interfacing activity noise in all parts of the business (as is the case in all organizations). Inability to achieve proper stock rotation in the finished goods warehouse was leading to write-offs of out-of-date stock, much of this being due to errors in recording locations. Problems with availability of fork-lift trucks, arising from lax maintenance and poor battery-charging discipline, was reducing the availability of equipment and therefore warehouse throughput. Various mistakes were being made in despatch of goods because team leaders, who had access to the required paperwork, were unavailable. Instead, they were busy walking around the warehouse looking for lost stock to fulfil orders. Their absence, and the resultant errors, in turn led to returned goods that had to be sorted and returned to stock or written off and destroyed; credit notes needed to be prepared and issued; the resultant customer complaints needed action by sales executives; and, inevitably, there were costly redeliveries, often with additional discounts to 'compensate' the customers, including all the major supermarket chains, for the loss of earning from empty shelf facings. The interfacing activity noise in the factory was also much in evidence. There were large losses of throughput time due to faults with bright stock (new, empty cans); variations in flow rates; communication problems resulting in cooked product being dumped because the filling department was not ready to receive goods; recipe errors resulting in dumping of product because of inability to find the right raw materials due to overcrowding in the small holding area for raw materials on the cooking department floor; etc.

From this interfacing activity data it was easy for us to deduce the activities that the 30 per cent of staff who had been made redundant used to do when things were running so well (before the downsizing). They were without any doubt inspecting in quality. They were checking and correcting to keep everything working smoothly, otherwise the business would have been unable to achieve such high performance and profitability levels before the downsizing. Probably the staff who had been made redundant had been doing interfacing activities such as checking goods were placed in the right slots in the warehouse; checking the fork-lift truck maintenance actually happened and that the trucks were all plugged in to charge each close of business; checking orders were complete; taking stock to inform production planning of what needed to be expedited; checking to see that the raw materials were all ready and accessible to the kitchen staff; etc. When they detected an issue they fixed it by doing the necessary work around interfacing activity.

However, the world had changed irrevocably six months ago. The trick now for implementation was not to put back the 30 per cent staff resource, a route that would have taken perhaps years to achieve as the experienced and often more capable staff were no longer there. They were the ones who would have easily found other jobs elsewhere and had volunteered for the redundancy package. Recruiting and training to replicate the past was just not practical, nor would the HO-sponsored director of manufacturing have been able to support it. The solution was to do the right core activities in the key places to ensure that the errors and omissions that caused so much mayhem downstream did not occur (Figure 5.3 on page 104). Paradoxically to the managers, but not to you the reader, a 20 per cent to 30 per cent noise level would indicate further, significant potential for saving as well as eliminating errors, omissions and overtime – and relieving stress levels!

The team of staff nominated by the union insisted, as expected, on being closely involved in the activity categorization and therefore the quantification of the waste. This delivered a signed-off database showing that 32.3 per cent of, say, 500 people's time (equivalent to 162 full-time staff) was engaged in interfacing activity noise – rework, duplication and unnecessary chasing, and its downstream consequences, which would not be needed if each task was done right first time, on time.

Now we had the data, and a meaty noise level to fund the change, we had another hurdle to jump. The downsizing had destroyed any remaining trust between staff and managers. The team fed back that there was a strong expectation by everyone that the data would be ignored by managers. This proved not to be the case, but this was not the point in the project to relax. The director of manufacturing and the members of his management team, somewhat surprised by the level of interfacing activity noise in their operation, were then very keen, perhaps overly keen indicating incredulity, to see an analysis that would highlight the major drivers of waste. They challenged us to do the analysis (which was actually done largely by the InterCo team) and then to get the staff to propose simple, low-cost solutions that could be quickly implemented. The managers really expected the team to come back with ideas to spend money, a great deal of money, to fix the noise. As usual, many of the most beneficial improvement required no capital expenditure, just behavioural, and therefore procedural, change.

The managers at this point exercised their right to undertake and control the implementation of the staff's recommendations. So let's take two or three examples from the dozens of ideas driven by the interfacing activity data to illustrate what happened, how things could have been and what was needed to implant the deployment culture.

First let's examine a simple, low-cost, low-risk, high-payback initiative proposed by the woman (we will call her Barb) who operated the automatic depalletizer for bright stock cans. Barb's station was next to the depalletizer. Her job was to ensure that the depalletizer arm swept (at high speed) each layer of new empty cans from the pallet onto the moving belt of the massive, high-speed line for the cans to be washed, filled, closed and sterilized and to ensure that the depalletizer was kept supplied with pallets of bright stock.

The 30-page consolidated interface map for the whole line (eg Figure 7.2 on page 144) revealed that a huge amount of staff time was being spent on clearing jams and doing the steps necessary to clear down to enable a restart. Every time the line stopped, the staff at each station had to remove cans to enable a restart. This obviously wasted line capacity because it created a bottleneck limiting production that wasted many operators' time and caused significant product, can and closure waste. The production managers were approached on the matter and the staff team came away informed that there was little opportunity to reduce the stoppages and therefore it was not worth investigating further. The managers had argued that they had spent many thousands of dollars in conjunction with the manufacturer on modifying the line to reduce jams and it was their view, confirmed in their minds by their benchmarking, that the line was set up to operate at its optimum – 'but the team can try if they want to get ideas to reduce the downtime'. The team took on the challenge with some almost instantaneous gratifying and frightening outcomes.

As described previously, interface mapping is done by each team. Consequently, the data showed all the activities undertaken and quantified the resource consumed by each, as well as showing who carried out each activity. It is therefore easy to see who to invite to an ideas meeting to discuss the problem of line stoppages – in this case, all those who had recorded anything to do with high-speed line jams and restarts were invited to the meeting. All were keen to participate. It turned out to be a very short but very, very, focused meeting. Everybody filed into the room and picked up their copy of the line interface maps, which had, of course, been consolidated together to include their bit for the end-to-end process. They spent a few minutes discussing it among themselves – checking their bit was as they had documented and agreed it and looking at the impact of what they did on everyone else. In other words, they were looking at data they could read and from it understand the end-to-end line activities and the interdependencies.

One of the line operators asked why the line had to be stopped so often 'because every time the line is stopped and started it causes a surge in cans so I have to either clear the cans before a restart or have to stop it immediately it restarts to deal with the jams the restart causes. The restart surge always causes a can or two to fall over.' All the heads around the table began nodding in agreement as he spoke and then everyone joined in airing their restart issues. Barb, who had been sitting quietly off to the side listening attentively to the discussion but saying nothing, hesitantly raised her hand. Everyone, seemingly in slow motion, turned to look at her. 'I'm sorry', she said, 'It's all my doing. The depalletizer arm often knocks cans over because of creases in the packaging material between the layers on the pallet so I have been told I have to stop the line to pick the can out.' Barb paused then rather wistfully went on. 'If only I had a stick with a magnet on the end, rather like the ones used by my toddlers in their fishing game, I would be able to flick the overturned cans off the line without hitting the stop button nearly all of the time.' Everyone stared at her and then to her obvious alarm started to clap. A look of extreme embarrassment, lasting for a few seconds, spread across Barb's face, then she just broke out into a huge smile as she realized everyone was right behind her idea.

The story did not end there as we shall see later, enthusiasm without the management principles needed to establish a culture for deployment of change can become out of control and be extremely unhealthy. One of the meeting attendees was from the maintenance department (we will refer to him as Dave) because he too had recorded activities associated with dealing with jams on the high-speed line. Dave volunteered that he would take the idea forward from there. He said he would prepare the required authorization paperwork for managers to sign and, once he received approval, he would get a stick made up with a magnet on the end of it for Barb to try out. He thought the stick should be available by Wednesday morning.

Now fast forward six weeks. By coincidence we meet Dave in the corridor as we walk into the plant and we ask how the stick idea is going. 'Still with management for a decision I think,' he said with a sigh of resignation. 'I wrote it up on the day of the meeting, asked around the maintenance shop, and we put a cost in for less than $100 for the stick complete with a strong magnet to be fabricated. It's been with management now for six weeks and I am still waiting to hear. You know, the annual benefit to one-off cost we worked out from the activity data and put on the authorization document was well over a thousand to one just considering increased capacity alone, without trying to work out how much we will save on maintenance by cutting out all that stopping and starting we have been having.' 'Mind you,' he said, 'the incidence of stoppages has dropped beyond recognition.'

We were disappointed by what we had just heard and made a mental note to follow up with the director of manufacturing as we walked round the corner and up the stairs to go into the team room. As we entered the team room we were surprised to find everyone in a huddle. 'Have you heard? Barb is in hospital, an industrial accident apparently. She fell on the line this morning and was nearly crushed by the hydraulic ram which is there to seat the cans properly before the washing stage.... She was apparently very lucky, just badly bruised, saved by the safety guards.' We felt sick and began to worry about the project, the very enthusiastic union-nominated team and the splendid, self-effacing Barb. What could possibly have happened?

Immediate investigation revealed three things. First, the authorization document was indeed still in a manager's in-box, unread, awaiting approval. Second, surprisingly, the line downtime had been appreciably reduced because of a remarkable reduction in stoppages since the meeting when Barb put forward her idea. 'Why?' we wondered, and hazarded a rather worrying guess that proved not to be very far from the truth. Third, we discovered what had really happened since the implementation had been passed to managers through their authorization document. It turned out that Barb had left the meeting and by the end of the week had enthusiastically put her suggestion into action without the benefit of her magnetic stick. She had ignored company procedures (and therefore health and safety policies) and had begun leaning over the line to right or remove fallen over cans as best she could by hand and had indeed almost eliminated the frequent line stoppages. She had, however, just that very morning slipped and overbalanced, falling onto the cans on the line because some oil had leaked onto her steel platform from the depalletizer. She had been lucky not to have partially been carried under the hydraulic ram that would have crushed her.

Needless to say that when Barb returned to work a week later her magnetic stick was waiting for her – the team, who were supposed not to be engaged in implementation, had seen to that. Authorization had apparently taken just a matter of minutes, fabrication less than an hour and the procedures had been revised and checked within a day. Whatever were the management doing with their time one had to wonder? A $100 investment had fixed a problem that had defeated the best brains who supplied high-speed lines for years.

Moving on to another initiative then, part of the downsizing implementation, now six months old, had been to reduce significantly the number of management positions in the hierarchy of the manufacturing plant. One of those implemented had had the effect of increasing the organizational separation of three key departments – preparation and cooking, filling and packaging – by eliminating positions. For hygiene purposes alone these three departments obviously needed to synchronize their activities carefully so that raw, prepared and cooked food was not left waiting too long. Difficult geography at the plant further exacerbated the imposed separation and would have spawned many situationally necessary interfacing activities. The food preparation equipment was located on the ground floor and prepared ingredients were transported in tubs by lift to a very restricted holding area on the third floor where the steam-cooking vats were located. The filling department was located on the second floor, directly below the cooking vats so that product, when ready for filling, could be dropped down to the canfilling heads onto Barb's high-speed line. The filled and closed cans then passed through a sterilizer before being labelled and packaged by machinery located on the ground floor. The increased turnover of staff, attributed to the step increase in work pressure resulting from the downsizing, had further exacerbated the situation because skill levels in each department were gradually being reduced as permanent staff who left were replaced by temporary workers.

The functional activities such as receiving materials; preparation (peeling, dicing, etc); transport; cooking; and testing were found in the interfacing maps to be exactly in line with the strategic aims of the business and with the activities specified by the downsizing consultants. However, as everyone knew, the plant throughput, service and costs were wildly out of control.

The interfacing activity data in the interfacing maps painted a different and rather more informative picture. The interfacing activities were dominated by just a handful of major noise drivers (noise drivers causing the waste of large amounts of accumulated time in the end-to-end process). One of these described and quantified the dramatic level of effort devoted to coordinating the interactions between the three departments – effectively the three floors. In spite of all the time devoted to coordination, interfacing activity errors and delays were occurring frequently. The interfacing activity data described and quantified routine happenings such as product would be ready in the cooking department but staff in the filling department weren't set up with the right cans to fill so product in huge quantities (for example a boiling vat full) were all too frequently being dumped to waste. This was obviously costly. Raw materials were wasted and, equally seriously, irrecoverable time for preparation and cooking processes was being lost, leading ultimately to stock shortages. This high product wastage in turn drove huge interfacing activity noise in emergency ordering and handling of ingredients, agreeing and making product substitutions with customers, making multiple deliveries, generating credit notes, authorizing discounts, etc.

Now add in the risk to this rather unfavourable situation. Vats full of boiling liquid were being dumped through temporary piping (the plant had understandably not been plumbed to routinely dump such large quantities of product) down from the third floor, above the heads of staff working below. Yet another example of the points made in Chapter 1 for the medical, transport and petrochemicals industries – unmanaged interfacing activity, particularly noise, can easily lead to death, and of course Barb's narrow escape was at the front of our minds.

As with Barb's solution, all the people who had variously documented elements of the coordination activity were invited to an ideas session. Again, the meeting started with a short period to allow the attendees to examine the end-to-end interfacing activity maps. From observing the meeting it was evident that the time they had spent documenting all their own activities had been valuable because they were all now able to read the end-to-end interfacing maps and thus understand exactly how their colleagues in the other departments were responding to their actions and, in turn, doing things that caused them grief. This prompted them immediately to start to think about some solutions. A number of key ideas quickly emerged and these were evaluated by volunteer attendees using the interfacing activity data in the maps to quantify the benefit, with the input of a little support from the team. These were passed through to the authorization system set up by the management team.

Two ideas are described here to set the scene further for the discussion of the management principles needed to establish a culture for deployment of change.

The first idea presented was a simple and straightforward 'no brainer' highlighted by the availability for the first time of interfacing activity data. The idea was to relocate the steam valves on the cooking vats. One of the functional activities was to turn on the steam valve for each of the vats to begin cooking and a further functional activity obviously followed, namely, turn off the steam valve when the product was cooked to the recipe's specification. However, the turn-off activity had attracted a number of bizarre interfacing activities – locate a wooden lever; ensure it is not contaminated; attach the wooden lever to valve; seek assistance if required; and, if product has been cooked over specified time, set up for disposal; oversee disposal; and, lastly, prepare the vat for the next batch (see the explanation below). The interface mapping data had here as always linked the interfacing activity noise steps, including the waste creation, to the underlying operation of the steam valves. These unexpected interfacing activities raised questions that brought to light a very real problem that had existed since the plant had first been opened. The documentation of the interfacing activities now prompted a simple cost-saving solution that increased throughput, reduced waste and eliminated a very real workplace hazard.

The small steel valves on the high temperature steam pipes (used to meter steam into the vats to cook the ingredients) were located about 10 cm above the ingredients. Turning them on was easy when the ingredients were cold. Turning them off was not. It was far too dangerous to turn off the valves by hand. The stainless steel valves had by that time reached the temperature of the steam, way above boiling point and were too small to grasp easily, especially as they were located just 10 cm above the boiling, bubbling product. A makeshift wooden lever had therefore been fettled and was normally used to turn off every steam valve. If the valve jammed (noise) – a not uncommon experience – assistance (noise) was sought from a colleague and with the new, lower staffing levels, finding this person (noise) could take time and the food could spoil before the steam valve was closed. The product then had to be dumped (more noise) and the whole process replanned and repeated all the way back to ordering and preparation (even more noise) to replace the lost production.

The delays in the management system that had led to Barb's fall had by this time been fixed. The implementation of management principles needed to establish a culture for deployment of change had thus advanced. This easily cost-justified change was enacted promptly and the steam valves were relocated to the side of each vat, reducing hazard, saving all of the quantified hours of the operator's time and the change was another step on the road to bringing the out-of-control waste back to best-practice levels.

A second, more complex proposal, however, could well have provided the script for a *Mr Bean* sketch if it had not been addressing such a serious cost and throughput problem. The need was to eliminate communication errors and delays between the three floors. The proposal from the staff's ideas meeting was to install personal radios operating through a base station so that the team leaders and key operators could communicate directly with each other. It was seen as a relatively quick and medium- to low-cost way of eliminating the swathes of ineffective interfacing activity introduced by the downsizing reorganization and benchmark-driven reduction in supervision (didn't anyone in the downsizing team know that interfacing activities are situational?). Again, although there was a strong financial case and a business imperative the initial decision on the equipment to buy took some time, but this time with good reason as radio communication in an environment where there is a lot of steel is notoriously difficult. Various trials were needed and carried out to ensure the selected product would work. Appropriate equipment was ordered and installed quickly but weeks were to elapse before it was to be used to effect.

It was tried by the staff for a shift but it didn't work at all. All people heard using the radio headsets was static. No one anywhere in the plant was willing to volunteer to take the bad news to management after recent experiences. As a consequence, several weeks elapsed before the problem was discovered by the production managers and investigated. It turned out that the installers had been instructed by the maintenance staff (who had not been involved in the evaluation) to install the base station in a convenient spot for maintenance, far from the steam-laden atmosphere in the operational area. The equipment was quickly relocated and was first used successfully on the next shift. Mr Bean then returned to the plant. At handover, staff on the incoming shift were briefed on using the radios but the headsets were nowhere to be found and certainly not placed on the chargers as was required. It was assumed that they had all been taken home by the members of the last shift or possibly stolen. Everyone shrugged their shoulders and got on with their jobs. Again there was no follow up and management was not informed.

In the end, after over a fortnight, the situation was referred back to the team by management in the form of instructions to raise a supplementary authorization document for the purchase of more headsets. A team member decided again to use his initiative to do more investigation and convened another ideas meeting with the attendees at the original ideas session. It lasted only minutes. The outcome, implemented that day, was that the box of foam disposable ear piece covers that came with the radios was quickly located and issued. The headsets reappeared on their chargers at the end of each shift. Mr Bean was again to return to the plant when the box of disposables was used up. No one in the management team, managing the implementation, had thought to include them on the list of consumables, which would have meant that supplies were checked and replenished routinely. But we will revisit this later in the chapter.

Exploring the deployment culture management principles

Our international research had identified the third segment of management principles leading organizations follow to support ongoing deployment of change in their business processes. These principles (described in Table 8.1 on page 151) are:

- relating the micro to the macro;
- establishing a learning culture;
- embracing change;
- supporting distributed leadership;
- measuring and reporting;
- being up front;
- gaining alignment.

Using the InterCo example, it is instructive to explore each of these seven management principles and develop recommendations for the changes managers should perhaps have made to implant the change culture in the business.

Relating the micro to the macro

Leading organizations, our research showed, strive to achieve one of two objectives associated with relating the micro to the macro. Some organizations went all out to ensure that each member of their organization, and therefore each work team, understood how the activities they carried out connected with, and contributed to, the 'big picture' of business success. Other leading organizations worked hard to ensure that each of their first-line managers, the team leaders, had a sound understanding of how his or her team-based work effort contributed to the overall organizational success.

This meant that either each staff member or each first-line manager had to be able to relate the micro (functional and interfacing) activities they routinely carried out to the outcome to be delivered by the key business processes in which they played their part.

To be able to achieve these objectives the employees involved would need to access in some way the activity documentation, that is the functional and interfacing activities they routinely undertake, and be able to relate them to the overall business goals. In order to do this they would need to be able to make use, formally or informally, of a strategic codification system such as the XeP3 CSDN framework proposed in Chapter 4 applied to procedures based on interfacing and functional activities. Assuming that this activity record existed in these leading organizations, and if it were strategically coded, then there would be a high degree of clarity in what each member of staff should be focused on doing (each person's core and support activities) and what the member of staff should be prompted to eliminate (his or her noise activities). Obviously, the culture in the business would need to encourage and support them to propose and follow through the justification and implementation of these changes. In other words management needed to create a culture of distributed leadership and provide the training and data to inform staff of how processes worked.

In InterCo this micro to macro linkage had clearly never been established. The process maps prepared by the downsizing consultants and tabled by the management team ignored three out of four of the activities routinely carried out (before downsizing) in the plant so how could it possibly be done? If it had been done then the importance of the jobs carried out by staff who had been made redundant would have been recognized and the necessary changes innovated to allow them to be phased out without damaging the reputation and service levels of the business. The missing activities were, of course, the interfacing activities where most of the noise activities resided. As stated earlier, these noise activities absorbed, as certified by the staff themselves, 32.3 per cent of approximately 500 people's time or the equivalent to 162 full-time staff.

There was simply nothing in place to encourage the staff or the management team to seek to link the staff micro to the business macro by reducing the noise or to ensuring that performance-driving activities (if they were known) were actually done. For example, finding the wooden lever to turn off the steam valves never appeared in the procedural documentation. It had either been missed by the HR specialist who had written the procedures or, more likely, this fettling procedure had been invented of necessity by an operator weeks after the original plant procedures had been written – and the operator would not have had the devolved authority even to seek to change the procedure. Further, the consultants would probably have been focused on getting their functional process maps together, a not insignificant undertaking, for their purposes. In the unlikely event that any of the consultants had ever had experience in industrial cooking there would have been little chance that they would have been visiting the cooking floor and been in the right place to observe the hazardous practice when it occurred. The staff on their part had not thought that the practice should be in the procedures as they regarded it as 'something that needed to be done to do our job'.

The staff in InterCo were not encouraged to make proposals. Members of the management team saw change and improvement only through the lens of capital expenditure. It was indisputably their role to evaluate capital proposals and capital expenditure. It was their belief that capital expenditure was the only thing that needed to be managed to get strategic change (see Chapter 1 for the historical reasons why this thinking so often occurs). The management team's complete lack of awareness of interfacing activities and their importance ensured that even an obvious beneficial change or hazard would remain hidden from view unless an accident occurred to draw attention to it, or possibly an enthusiastic new manager or a new Lean, Six Sigma or occupational health and safety specialist stumbled over it. As a consequence, in InterCo there was no understanding of the existence of the interfacing activity opportunity and therefore there was no association of the subsequent product wastage, product rework and plant disruption caused by the difficulty in turning off the valves.

Again, the time staff spent stopping and starting the line had been in the hitherto hidden interfacing activities. Managers were absolutely confident that there were no opportunities to make technical investments to improve uptime. They and their technical experts had exhausted every possible opportunity for cost-justified capital expenditure to improve line uptime and reduce breakdown, including benchmarking. In contrast, as soon as Barb understood the implications of following the documented procedures (in her case the impact of frequently stopping the line whenever a can fell over), she could not help herself from blurting out the all too obvious, to her, solution. Her innovation inspired by interfacing activity noise data provided the solution to a throughput problem that the whole company had lived with since the high-speed line had been first installed. Barb's solution saved the company in the first few months more than the cost of her entire lifetime's employment. Clearly, changes to management thinking and practices were needed. Managers themselves also needed to embrace change, adopt a learning culture and think about distributed leadership, as referred to below.

In a similar vein, Pensions (See Chapter 3) spent nine months documenting their 15 business processes at a high level and managers were easily able to relate what was being done (the functional activities) to their defined strategy. However, managers were unable to identify any meaningful opportunities to deliver beneficial change because they were unable to relate what was actually being done by their staff – the micro (interfacing) activities – with the macro picture. After spending just three weeks getting their staff to document what they really did, including making visible the missing 1,729 interfacing activities (out of a total of 2,609 activities at the micro level) managers were able to pinpoint opportunities that could release up to US $921,000 per annum out of a salary bill of around US $2.303 million from just one of their 15 business processes.

So what should InterCo have done to install the principle of relating the micro to the macro? First, the company should make visible to all staff and managers what is really happening every day in the business by interface mapping all of the actual interfacing and functional activities. So managers should support employees to participate, part time and once per year, in the interface mapping of the business using a proven interface mapping tool.

As part of this interface mapping managers should include a significant training module to enable the staff who provide the data on what they do forensically. That is to use a strategic coding framework (such as the CSDN approach described in Chapter 4) to pinpoint noise and core activity and thus directly link what each person does to the organization's strategic intent.

Everyone will then actually have linked their personal work (the micro) to the company's (macro) goals.

Establishing a learning culture

There is a widespread, and as many people would now say, a total acceptance that learning for all employees is critical to best-practice firms. Well yes, but what is meant by learning? One of the world's largest banks operated staff training programmes designed, prepared and promulgated by their expert HR teams which addressed just 3 per cent of the drivers of noise affecting customers and wasting resource. This interfacing activity derived finding was so sensitive that it was buried by the requesting executive.

We found something a little different to what was happening in this bank in the leading firms in our research. We found that the employees in these businesses worked actively to transfer knowledge to others and did not feel threatened by knowledge transfer. These firms had recognized, formally or informally, that interfacing activities occur, are largely invented by the staff doing the work and need to be recognized. New staff need to be trained in their practice. Further, learning requirements in these firms were directly driven by the need to develop their strategic capabilities; that is, to achieve strategic alignment of their business processes. In other words, the training agenda was not driven by external agendas such as national training and workplace reform, awards, union influences, etc, but from an understanding of current business process needs and then, having understood the needs, it addressed them directly.

In InterCo we were initially stopped dead in our tracks by the meeting called by the union representatives before the work could begin, when someone yelled out angrily that no training had been undertaken there in the last year (training had been seen as a discretionary activity that had been downsized). In the light of this, look at the opportunity for training revealed by noise elimination in just the three examples again below.

Visiting Barb again, her standing instructions in the company procedures needed to be revised to reflect what she was actually now required to do. This in turn would prompt revisions to the training given to new line operatives who could be required to do Barb's job. The procedure needed to be changed to state that the line should only be stopped as a last resort (this became one of a number of core drivers of output for the whole plant and should therefore not be left to chance). Further, to enable this, when cans fell over they should be flicked off the line using the equipment provided, the magnetic stick. Some might dismiss these revisions as bureaucratic and unnecessary even childish. However, events confirmed that issuing these new standing instructions and providing the training were absolute necessities. How to use the magnetic stick was perhaps obvious, but the imperative of never, ever attempting to right cans by leaning over the line was essential to avoid the risk of a life-threatening fall, which could easily place body parts under the hydraulic ram. At this point it might be instructive to read the example of wrong-side surgery again (case study 1.1 in Chapter 1), if you are still of a mind to leave the interfacing activities undocumented, unanalysed and therefore unmanaged.

Similarly, and at the most basic of levels, attention to detail in revising procedures, policing them and training the operatives in the use of the disposable foam earpiece covers on the radio headsets would have delivered the high payback much sooner from the radio investment, ensured that the practice would not be abandoned and ensured compliance to basic hygiene practices. Finally, the extension of the procedures to purchasing would have placed the foam earpiece covers on the list of consumables and this would have obviated the need for Mr Bean's third visit. This visit took place when the box of disposable earpiece covers was used up and this generated much new noise in getting supplies urgently and disrupting production as the headsets were not used until the covers were delivered.

InterCo was not exhibiting the principle of establishing a learning culture. Here is a list of recommendations for InterCo to install this management principle:

- Use the output of the interface mapping exercise that is required to achieve the link between the micro and the macro to update the company's procedures and form the base record of the company's business processes used to manage change. Using this interface mapping output in this way will embed in the business both the principles of relating the micro to the macro and of being disciplined (Chapter 2)

- Encourage employees to highlight, address and actively support changes that eliminate (and not transfer) interfacing activity noise and establish a new business process and training to support the staff's involvement.

- Ensure that the training and competency agenda for the business is firmly built on addressing the major situationally generated interfacing activity noise as well as reflecting industry standards.

Embracing change

Leading firms are as good at executing ideas and strategy as they are at formulating them. They strongly embrace relevant change and have strong project management and change experience. Our research also revealed that the leading organizations were good at what one of the participants rather uniquely described as the 20/80 rule – 20 per cent of the effort to be spent on design, 80 per cent on implementation.

In contrast, the lagging companies, to the extent that they were even interested in change, spent most of their effort on defining the problem, in fact any problem strategically relevant or not, and then grossly underestimated the effort required to implement and over-delegated the actual implementation.

It almost seems churlish at this point to revisit InterCo again. We have already demonstrated that the managers were not open to different ways of doing things, as their change focus tended to be on capital projects as illustrated by their attitude to the issue of line stoppage. Nor were they aware of a multitude of opportunities, such as the steam valves, hidden from their view because they did not have a process in place to make them visible – appropriate interface mapping, a strategic (CSDN) coding system and a staff mechanism to encourage staff and managers to get involved. The management team were clearly surprised by the improvements that came quickly from the many innovations resulting from focusing staff on pinpointing and quantifying the interfacing activity noise by supporting them to use the interface mapping and the CSDN framework. Further, it became obvious that the staff-generated interfacing activity data provided indisputable evidence that there were further, significant productivity gains, at the same time addressing the many process weaknesses incurred by the downsizing.

Certainly, as with managers in the lagging companies in our survey, InterCo management, when they engaged in change, invested a lot of time in evaluation, for example with the radio headsets, and too little time on implementation. Their project implementation skills needed to be improved, but project implementation skills in engaging with their staff and in monitoring and supporting, not doing it themselves.

Finally, in considering the management principle of embracing change, lots of latent staff energy was just waiting for encouragement to become engaged. There was the insistence, through the unions, in using real data collected from those actually undertaking the work. Many low-cost, high-payback process and procedural innovations emerged almost effortlessly from the staff once they were given the tools (interface mapping, the CSDN framework, the software tools, the meetings and the suppression of the cloying management influence). The staff and managers both just could not wait to see the end to the waste, disruption and uncertainty that had resulted from the inappropriately conducted downsizing programme. However, the staff embraced the process they were given while the managers remained as slightly bemused bystanders.

These are recommendations for InterCo managers to install the management principle of embracing change:

- Provide training in supporting change initiatives, not just traditional project management.
- Incorporate managing interfacing activities, and particularly the negative performance impact of interfacing activity noise, into the company's management development programme.
- Adjust the management team's incentive and promotion schemes to reward managers for actively supporting (not taking over) properly justified and prioritized change initiatives.

Supporting distributed leadership

The great majority of all problems can be resolved at the first level of supervision they encounter and the examples recounted from InterCo would be consistent with this view. However, this can only be done if the authority and accountability for those changes has been correctly and fully delegated. Our international research revealed to us that the senior and middle managers in leading companies are spending less and less of their time running the organization and resolving operational issues. They have been devolving responsibility to individuals and work teams who have been given, and accept, increased decision-making authority within agreed parameters to ensure that strategic alignment of business processes is firmly seen to be the goal. In other words, our research revealed that a new business process is being established in these leading companies to enable their more junior managers and staff to resolve business process issues where the scope of the change is within their remit, or within the remit of themselves and their immediate peers. Obviously, changes that have a wide span, perhaps affecting how customers need to interface with the business, involve significant capital spend or would affect safety or environment policies are required to be referred to higher levels.

This emerging trend is certainly welcome and begins to address the increases in complexity from outsourcing, partnering and cost pressures referred to in Chapter 1. In many of these leading companies the senior managers had therefore learned how to 'let go' even though most of them had gained their positions through 'troubleshooting' and close personal management of change and other difficult issues.

The principle of supporting distributed leadership should not be confused with establishing empowerment. When InterCo retained us to address the all too obvious problems from the downsizing they authorized us to work with their staff to help them to document their interfacing activities, then apply our strategic CSDN framework and finally propose solutions. We were therefore immediately able, with management's blessing to empower the staff to undertake these steps. However, members of the management team very specifically reserved the right to deal with all implementation proposals. They were not prepared to work within the principle of supporting distributed leadership to accomplish the task. They recognized that they had no process to do it. Thinking about the situation, in their position at that time, it is unlikely you would have risked it either. After all, the management did not understand the need for, or possess, an established business process to support distributed leadership and they could hardly be expected to devolve it to us, management consultants, given their recent downsizing experience.

However, as we have described perhaps a little mischievously already, this retention of control brought Mr Bean to life in their business. In Figure 8.1 (which first appears as Figure 3.6 on page 74, derived from a manufacturing company similar in size to InterCo) the real problem is shown to be the management need to address these very issues. The managers who reserved the right to manage the implementation were typically in positions 4 and 5. How could anyone know, understand and manage some 1,934 activities within the broader context of a department, let alone 18,725 in the context of the business when only one in four of the activities had been documented.

FIGURE 8.1   Why leading companies should make use of distributed leadership

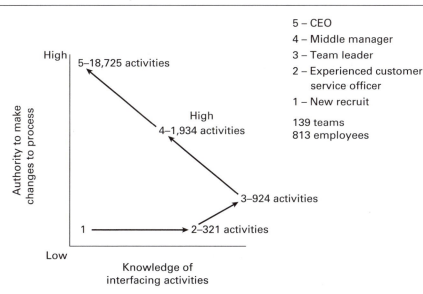

So when the members of the management team examined the large mound of information from the staff's effort on interface mapping, they readily acknowledged that they really did not have enough awareness of exactly what had been happening in the day-to-day business to be able to identify the problems and address them even one by one. Worse still, they recognized that the plight of their business demanded that many of the emerging changes should be tackled simultaneously. They did not have an answer and their implementation of initiatives such as deploying the radio communication system demonstrated both the absence of process and dearth of experience, both to themselves and all involved.

The gap, perhaps better described as a chasm, illustrates the imperative to adopt the principle of supporting distributed leadership in order to manage the depth and breadth of the change facing a company. The managers of InterCo needed to empower their staff first to provide the information platform for distributed leadership, and then ensure that the employees were willing and able to accept the responsibility for introducing and implementing improvements. In InterCo this meant managers had to change their behaviour to enable the enthusiastic workers to use their new-found, documented, knowledge of the company's process weaknesses from the micro-to-macro data and workshops. By using this knowledge, staff could achieve the required learning focus as well as look to managers to embrace change by getting out of the way and supporting them.

So what does distributed leadership consist of? It has a number of characteristics. The most obvious one is that decision making for change is delegated down the organization, that is, managing change is one of the tasks every manager and team leader (and in some of the leading companies, every employee) does daily as routine. This means that a number of things need to be in place to create a routine business process that builds capability for change. These include the provision of the interface mapping data and training on how to use it so that relevant change that links the micro to the macro is identified and justified. Policies are needed that define authority limits and a referral mechanism to support them, as well as incentives and measures, are needed to encourage managers and staff, to participate.

Here are the recommendations for InterCo to install the management principle of supporting distributed leadership:

- Review the already existing authorization documentation.
- Ensure that the documentation includes accountabilities for delivery, implementation of key milestones and dates and evidence that implications and interactions with other initiatives had been considered.
- Demonstrate interest in and actively support a process to allow the staff to use interfacing activity data to pinpoint, justify and deploy change in business processes.

Measuring and reporting

Measuring in particular, with its associated reporting, has in our experience played a major role in the success of achieving every major performance gain in organizations. The Balanced Scorecard concept, first presented by Kaplan and Norton in 1992, was a significant leap forward and deserved and achieved almost universal recognition.

Some of the most effective process realignment programmes we have been involved in have been with organizations where measuring has been taken to a new and exciting level – the measurement of input core activity through the use of behavioural change indicators (BCIs) to operationalize the outcome KPIs at the team level. We introduced BCIs and their potential to encapsulate an organization's 'DNA' in the last chapter. However, the need for living by the principle of measurement of outcomes and reporting of progress to agreed plans provides the foundation for all process change and will be discussed here in the context of InterCo.

We found in our research that best-practice organizations make extensive use of a range of both non-financial and financial measures. The measures used by leading firms relate to business strategy and positioning, business goals, operational goals, organizational goals and external stakeholders. We found that in these leading organizations, the measures are typically transposed into KPIs that are attached directly to each key business process: that is the set of processes through which the organization delivers its products or services or achieves other specific goals such as alignment of business processes. These KPIs might be used to measure particular aspects of key delivery processes such as the progress of reduction in transactional costs of holidays in the competitive wholesale travel industry; or the cycle time and variation reduction in a regulatory body which was keen to eliminate the 300 complaints it was receiving each and every week.

In InterCo the KPI measures were applied at firm level (not individual business processes) or they were specific project measures (for example, being on time and on budget not being linked to outcome achievement). Clearly, attaching measures to the business processes that deliver products and services to customers, or achieve other specific organizational goals, provides a mechanism to avoid the pursuit of functional goals. The application of KPIs to specific business processes therefore strongly underpins adherence to the management principle focusing on strategic intent (described in Chapter 2) of ensuring integration of effort. Further, it keeps the focus on the business outcome and, in our experience, neatly and completely eliminates the propensity of many engaged in change to strive to substitute the easier-to-achieve budgets and delivery date goals for outcome achievement.

As an example of where this principle was not followed consider InterCo. The goal of the production process was to keep up with demand. To do this it needed to reduce stoppages and wastage on the high-speed line. Managers attached no urgency to Barb's widely applauded proposal. It was in the approval and evaluation system, and that was all that seemed to matter. The radio communication proposal was made directly in response to the need to address the unacceptably high product wastage. Here managers efficiently evaluated the options and selected a suitable radio system, tasks they recognized as their own. They then delegated implementation, with the result that the desired business outcome was not delivered although what they measured, the timescale and budget targets, were met. As a consequence of the lack of focus on outcome, the radio base station was installed in the wrong place. It took weeks before it was relocated only to find that the headsets all disappeared. InterCo managers demonstrated the difference between achieving budgets and deadlines and achieving outcomes. They demonstrated that outcomes were much harder to achieve and their project-based measurement system did not highlight the shortfalls.

These are the recommendations for InterCo to adhere to the management principle of measuring and reporting:

- Allocate and, where necessary, transpose the company's KPI measures to each business process.
- Measure outcome achievement before adherence to budget and delivery date for change initiatives.

Being up front

Being up front in the leading companies meant being open, honest and acting with integrity in all areas of business activity. We found that leading companies do not make promises to customers, employees or stakeholders that they cannot keep and thus they place a high value on building trust and relationships.

InterCo could not be rated highly. There was the evidence of the initial distrust exhibited in the union meeting; the general expectation that nothing would happen after all the work that the staff did to document, codify and analyse their functional and interfacing activity; the delays on supplying Barb's magnetic stick; and the dozens of other proposals left languishing in management in-boxes. If only the management team had displayed at the start Barb's dedication to her job and her commitment to her co-workers and the company.

Perhaps the issue is summed up by the comment made by one of the operators in a leather-processing factory who when challenged by a colleague who pointed out that changes could mean the loss of her job, said: 'I work on the afternoon shift here and I am pleased to have my job. Every morning I walk my children to school past these factory gates. In future I would like to think that even if I do lose my job, then I was one of the people who contributed enough to enable this factory to continue supplying leather to our customers, so that you and others kept yours.'

These are the recommendations for InterCo to adhere to so that it lives by the management principle of being up front:

- Adopt the passion and commitment displayed by many of the staff.
- Focus the measurement on outcomes, not on following process.

Gaining alignment

The leading organizations in our survey demonstrated that there was good alignment between employee behaviour and stated company values. InterCo's management seemed content to operate in an environment where they and the staff rarely, if ever, worked together to address common goals. Clearly, the improvements and opportunities available in reducing interfacing activity noise and correctly implementing training to do so, deploying core activities, embracing change and driving forward on the principle of being up front would all lead to stronger alignment in the organization. Further, and of great importance, the process improvements at the work level, and the forward movement with regard to principles related to culture and change become fully self-reinforcing, leading to improvements at the shop floor level becoming integrated with improvements at the 'top floor' level.

There are no losers in this forward progress: all stakeholders gain significantly. Once this is clearly communicated, and the cynicism that overhangs from taking the wrong steps in the past is overcome, then resources are freed up. They can be reallocated from wasteful interfacing activity noise to performance-driving core and effective support activities, with compliance being monitored through carefully considered discretionary activity. This then defines the new management job – to understand that the real problem in the workplace processes is the failure to acknowledge and deal systematically with interfaces.

The alignment that comes with this realization is liberating for all concerned, and more importantly, it leads to improvements that create significant business value.

Contrasting approaches

We cannot end this chapter without contrasting the way that two very different companies addressed their strategic business goals. InterCo's business had been, until downsizing, one of the best performing units in one of the most successful companies in the world. What had gone wrong? Simply, they were not set up and had no process for managing wide-ranging systemic change to their processes and because of their success they saw no need to establish one. They had historically managed their brands extremely well but had used, by their own headquarter's benchmarked measures, excessive staff to make sure that everything that was important was checked and corrected as soon as it went wrong – they had inspected in quality. When the benchmark-driven downsizing was implemented, albeit poorly, these crutches were kicked away and the absence of the interface management skills in the business became apparent.

The managers deserved much more from their corporate office. Prove that there was a huge opportunity by benchmarking, yes. But why did the headquarters take no account of situational differences and not diagnose the absence of the management principles seen in leading companies? Surely the HQ management team should have been helping the managers and staff in their subsidiary to achieve the corporate goals through learning and support for the journey they were about to embark upon?

The situation InterCo senior managers found themselves in is not uncommon. It can be triggered by the severe price competition that has often resulted from globalization. It happens in many businesses where the managers have not been pressured to achieve excellence in their business processes so they gradually become uncompetitive. The first sign of trouble appears as margin erosion or, in InterCo's case, margin erosion in the overseas operations that drove the corporate managers into a benchmarking frenzy. The managers then turned to help from consultants. Now they were at a crossroads without understanding. They could adopt 'gardening' approaches and 'trim back' or they could look to the principle-based management found in the best practice of managing business processes.

Because of their lack of understanding of the importance of managing interfacing activity to raise productivity, customer service and employee satisfaction, as well as presenting the opportunity to free up time to focus on driving value activity, they opted to 'trim'. Like the motorist who lost his keys, they looked for solutions where the light was shining, not where the keys were dropped. Benchmarking offered InterCo a potential quick fix. Its HO management decided to trim to get competitive without spending much time on thinking through the consequences of ripping out resources with no understanding of the critical interfacing activities they were doing. Imposed downsizing rarely rectifies the situation: in this case it merely destroyed morale, damaged service to customers and reduced revenue.

Benchmarking correctly showed that most elements of the business were carrying unnecessary resources. No interfacing activity data was available and no one was aware of the value it would add. It would have shown that much of the deemed surplus resource was absorbed in checking and correcting interfacing activity at every point in the process to compensate for all the day-to-day errors and omissions endemic in every business. So instead of learning what needed to be changed in each process, training the staff in what was required of them and managing each change so that everything that mattered was right first time, resources were suddenly and catastrophically removed. The result was similar to that achieved by turning off the safety systems at Chernobyl nuclear power station. InterCo's processes suffered a catastrophic melt down.

By contrast, a large (1,200-person) mail-processing centre, in an industry not known for innovation, faced similar issues in an environment much more influenced by union involvement. Debbie Spring, the general manager, did something quite different. The operation interface mapped its business processes and isolated the key drivers of its 32 per cent noise – one-third imposed on themselves, two-thirds presented to them at their interfaces by their customers in the form of mail-presentation issues. The mail-processing centre carefully planned how to implement change. It first marginally increased resources to add additional interfacing activity to fix the huge received input issues. These additional resources checked and prepared all incoming mail from post offices and mailing houses to ensure it would present properly at the high-speed sorting machines – the centre thus eliminated its largest noise driver. This enabled the operation to demonstrate that it could achieve large productivity improvements and 24-hour delivery targets for letters by eliminating many interfacing activity noise activities that were endemic to the centre. The centre then went on to progressively address its other 'top of the Pareto' opportunities list, as priority noise drivers.

In addition, the extra interfacing activity information at entry of the facility had allowed the centre to identify all the post offices and mailing houses that were causing the problems in the presentation of incoming items. The management team defined new core activity, to train the worst offending mailing houses and post offices in mail preparation, and transferred and trained the staff needed to deliver this programme. As the worst post offices and mailing houses got their presentation right, the introduced interfacing activities were reduced eventually to an oversight role performing discretionary activity.

Debbie Spring encouraged her staff first to introduce additional core mail-sorting activities at the external interfaces to prevent noise entering the facility. This gave a huge payback. The centre then progressively addressed its internal interfacing activity noise drivers to get the plant operating at maximum efficiency. It 'banked' its largest gain. Time was then taken to move core activity gradually across to train the centre's customers (the bulk mail houses and post offices) to present items properly. Finally, the centre was able to introduce a small compliance team to ensure that the massive gains were locked in.

Multi-organization process management

This example shows some further important initiatives that are possible for organizations that use interface mapping. The top-down and bottom-up changes and synergies referred to are not just applicable to your own organization; they can, and should be implemented across the whole supply chain (just as the mail-processing centre was able to improve its input from another business unit or organization). The interface mapping process is easily extendable to supply chain interfaces and can readily be applied – without having to start again. It is simply an obvious and logical progression. Once the opportunities are identified, then the question clearly arises as to how best to influence supply chain partners to recognize and then implement improvements, usually because of the mutual benefits that are waiting to be captured. Engaging them in interface mapping addresses the cultural barriers between organizations as effectively as it does between divisions as described in Chapter 6.

Summary

The fully integrated approach of process improvement through fully mapping an organization's interfacing activities and then prioritizing the interfacing activity drivers is best done through connecting these works explicitly to the high-level principles associated with change management. Clearly, this must include all activities, especially interfacing activities, where large, previously hidden, benefits arise. In the case of InterCo, the principles it would have needed to accomplish its productivity gains and simultaneously preserve or improve its performance are summarized in Table 8.2. These would be likely to be relevant to any organization seeking to embrace operational excellence through strategic alignment of business processes.

TABLE 8.2 Summary of actions needed to implement the seven management principles associated with achieving change

Management principle	Action required
1. Relating the micro to the macro	• Make visible what is really happening to all staff and managers by introducing the participative use of interface mapping of all interfacing and functional activities • Train staff to use an activity strategic coding framework (eg XeP3's CSDN) to pinpoint noise and core activity and thus provide the mechanism for micro to macro
2. Establishing a learning focus	• Use the interface mapping output to update the company's procedures to cover what is really done, not just what is supposed to happen. Use this as the base documentation of the company's business processes. Use it to manage change and keep up to date • Encourage employees to eliminate noise by giving them the tools and training them to propose and implement justified changes • Base the training and competency agenda for the business largely on achieving business process alignment
3. Embracing change	• Incorporate interfacing activities and their negative and positive performance impact of noise as a key element of the management development programmes • Adjust the management incentive and promotion schemes to reward support of properly justified and prioritized change initiatives – not hijacking them
4. Supporting distributed leadership	• Provide authorization documentation to include cost benefits, accountabilities for delivery, implementation milestones and dates, and evidence that implications and interactions with other initiatives and other parts of the extended business have been considered • Demonstrate interest and actively support and provide guidance on business priorities and customer needs
5. Measuring and reporting	• Allocate and, where necessary, transpose the organization's KPI measures to each business process • Measure outcome achievement of change initiatives ahead of measuring adherence to budget and delivery date
6. Being up front	• Get focused on what you and others can do for the business • Encourage openness, helpfulness and honesty
7. Gaining alignment	• Management should focus on developing and deploying an improvement process based around engaging the staff in documenting everything they do, identifying the major divers of interfacing activity noise and supporting the staff in proposing, refining and deploying change proposals

Using interface mapping to deliver performance

09

Objectives

This chapter draws together how interface mapping, through the use of activity categorization and the new business 'genomics', will enable your organization to implement the management principles and thereby attain and maintain the strategic alignment of your business processes and place you firmly alongside GE, Motorola and Toyota. The capability to implement change clearly comes from having a forensic knowledge of the operating landscape of the organization, without which one is left not knowing the starting point and therefore not knowing what to change from, except in vague terms. Detailed process knowledge, down to the activity level of the organization's 'genomes', gives precise knowledge about where you are starting from, and hence where is the 'bang for the buck' best available to drive change.

It is a documented fact, and we expect it will accord with most professional managers' experience that many, even most, change initiatives fail to deliver sustainable advantages. This chapter further sets out the connection between the high-level principles common to the world's best companies and the interface mapping approach which, among other things, takes out the otherwise high risk of initiative failure, and provides full clarity of the forward improvement path. Delivering strategic change involves connecting the top-down principles to the bottom-up operating map just as the GPS software uses its road interfaces data to develop the optimum route.

Introduction

As described in Chapter 1, there are two complementary components to business strategy. The first and by far the best understood is the need to position the business in its market space equipped with the apposite resources that are seen to be needed to deliver the desired strategic outcomes. A positional business strategy alone, however, leaves organizations vulnerable to cost and service attacks from more aligned market players, as many organizations have found to their cost. The second component of business strategy is the realignment of resources to build strategic capabilities in such a way that the staff and managers are able to conduct the appropriate activities to achieve the strategic goals and meet customer and other stakeholder needs. That is, the staff are managed to conduct the right activities in the right sequence to operate the organization's business processes consistently and efficiently to achieve sustainable competitive advantage.

As we catalogued in Chapter 1, the approach and tools for defining a positional business strategy have been widely known and practised since the mid 1960s as a result of the efforts of strategy gurus such as Porter, the growth of the business schools and the work of the major management consultants. The first tiny glimmer of theory underpinning strategic capabilities did not appear until much later. Further, and as we have argued in Chapters 4 to 7, ignorance of the strategic role of interfacing activities in pinpointing misalignment and discontinuities has prevented most organizations from strategically aligning their business processes. The result is that building fit-for-purpose strategic capabilities is way beyond the reach of most management teams. On the other hand, GE and Motorola have demonstrably been successful in achieving strategic alignment of business processes using the tools they themselves have developed and released to the business world. These tools, Lean and Six Sigma, have become almost the industry standard but clearly have failed to deliver in the wider context, where 33.6 per cent of the average organization's staff are still engaged every day in noise that destroys customer service and performance and is buried in ignored interfacing activities.

Our international research shows that GE and Motorola exhibit the characteristics of leading organizations and manage by the excellence principles described in Chapter 2. We therefore draw the obvious conclusion that the success of Six Sigma in GE must be in large part due to the management principles that underpin the deployment of the company's strategy, as well as the widespread use of the Six Sigma tool it has developed and generously released to the world.

We saw no value in entering into a long discourse in the mechanics of executing change initiatives. The steps required – define, agree, plan, deploy, etc – are almost certain to be well known and in use in your organization, be they part of your Lean, Six Sigma, quality, BPR or the original framework of plan, do, check, act (PDCA), which was proposed by Dr W Edwards Deming in 1950. The spotlight must remain on the management principles (described in Chapter 2) and how their use creates the framework for the successful application of tools, such as Six Sigma, to build strategic capabilities. First must be adherence to the management principles focusing on strategic intent. These ensure that an organization conducts thorough analysis of current business processes to determine exactly what change needs to be done to align business processes and set strategic priorities for implementation. As we have already argued in Chapter 6, this means mapping, measuring and then using interfacing activity data to pinpoint and quantify the gaps and opportunities by addressing the principal causes of noise. Second, the prioritized changes need to be deployed by developing and embedding a process for ongoing strategic alignment of business processes that becomes part of the day-to-day routine. Taken together, adherence to these management principles has the potential to exorcize both guesswork and excessive use of judgement and experience from driving an organization's agenda for strategic change.

Relationship between interfacing activities and the management principles

Chapter 2 described the management (excellence) principles derived from international research. These were presented in four segments (See Table 2.2 on page 36). The four segments are:

- Segment 1: Having the desire to be out front – managers wanting their business to be the best.
- Segment 2: Focusing on strategic intent – the management team establishing a clear definition of all activities the staff and management need to carry out routinely to achieve the organization's strategy, and a clear definition of the changes needed to achieve strategic alignment of business processes (through, we have seen from Chapter 2 onwards, pinpointing the functional and interfacing activities).
- Segment 3: Driving the change through – managers creating the environment to foster and drive change thus enabling them to drive it through and to achieve continual strategic alignment of business processes.
- Segment 4: Resourcing for the medium term.

The first segment of these principles requires little further explanation. As managers, you have to want to be out front. You have to want to release much of the cost (around US $25,000 per person employed per annum) of interfacing activity noise as this imposes a 50 per cent burden on the people cost of transactions in your business. You will also want to transfer this resource to productive value-driving core activity or revenue-accretive support activity.

The second segment of management principles has been the focus of much of this book. We have described the role of interfacing activities, how to map and measure them and their impact on business performance in Chapters 3 to 6. Chapter 7 was used to describe the framework needed to support strategic analysis of the interfacing and functional activities. This chapter also demonstrated how the new business documentation framework enabled the management principles focusing on strategic intent to be established within a business.

The third segment was addressed in Chapter 8 by making use of the experience from InterCO. A set of recommendations were developed that would have enabled the managers to install these change-enabling management principles in their business (see Table 8.2 on page 176) to avoid the implementation catastrophe they were forced into.

The fourth and last segment was that a business needs to take a longer-term view of resource planning in order to align its business processes. We examined cases illustrating this. FinCo made investments to build its capability for change in order to decouple its cost of doing business from zero-profit business growth. Then we saw how the mail-processing centre made up-front investments by injecting discretionary resource to quarantine its incoming mail compliance issues to enable the centre to align its processes internally. It then reinvested a small part of the harvested noise to work with customers to fix the incoming mail compliance issues. The result in both cases was dramatically improved customer service, large measured increases in utilization of resources and increased profitability in the business.

Installing the principles and aligning business processes

The various elements now need to be drawn together to describe the steps necessary to achieve the goal of embedding these 14 management (or excellence) principles in the business so as to install a new business process to deploy changes in strategic alignment of business processes. This new process will provide the mechanism to plan what needs to change to achieve this.

Table 9.1 lists the 14 management (excellence) principles and their characteristics from Chapter 2. Each management principle, or group of management principles, is taken and discussed in turn.

We provide a comprehensive outline below of each of the principles as introduced in Chapter 2; however they now are re-expressed for you with the knowledge in mind of the importance of interface mapping a business's processes.

TABLE 9.1 Embedding the 14 excellence management principles in a business

	Management principle	Characteristics of the principle (from Chapter 2)	Interface mapping	Strategic categorization	Cartography
1	Being out front	The organization strives to lead the pack in all industry standards and practices: safety, customer service, product and process design, environmental management, etc	?	?	
2	Ensuring integration of effort	The organization is focused on creating value and managing processes, not on functional needs and hierarchies	√	√	√
3	Being disciplined	The organization invests in policies, procedures and standards and applies a strong system perspective in everything it does		√	√
4	Creating customer value	All employees understand the set of order winners and actively strive to enhance creation of customer value	√	√	√
5	Being time-based	Time is developed as a critical organizational value. The business practises the principles of time-based competition	√	√	√
6	Creating strategic capabilities	Business and organizational capabilities are defined and prioritized and drive critical development and investment decisions	√	√	√
7	Relating the micro to the macro	All employees know how their particular activities and individual efforts contribute to the 'big picture' of business success	√	√	√
8	Establishing a learning culture	All employees demonstrate a willingness to develop skills and knowledge and are involved in a learning/development programme	√	√	√

(Continued)

TABLE 9.1 Embedding the 14 excellence management principles in a business (*Continued*)

	Management principle	Characteristics of the principle (from Chapter 2)	Interface mapping	Strategic categorization	Cartography
9	Embracing change	All employees demonstrate a willingness to embrace and accept change as an essential part of doing business. The organization excels in implementing new ideas	√	√	√
10	Supporting distributed leadership	Individuals and work teams are assigned, and accept, responsibility for operational decision making and performance improvement	√	√	√
11	Being up front	All employees demonstrate integrity and openness in all areas of their work and dealings with others. Relationships are highly valued	√		
12	Gaining alignment	There is good alignment of employee behaviour with stated company values and direction at all levels in the organization. Employees are involved	√	√	
13	Measuring and reporting	The business measures and reports to all employees the financial and non-financial performance information needed to drive improvement	√	√	√
14	Resourcing for the medium term	The business is able to balance effectively short-term operational and medium-term development and growth issues and requirements			

Having the desire to be out front

This is the prerequisite to mounting any change programme that has the objective of building strategic capabilities by strategically aligning business processes. Members of the management team have to want their company to be a leading company and have to be willing to change the way they think and behave as necessary to achieve this. They will first need to become comfortable with role duality. They will need to recognize that business strategy is as much about managing the detail of the deployment of strategically planned change to their organization's business processes as it is about positioning the business in its market place. Inevitably, this will require management and staff to set their agendas based on business priorities and avoid individual or functional rivalries or myopia.

In our experience, management teams inevitably hold differing views. Some will argue that change is required, others that change is unnecessary. Those who accept that change is needed will hold different opinions on what needs to be addressed. Yet others will differ on how change should be undertaken. If profitability is an issue, then some managers will feel that the need is to cut costs by reducing staff and perhaps want to start a benchmarking exercise to highlight where the business is behind and then take the recommendations and get it over quickly. Others might interpret the same symptoms as a customer service issue, in which case they might proffer strong arguments that the business should undertake customer surveys or use focus groups to find out more about the nature of the failures. Others may interpret the same symptoms as evidence that the business has an employee satisfaction problem that is having an adverse impact on performance. The HR department would then be recommending that an employee survey be undertaken to understand the issues better. Every one of these different interpretations is likely to hold merit and, indeed, every single one could be right. The company's performance could well be suffering from issues of productivity and customer and employee satisfaction all at the same time because of non-alignment of interfacing activity in the strategic business processes.

The big risk is that the decision makers could interpret the problem through the lens of their own experience. Clearly, a thorough analysis is what is really needed. So what are the common mistakes made at this point? If managers commit to a specific investigation, for example focused on customer service or benchmarking or employee satisfaction, they demonstrate that they are paying lip service to the management principle of being out front. Commissioning a particular type of study indicates that they already know the specific direction of the solution and are looking to find a quick fix rather than wishing to really understand the firm's ills and opportunities. By commissioning such a study they signal that they do not want to be up front and would rather remain in their existing paradigm and that they have little understanding of how to tackle what is almost certainly an issue of strategic alignment of the interfaces in the business processes.

If the management team commissions such a study the outcome will probably follow a traditional course. First, action will be postponed by at least three months to allow a study to be commissioned, the work to be done and the report delivered. Second, when the report is presented there will be enormous pressure to adopt its recommendations – after all, managers would lose face if they did not proceed and inevitably the report would have been expensive. So a budget, time frame and steps are agreed to implement most of the recommendations. The hare is set running and sight is lost of the original objective – strategic alignment of the business processes to achieve specific business outcomes. Unfortunately, the report is likely to be correct but not complete because of its narrow focus. As a consequence, its recommendations are likely to address symptoms of poor alignment of business processes rather than root causes. As we have already demonstrated, problems in alignment of business processes always affect customer service and employee satisfaction and productivity, distract managers from their core tasks and cause shortcomings in performance. The outcomes from such an approach are likely to be positive but below expectations and a significant amount of new resource is more often than not required. More importantly, this approach will postpone addressing root causes, possibly for years.

The need is to study the mechanisms by which strategy is delivered, the business processes, not a particular attribute. Paradoxically, the alternative approach of looking at the business processes completely would take just three weeks, not three months, and would enable management then to detect and prioritize everything that is not aligned. The result, from addressing root causes, will meet expectations and in most organizations resources levels will not need to be increased, in fact, they are likely to fall. However, we are not saying that using customer service or employee satisfaction surveys is wrong. Rather that they should be sharply focused to respond to a well-defined issue of key strategic processes. We are advocating a sensible, structured and orderly approach of 'Ready, Aim, Fire', in which the first step, 'Ready', involves wanting to be out front, and then knowing where to focus improvement efforts, which means understanding interfaces to achieve a good 'Aim'. We are against the approach of 'Fire, Ready, Aim', or even worse the approach of 'Fire, Fire, Fire', as if doing anything is likely eventually to work.

The 'right approach' would be first to carry out interface mapping across the business to uncover all the issues, where each issue originates, how each issue affects business performance and who is affected by each issue. This would have three advantages compared to mounting a symptoms-driven investigation:

- It would engage the staff to get their buy-in. After all, it is the staff themselves who will ultimately have to change what they are doing to deliver the required outcomes.
- It would uncover the causal factors not just confirm the symptoms. As has often been demonstrated, problems with delivery to customers

are often issues relating to customer input interfacing, symptoms of non-integration or errors or omissions elsewhere.

- Further, if interface activity noise levels are significant (and they will be), this alone could provide the 'crisis' that would spur the management team to take action.

Ensuring integration of effort

The achievement of this principle requires that the organization's priorities set the agenda for everything. The pursuit of personal or functional goals rather than focusing on the company's objectives gives rise to significant organizational dysfunction. These dysfunctions will not feature in the functional activities and therefore will not be revealed in process maps, job descriptions and procedures. They will show up instead as interface activity noise in the interfacing activities that have to be structured by the staff to enable the passage of transactions through the business. Non-aligned goals inevitably result in noise in these interfacing activities from chasing up delayed information or work, or from rework.

For an example of the absence of the principle of ensuring integration of effort, take a call centre business where the practice was for senior managers to make an unauthorized request for IT service relatively frequently. The normal workload was immediately interrupted and the work that should have been done was delayed. Complaints about delayed work had to be handled (noise) and the time committed to the abandoned, authorized job was wasted as the job had to be started again from scratch (noise). Work often had to be rescheduled (noise). Further, the work that jumped the queue was usually rushed so it was inadequately investigated and unplanned consequences were experienced. This led to rework of the change (noise), correction work to reverse the transactions or restore files (noise) and customer change delays requiring additional liaison and negotiation (noise).

The business 'genomics' enables the accumulation of noise by causal factor (noise driver). This highlights the pockets of activity in the business where effort is not integrated. The higher the level of noise, the more serious will be the lack of integration. Alignment can therefore be achieved by eliminating the noise by addressing the causes. This would lead to replacing the functional or personal agendas by the organizational aims. In the example quoted the senior managers as a group agreed not to use back door requests and the number of unplanned requests received in IT per month was made a board KPI (coincidentally where the board members were the principal culprits).

The solution therefore lies in the adherence to the principle of gaining alignment by adhering to one set of goals, those of the company. Interface mapping captures the interfacing activity. Strategic categorization enables the noise to be identified. The cartography that supports the 'genomic' framework enables the impact of particular causes of noise to accumulate across the business so that strategically important non-conformity with the principle of ensuring integration of effort is easily identified and its impact quantified. The causal factors are always obvious from the activity so the focus for implementation is on gaining agreement to the required behavioural change and monitoring that change.

Being disciplined

The principle of being disciplined requires the organization to invest in policies, procedures and standards and apply a strong systems discipline to everything it does (see Chapter 2). This means keeping process documentation up to date and using it to both operate and change the business.

The overarching issue here is that organizations commonly only document functional activities. Functional activities define what has to be done to deliver the strategy on the assumption that there are no issues in the effort spent on achieving the interfaces between the many individuals involved in the business process or value chain. In practice, as we have outlined earlier, our research shows that up to three out of every four of the activities carried out by staff are interfacing activities. The noise elements of these interfacing activities absorb routinely 33.6 per cent of everyone's time and are responsible for failures in customer satisfaction, staff satisfaction, productivity and focus. This failure to document interfacing activities between personnel means that the most complex elements of a process are never visible to management. The significance is that three out of every four activities undertaken by staff cannot be, and therefore are not, managed. The design of the sub-processes to handle the inevitable errors, and variations that occur, are therefore being left to the least experienced, lower levels in every organization without oversight.

A generic example, so commonplace and so very close to many real examples we have seen and worked with, brings the point into sharp relief. A document (an order, insurance proposal, specification, etc) is received by a customer service officer (CSO). It does not have a customer number on it so it cannot be input to the system. The CSO, in order to interface, has to find the missing information (noise), which may involve phoning people (noise) only to have to phone back later (noise and delay). He or she may have to field requests from a colleague in another department who is wondering why the information has not arrived (noise), and so on. If the interfacing activity concerns the transmission of something that cannot easily be held up – for example in a medical context: blood plasma, sterilized instruments or information on where surgery should be performed – failure to manage the activity could easily be fatal. At the very least, failure 'costs' the organization in terms of direct productivity and responsiveness, hence customer service and satisfaction.

A leading organization, such as GE, manages this situation by ensuring that all managers are held accountable for improving their business processes. GE's managers therefore have an unusually high awareness of process disruptions.

A key to establishing the management principle of being disciplined in an organization is to document every activity that is undertaken using interface mapping. This will quickly provide the information fundamental to installing this management principle as well as providing the essential information base for managing business processes. Interface mapping captures the interfacing activity. Strategic categorization enables the noise to be targeted, and the core activity to be understood and monitored. Discretionary activity is essential for risk management practices to be understood. The 'genomics' enables the analysis across the business to be undertaken and procedures and process models to be generated.

Creating customer value

This principle requires all employees to understand how the various activities they undertake align with their customers' expectations and calls for them to strive to enhance customer value. There are two distinct actions required to be able to meet the necessary conditions. The first is that everyone in the business needs to understand how the activities they carry out affect their customers. The second is that there is sufficient dialogue with the customer so that the value-driving activity reflects the value drivers (core activities) for both their organization *and* that of their customers.

Implementation of this principle stems naturally from the work needed to implement the previous two principles of ensuring integration of effort and being disciplined. The interface mapping will have captured the interfacing activity and strategic categorization will have enabled the interfacing activity noise to be targeted and the present core activity understood. The 'genomics' cartography enables the work to be done and improved across the whole business. A further step is then needed to understand what drives value for the business and what drives value for the customer. A carefully targeted customer survey will allow the customer to pinpoint the critical service activities that are undertaken and provide a competitive performance rating. Exploration of these critical service activities with the customer, together with an extension of interface mapping into the customer's organization, allows needed core activities to be determined and implemented.

Being time-based

Operating by this principle means that the business uses time as a critical dimension to eliminate delays and waste from its organization. In other words, this means eliminating the activities that reduce the responsiveness of the organization – drivers of interfacing activity noise.

Implementing this principle calls for the removal of the main drivers of interfacing activity noise from the business. This would include addressing errors and the associated delays in order taking, order processing and delivery. An example in public policy formulation illustrates how the principle applies to more complex transactions. An analysis of activity in a large health policy unit revealed noise levels absorbing over 60 per cent of the total effort. Two-thirds of the noise was driven by style and grammar rework, pointing to the need for targeted training and the generation of standards for articulation of policy. Such analyses in intellectually demanding areas have led to initiatives such as: increasing the capability of the staff undertaking the jobs by employing people with higher skills and experience to reduce the number of iterations (noise); investing core effort in defining and agreeing requirements clearly before work is undertaken, to eliminate rework (noise); and co-locating design teams and databases to enable joint development while removing the need to iterate (noise).

Implementation of this principle stems naturally from the work needed to implement the principles of ensuring integration of effort and being disciplined. The interface mapping will capture the interfacing activities. Strategic categorization will enable the noise from these to be quantified. The cartography will enable analysis across the business. Implementation now requires the organization to use the data to address the higher-value noise drivers to eliminate delays and unnecessary activity and cost.

Creating strategic capabilities

The research demonstrated that leading organizations understood the need to build strategic capability by managing the interfaces to complement their positional strategy. They built their strategic capability by pinpointing gaps in their process alignment, developing solutions for them and deploying the change efficiently. They defined their change needs in accordance with the four management principles focusing on strategic intent: ensuring integration of effort, being disciplined, creating customer value and being time-based. They set up the mechanisms for deployment in accordance with the principles described below.

Relating the micro to the macro

The leading companies demonstrating this management principle were able to show that they had succeeded in tying the activities their employees undertook to the strategic goals of the business. In particular, all employees knew how their particular activities and individual efforts affected and contributed to the 'big picture' of business success, including how their activities affected others.

Many organizations have instituted programmes with this goal in mind. The programmes have included empowerment; team-based working and voice of the customer for the staff, as well as management by objectives (MBO); the Balanced Scorecard; customer surveys; and benchmarking for management. All of these programmes set out to raise staff's or managers' awareness of strategic goals so that they can theoretically adjust the activities they undertake to align with strategic goals. However, all of these approaches are indirect. They leave staff or managers to use their judgement to decide which activities need to be changed and how the required adjustments will be effected. These approaches, while benefiting from being close to the action, are yet another example of the use of guesses, judgement and experience to define change – analogous perhaps to building a house without plans and specifications.

Interface mapping, strategic categorization and the use of the new 'genomic' framework offer a precise mechanism to link the micro to the macro. The first step is interface mapping, which by definition requires the staff doing the work to document and quantify all the activities they routinely undertake. This mapping is conducted by each team and includes steps to validate the activities and gain team certification that the data is a complete and accurate record of everything that is done. This has a number of implications:

- There is wide understanding. The language used is the everyday language with which the members of each team are familiar and staff generate it themselves.

- A complete and accurate record is made. The staff certify that the documented activities embrace everything they do.

- Functional and interfacing activities are included. There is no attempt to restrict the activities that are documented.

- The record is quantified. The team resource is allocated across all the activities that are documented.

- The outcome is that a base line that everybody understands and agrees has been established.

The next step in the three-week documentation process is to categorize strategically each of the 196 activities (see Table 5.2 on page 95) that each team on average undertakes. This is always an exhilarating process preceded by a short training session on how to identify the four categories of activity. The area that creates the least debate is the identification of interfacing activity noise. The people in the team experience first hand the consequences of errors and omissions elsewhere in the process. They are the people who have to chase others to get missing information and to obtain corrections then redo the work. They therefore grasp the concept of interfacing activity noise immediately and quickly code up the relevant activities. Our experience demonstrates that no external person – manager, specialist or consultant – has ever matched the performance of those doing the work in this coding task. The result of the noise coding is that every disruption to the smooth flow of a process is flagged in the database and, much more importantly, in the mind of the employees undertaking that task. The outcome in every one of the 400 applications of interface mapping is that the staff can hardly wait – they want to address the causes of the interfacing activity noise there and then.

The area that creates the most discussion is the coding of core activities, which on average occupy just 3.3 per cent of people's time. The most common misunderstanding is caused by an overwhelming desire to relate role to core value-driving activity as, for example, in the statement, 'I am an accountant therefore everything I do, other than noise, must be core activity,' as explained in Chapter 6. The debate that takes place on core is therefore absolutely fundamental to the success of implanting the management principle of relating the micro to the macro. This dialogue permits staff and managers to agree and understand which activities (around 6 out of 196 in the average team) deliver strategic outcomes. Core activities are those activities that provide strategic outcomes to the organization's stakeholders. They include the activities that increase customer value as well as those that eliminate the major drivers of noise.

If this debate were not to occur, and the misconception that role defines core is allowed to persist, then organizations would remain stuck in the value-adding paradigm where over 60 per cent (see Chapter 6: 3.3 per cent core, 48 per cent support and much of the 14.5 per cent discretionary) of the work they are doing would be seen as value adding and therefore necessary. It would be impossible for most employees ever to know which activities drive the business outcomes. (The definition of core was explored in depth in Chapter 4.)

Implementation of this principle stems naturally from using interface mapping to capture the interfacing activities and then carrying out strategic categorization. Not only do the managers and staff know which activities drive strategic outcomes, they really want to get stuck in and eliminate the interfacing activity noise and, by so doing, agree which activities drive value for the business.

Establishing a learning culture

Our research shows that all employees in the leading organizations demonstrate a willingness to develop skills and knowledge and are involved in a learning or development programme. This is born from always being dissatisfied with performance and business processes, coupled with the understanding that improved knowledge can be translated into improved business processes and thus improved performance. We also note in these leading organizations that employees do not feel threatened by knowledge transfer to others but rather believe that shared knowledge is an important ingredient to their organization's future prosperity.

Learning and employee development is an objective commonly encountered in most organizations. Initiatives can be wide ranging. New staff induction programmes, training and development and management development are examples that are virtually always found. Some organizations use technology alliances to keep up to date with new developments. Other organizations sponsor research and fund tertiary courses for their employees. In parallel with these initiatives, government-sponsored schemes and development programmes associated with professional bodies make significant contributions to learning and development.

So what is different about this principle as applied in our best-practice organizations? The critical difference is not to be found in the nature, or the depth and breadth, of the training and development undertaken. The difference is in how the need for training and development is determined and how they are delivered. The primary driver of this learning focus is the need to develop the firm's strategic capabilities by aligning its business processes. If a key issue is in the quality of components received from suppliers then a focus is placed on learning about supplier interfaces. If a key issue is the level of errors and omissions internally then the primary causes in the interfacing activities are addressed. Staff and management development programmes are then adjusted to feature these new elements. The most important point we are making is that forensic diagnosis comes first: following a full interface mapping process one can know where to focus the learning so as to achieve impact; otherwise it is a guess, perhaps an educated guess, which may not be correct.

Interface mapping, strategic categorization and the use of the new 'genomics' framework offer a precise mechanism both to promote and target learning. Interface mapping is fundamentally a discovery process aimed at cataloguing every activity undertaken in an organization. Strategic categorization, as outlined in the previous section, enables staff and managers to understand which activities drive the desired strategic outcomes and which destroy value. The new cartography allows these elements to be understood in the context of business processes and thus allows priorities to be established. Further, the cartography allows staff to see the impact of their actions on others in the process and thus work with them to develop solutions. Finally, the cartography also allows the organization to monitor implementation to ensure that the desired results are achieved in each of the many affected teams.

Implementation of this principle stems from the analysis undertaken as a result of using interface mapping to capture the functional and interfacing activities, carrying out strategic categorization and analysing the results by business process using the 'genomics' framework. Staff and managers use this base-level work to understand the activities they undertake and the impact these have on the other parts of the supply chain and the business outcomes. They are able to make use of this understanding to prioritize change needs and develop training solutions to address the priorities, in many cases without outside assistance or resource. Where the solution affects other parts of the business or other stakeholders, they are able to define further investigation needs precisely in order for the necessary work to be put into train. Where greater technical input is required, the information and understanding they have allows them to define larger initiatives to be tackled by the Lean or Six Sigma team.

A paradigm shift

At this point in this chapter you will have realized that the use of interface mapping, strategic categorization and the new cartography is a game changer. The information these elements provide enables strategic priorities to be quickly established and precisely defined. Further, the changes can be planned in many cases by the real experts – the people who actually do the work – which has the virtue of achieving wide engagement at the same time as eliminating the need for extensive communication and management of initiatives. The approach thus makes redundant most of the effort devoted to establishing change needs based on conventional process maps with the liberal use of judgement. It helps very much with the avoidance of fads too.

This fundamentally alters the nature of most change programmes. There is no longer any need to devote so much effort to up-front analysis on each initiative passed up for consideration, followed by close monitoring to identify emerging gaps and omissions that inevitably occur frequently in experience-driven change. The time freed up by the precision provided by interface mapping can be invested in tackling more initiatives at any one time. It is against this background that the four management principles of embracing change, supporting distributed leadership, being up front and gaining alignment are now discussed.

Embracing change

Best practice in the leading organizations included the principle of embracing change. The employees demonstrated a willingness to embrace and accept change as an essential part of doing business. Further, the organizations excelled in implementing new ideas.

The goals of interface mapping can only practically be achieved when employees are fully engaged in interface mapping and in subsequent strategic categorization. We have never encountered resistance from staff in 400 studies when they were asked to document everything they actually do. On the contrary, their involvement, even if initially restrained by concerns about the time it might take, turns from cooperative to enthusiastic when they realize that they are to document everything that they do including the frustrating interfacing activity noise that would have been swept under the carpet and ignored in previous conventional approaches to process documentation. The completion of the interface mapping therefore signals that staff and managers have already begun to embrace change. Further, staff now understand how each of them contribute to the overall strategic goals of the organization, and, more importantly, where the opportunities lie to increase the performance of the business.

Supporting distributed leadership

In the best-practice organizations in our survey the individuals and work teams are assigned, and accept, responsibility for operational decision making and performance improvement. This enables the more senior managers to focus more of their time on strategy – both ensuring that the organization strengthens its position in the market place and that the organization builds an effective process to create strategic capabilities. They focus on creating opportunities for growth and resourcing for the medium term.

The principle of supporting distributed leadership goes beyond empowerment. The employees are engaged in two ways. First, they are engaged in the analysis process in the business to determine the process change needs. They then go much further. Their achievement of the management principle of relating the micro to macro gives them the knowledge to take part in determining the location, nature and priority for particular change initiatives they can then follow through and implement within the framework established by senior managers. Our experience demonstrates time after time that they are very good at doing it given their new-found ability to see the end-to-end business process in the interface maps.

Interface mapping and strategic categorization give employees the information they need to quantify and describe the opportunities they now know need to be implemented. Measures based on the 'genomic' framework can then be used to monitor progress and keep documentation up to date.

Being up front

This management principle found in leading organizations is in evidence when employees demonstrate integrity and openness in all areas of their work and dealings with others. Relationships are highly valued. Employees can make promises that affect customers, safe in the knowledge that they do know which activities drive performance increases and confident that their colleagues in other parts of the business share the same framework. Equally, short-term expediency is avoided. Problems will not be glossed over and passed on for some other person in the business to eventually resolve at a cost to customer satisfaction and productivity, etc.

While being far from the complete answer, interface mapping plays an important enabling role in embedding this principle. In almost every application of interface mapping in which we have been involved we take particular care to set interfacing activity noise expectations. Managers, especially in more traditional organizations, are often assessed on efficiency. Efficiency can be judged in various ways ranging from objective benchmarking to complaints received. The issue with benchmarking is that well-managed organizations are often as good as or better than 'best practice' and this can lead to complacency. So better managers, confident in their benchmarking comparisons, can be dreadfully shocked to find between 30 per cent and 40 per cent noise in their operations resulting from poor interface management. Further, this 'poor result' may well be held against them by their superiors in the more traditional businesses.

Careful management of expectations avoids this glitch. It becomes a mechanism for opening up a previously closed culture to admit to problems, mistakes and inconsistencies: this lays the foundation for being up front. A significant noise level is in fact something to welcome and covet. It will provide a huge resource to fund improvement or growth at little or no cost;

it will provide a clear indication that competitive advantage can be built by investing in building strategic capabilities and it provides a platform to engage and excite staff to embed the 14 management principles required to build strategic capabilities in the organization and to take its place with the best organizations.

Gaining alignment

The leading organizations were differentiated by involving their employees and achieving good alignment of employee behaviour with stated organizational values and direction at all levels in the organization. The organizations that achieved this principle had built shared common values and a shared strategic intent.

They had used many of the common techniques to accomplish this, such as vision workshops, management development programmes and sophisticated use of communication, including their in-house communications approaches. The difference from common practice, as for the learning focus principle, lay elsewhere. It did not lie in mechanisms to generate difficult-to-apply shared common values. The difference was to be found in what the programme was focused on. The alignment for these organizations was the strategic alignment of business processes through the elimination of the major drivers of interfacing activity noise, the day-to-day encouragement to perform core activity and the consistent compliance to the essential discretionary activities. The values, in other words, revolved around the achievement of a seamless end-to-end business process by concentrating on the interfaces between personnel as well as doing the functional activities called for in the strategy.

Measuring and reporting principle

Best-practice organizations measure a range of financial and non-financial parameters. These measures are made available in reports to all employees to give them the information needed to drive improvement.

Virtually every organization relies on KPIs to monitor the performance of the business against targets. Some organizations have adopted the excellent Balanced Scorecard framework and allocated the KPIs to the relevant business processes. Non-financial KPIs are used to monitor performance outcomes of business processes, such as customer service, document turnaround times, safety, employee satisfaction, asset and plant utilization, stock turn and processed volumes. Senior managers are then in a position to see the evolving trends.

There is a big problem with KPIs, evident to anyone managing a business process. KPIs are historic measures; they can only indicate what has already happened. They do not predict the future. An analogy often heard is that using KPIs to manage a business is rather like driving a car with the windscreen obscured and relying on the reversing camera to steer. The advantage is that the driver will know that he or she has not run over anything yet and is able to confirm that the car is still on the road. The disadvantage is that the driver has no knowledge of what lies ahead – no inkling that schoolchildren have stepped out onto the road or that there is a severe bend ahead. Further, if the KPI trends show a deteriorating performance the manager has no indication of why this is occurring and has no other option than mounting an investigation to try to understand what has caused the problem – no doubt placing heavy reliance on informed guesses, experience and judgement.

What is ideally required are leading indicators, indicators which if positive will confirm how much value-driving activity is being carried out with a consequently predictable business outcome. Interface mapping and strategic categorization identify the activities that are being carried out and their strategic worth by team.

When change is planned to address, for example, a particular highly disruptive interfacing activity noise driver, a modest injection of new core activity will be required to ensure that the noise is prevented from entering the process. This new core activity will be performed by a specific team. A leading indicator can now be defined to monitor that the action needed to eliminate the penetration of the noise is being carried out. We call this leading indicator a behavioural change indicator (BCI). BCIs are team-, even person-, specific. They provide the mechanism to link the micro measures (the BCIs) back to the macro measures (the KPIs). The array of BCIs for each particular team can be likened to DNA. When all the BCIs are adhered to the strategic outcomes will be delivered.

Resourcing for the medium term

Leading organizations are able to balance effectively short-term operational and medium-term development and growth issues and requirements.

An examination of the activity footprint of senior managers all too often reveals that a high proportion of their time is spent dealing with interfacing activity noise issues as a consequence of the failure of the business to manage interfacing activity. These noise activities range from trivia to business-threatening failure. The trivia includes handling the ramifications for customers of simple delays and errors, perhaps by having to contact the customers involved, forgive fees, authorize credit notes and discounts to compensate for errors or having to write off valuable product. At the threatening end it has included protracted attendance at public enquiries as a result of fatal incidents, dealing with the consequences of poor lending decisions or developing major elements of software to address 'unanticipated' needs.

The key issue is that the leading organizations focus on establishing a process for developing strategic capabilities, within this framework of management principles, in order to have the freedom to focus on the business scenario, competitors' activity and technological developments. They can be confident that whatever change is needed their organization has the capability to make the change without messing things up.

Conclusions

When we first saw the principles common to the world's best companies, which we deduced from first-hand observation of many such businesses, the factor that was not clear was how to achieve an industry-leading position quickly and effectively. These principles are a lasting but high-level set of valuable guides for senior managers. Yet when executives find their weaknesses on these principles, which can be quite readily recognized, frustration often occurs because it is not clear what should be done to improve. This top-down recognition of such things as poor alignment, low level of embracing change, lack of discipline, poorly focused or lack of learning, etc, is a start. The key question managers want answered is what they should do now.

The answer is obviously to connect up a desire to move forward on these drivers of strategic capabilities, with the bottom-up process management that can only come with knowing (with the fullest facts and detail) where you are starting from. A full map, including the largely ignored mass of interface activities, is that starting point. It completes the connection between the high-level desire to improve strategy implementation, with the bottom-up capability to know what to change. And ultimately the 'devil is in the detail' to the extent that the process problems that cause many organizations to fail, or at best struggle, can be significantly driven forward.

Once the interface mapping is done, all the principles become self-reinforcing in moving the organization forward. With this 'organizational GPS' in place, the morale of the workforce goes up, confidence rises right around the organization and the destructive interfacing activity noise can be greatly reduced. All the principles are hard, sometimes impossible, to move forward without this organizational GPS in place, yet they are fully able to go 'onwards and upwards' with the focusing and change management capabilities in place, as delivered by the interface maps. As we have said, many organizations persist for years to implement one of the best-practice management principles because the focus is on the perfection of the implementation of the principle. The need is to focus on improving the business outcomes through managing the interfaces in the business processes. Properly using interface mapping as the organizational GPS guide provides an efficient and fast way to achieve the outcomes and deploy the principles. It 'short cuts' the whole process, changing it from a grind that should possibly achieve benefits at the end to an exciting managed discovery journey delivering outcomes along the way.

Finally the process we have described is not a one-off process: the use of the principles as integrated with the interface map becomes a living and recurring process in itself. It becomes clearly a core process, and can clearly make the organization more efficient in converting inputs into outputs, and able to be agile in adjusting to changes in the external environment and the internal strategy. Some of the companies we have studied and worked with, such as Toyota and GE, have taken decades to become as good as they are at implementing their version of the general principles in this book, as well as so very efficient from a business process perspective. The really good news is that it now doesn't have to take that long: Toyota and GE evolved relatively slowly (over decades) to their positions of organizational excellence, yet now a combination of the interface mapping process, combined with the explicit knowledge of the business excellence principles and their explicit pursuit potentially delivers a much faster journey.

Staying on top: maintaining business outcomes

10

Objectives

There just does not seem to be a generally followed approach in common use to achieve continuous, strategically focused, process management practices other than in leaders such as Toyota and GE. We will therefore describe in this chapter how to achieve ongoing, strategically focused change of end-to-end business processes to achieve and then maintain the business outcomes required to meet your business intent.

This challenging goal is achieved from two components that bring together everything we have talked about in the previous chapters. The first component is to make the day-to-day 'continuous improvement' programmes deliver strategic outcomes – thus bringing together strategy and continuous improvement to achieve continuous strategic realignment. We will explain how to achieve this using interface mapping and the management principles focusing on strategic intent (first described in Chapter 2). In so doing we will bring to life the management principle of discipline, particularly through investing in and making use of policies, procedures and standards. The second component is a tool to allow managers to make a change and move on, confident that all planned changes have been made, are delivering the expected business outcomes and are being maintained in force. Managers will then be relieved of much of the policing burden of change, such as checking to make sure that the new way of working is still being followed and staff have not lapsed back into their old ways. We will therefore further explore the operating-level delegation tool (BCIs), which work for each team in much the same way that the Balanced Scorecard has so effectively ensured that higher-level managers keep their eye on the ball for the business as a whole.

We begin the chapter with a brief recap of relevant elements of business processes and the functional and interfacing activities from which they are built.

Introduction

In previous chapters we have described the interface mapping approach for quickly documenting business processes each time strategic change is contemplated. We have outlined how to use the interfacing activity data to prioritize, plan and implement change to achieve the organization's strategic goals. We have also explained the advantages interface mapping has. It will always engage and excite the people who are doing the work. Staff will invariably welcome the help it will give them to overcome the many examples of interfacing activity noise that keep appearing in the business, waste their time and reduce their performance and job satisfaction. Further, properly documented interface maps will enable existing in-house teams to improve the breadth, yield and the delivery speed of their Lean, Six Sigma, quality or BPR initiatives by enabling all of the benefits across the business to be harvested. Finally, interface mapping will move any organization towards the achievement of the best-practice management principles because goals related to strategy, productivity, customer service and staff satisfaction will be delivered with surgical precision. Considering the high proportion of strategic initiatives that fail to deliver their desired and planned outcomes, this is quite an achievement.

Interface mapping as a tool is always available and can be quickly used to initiate strategic changes or tactical improvements to business processes, but is this as good as it gets? Well no, we are not yet at the end of the story. We have not yet described the approach to the complete implementation of the best-practice management principles. There is more to do if the business goal is to operate truly world-class, strategically aligned business processes. This chapter will argue that to achieve this goal, the need is to establish interface mapping as an ongoing process, a strategically driven continuous improvement process, which will in turn ensure that the best-practice management principles remain, uncorrupted, in your business.

Common approaches to business process change do not last

The way that strategic change is tackled in business today does not make it easy to achieve the strategically focused change continuum that characterizes the leading organizations, which may explain why they maintain their position out front. First, strategically motivated change is invariably episodic. It is undertaken at irregular intervals when strategic, top-down initiatives are mounted. Second, strategic change always seems to require a huge amount of effort because of the need for a lot of preparation and management effort to overcome inertia. Strategic change to business processes seems to involve months of preparation followed by months of process mapping (while ignoring most of the interfacing activity) before the planning and deployment can begin. Then comes the clean-up, the bug fixing and bedding-in required to allow time for a raft of new interfacing activities to be developed by the junior staff affected by the deployment to plug all the gaps and omissions. These new interfacing activities, as always, will absorb yet more of the business's resource. When one thinks of it, this very concept of how many organizations conduct major change initiatives sounds close to ridiculous. Yet it is all too common.

Continuous improvement, on the other hand, is an ongoing process with regular deployment of tactical changes. It depends for its success on identifying beneficial opportunities to change, gaining agreement to them and then deploying the changes. Each change will be confined to a particular element of a business process. While much overhead effort is spent on defining each problem, it never seems appropriate or justified to engage the whole organization in the preparations needed for strategic change. Projects are therefore rarely wide enough in scope to be strategic. Certainly, the effort required to collect the data in all the other parts of the business would be prohibitively expensive using the usual tools. Traditional process mapping alone would take months. So the focus tends to be confined to a particular part of a business process. This means that most of the potential benefit will not be attainable, as proved by the analysis in Chapter 5 (see Figure 5.6 on page 105), which shows that two-thirds of the benefit to be obtained from addressing interfacing activity noise can only be harvested elsewhere in the business. Thus the benefits that could be realized downstream and elsewhere in the business are never known and targets for customer service, productivity and staff satisfaction remain out of reach. Continuous improvement does deliver value though in the form of local, tactical improvement; however, it could be very much more powerful than it currently is in most applications.

It is therefore no surprise that there is such a high interfacing activity noise level (consuming on average 33.6 per cent of the staff's time in our database of 117 organizations). So, at present there is too much potential left on the table. Its very existence is the evidence that the strategic change and continuous improvement initiatives currently practised are either improperly focused or poorly executed. Focus and execution are the very areas the best-practice management principles address.

Continuous, strategic business process alignment

Imagine a different scenario, where strategically focused change takes place on a continuous basis in all parts of the business. Gone is the prolonged preparation, the endless process mapping and the interminable investigations, tweaking and fettling of the new initiative. Envisage instead a situation where a clean-up is no longer inevitable and where the staff and managers' effort is devoted entirely to the required changes. The result would be a leaner, fitter, strategically more responsive organization. This organization would be ranked with the best in the world. Further, using the approach outlined in the first nine chapters of this book, there is no limit to how much forward progress can be achieved.

Interfacing activities continually change

We have made the point many times through the book that interfacing activities are subject to ongoing change. We have shown that physical layout can require different interfacing activities to take place. For example, a multi-factory food company had one of its finished goods warehouses located away from its factories, on the other side of a divided highway – self-harm you probably think, and that would not happen in your business! But differences in layouts do not have to be major to have a toxic impact. Things as simple as the location of the photocopier or the insistence of a manager that he or she is the only person who can use particular equipment or sign-off an approval will significantly change the interfacing activities required as well as increase service cost and reduce the quality of customer service. The key is to know what and where these impediments are.

The most frequently encountered generators of change are the people involved. Employees continually change jobs and any new person, being human, will inevitably do some things differently, have a different interpretation of instructions and make different assumptions of what is required. The way employees handle the new person's output is thus likely to change. Critically, any such changes will affect the many interfacing activities for better or worse, and no one will know what these changes will be until the new face actually appears on the job. Legislation is another area that causes changes to interfacing activities. Different types of enquiries will be generated, requiring different information to be accessed by staff. Customers' expectations change, products and services change and partner organizations update their systems.

So change, as the saying goes, is the only constant. But is change really constant? Is this assumption really true for business processes? Let's visit some examples. A wholesale electrical company expanded the warehouse at the back of one of its stores and reduced the space available for goods inwards. The functional tasks carried out by the staff to receive the goods were unchanged. The interfacing activities, on the other hand, expanded. They now involved walking down the street to unload the goods from the larger trucks that were unable to get into the reduced-size loading dock. Staff also had to do extra interfacing activities to prevent water damage to packaging when unloading in the rain. The interfacing activities had changed radically, especially in the rain, increasing cost and the potential for damage to the goods with the promise of even more interfacing activity if the damage ensued. However, the functional activities, the unloading, updating the computer, signing for the goods and putting the goods away, had not changed at all.

Let's take another example. The ATM machine at a major bank branch was relocated to a more prominent position at the front of the premises. The older clientele then couldn't read the screen because of strong reflections of the sun from mid-morning to mid-afternoon – the very times that the older customers came out to use it. The branch's functional activities again remained exactly the same for the staff. However, they were now inundated with new interfacing activity, having to deal with lots of complaints (noise) about how customers used to get their cash easily from the ATM and the two cashiers had to handle a greater volume of withdrawals and deposits (noise driven by the relocation error) while the ATM serviced fewer customers.

Here's yet another example. A high usage range of spare parts was withdrawn in a 200-branch wholesaler without a replacement being offered. Again the sales or service functional activities did not change in any way but the 1,000 staff across the company tried to help their key customers by searching for an alternative supply of spare parts for them (noise) thus keeping other customers waiting. They would rather do this than lose key accounts to a competitor. They also had to deal with complaints and telephone enquiries (more noise) and the outcome – still a loss of business.

Then there was the new doctor who joined a major hospital. His prescriptions could not be read by the in-hospital pharmacist, and like other doctors, he was not prepared to use the recently installed computerized script system. Again, the functional activities did not change one bit but the pharmacist now had the added burden of spending a considerable time chasing the doctor on the phone (noise) or risk issuing the wrong drugs or be criticized for poor service which would in turn have increased bed occupancy (noise) because late issue of discharge drugs would mean another night in the hospital for that patient and the postponement of a scheduled procedure for another patient. The staff then had to deal with the complaints of the waiting patients.

To push home this point let's return to Henry Ford (Chapter 1). The less-skilled assembly-line operators did exactly the same functional assembly activities as the artisans they had replaced. They picked up parts and bolted them together. The big and strategically critical difference, the change that propelled Ford to dominance in his industry, was that in his system the assembly-line operators did not need to do any fettling of any of the parts. The parts interfaced with each other cleanly every time. There was no longer any need for the fettling (another name for interfacing activity noise). This enabled more than a tenfold increase in productivity as well as producing a more reliable product, with spare parts that would actually fit being readily available. Ford had focused his whole attention on managing assembly-floor interfacing activities, not the functional ones.

How does this alter the way we should think about change then? The things that change rarely are the functional tasks called for by the strategy, but they do change from time to time. The frequently occurring changes are found in the interfacing activities. These are the very activities we have shown need to be managed to achieve the strategic alignment that will deliver goals associated with customer service and employee satisfaction and, of course, address the 33.6 per cent waste. Further, it is only after functional changes have been deployed (the warehouse design, the ATM location, the parts catalogue, the new doctor) that the impact on the interfacing activities can be assessed. All activities must first be documented to enable things to be put in place to allow them to be managed. So if continuous strategically focused change is to occur then a frequently updated interface map is required, containing up-to-date data on both the functional and interfacing activities.

Up-to-date interface maps

The need for an ongoing programme

There are two important conclusions to be drawn. The first is that traditional process maps, primarily containing functional activities only, need to be updated when the strategy changes. Functional activities are not affected by the vagaries of day-to-day change nor are they situationally dependent. They are a catalogue of what staff and managers are required to do on the assumption that performing these tasks will provide the desired outcomes. This explains why there has been no call for frequent update of traditional process maps, procedures or job descriptions – frequent revision would add no value simply because functional activities rarely change. This conclusion provides a logical explanation of why a large communications company specifically required its process documentation to exclude all elements of process failure and therefore excluded the interfacing activities. The senior managers' error was making the assumption that a functional catalogue was all that was needed to enable them to drive the organization-wide transformation programme they were about to undertake. Their assumption, that focusing on managing functional tasks will deliver goods or services efficiently, or deliver strategic change itself, was very much flawed. This is an organization that delivered significant value destruction to its shareholders, in an industry in which growth (and hence opportunity) was little short of rampant. Its strategic position had been one of industry dominance, yet its lack of capability on the best-practice management principles, and its poor state of process capability, led it to underperform severely considering what would have been predicted based on its industry and strategic position.

If the requirement is to manage outcomes then how the work is done becomes at least as important as what functional tasks need to be carried out. The emphasis thus shifts to understanding and managing all the things that hold the process together, particularly the interfacing activities, as well as dealing with any changes in functional activity arising from a positional decision to change strategy.

The second conclusion thus becomes an imperative if the objective is to build competitive advantage through building strategic capabilities, or less loftily, to harvest the 33.6 per cent waste hidden in interfacing activity noise and deliver the desired outcomes for customer service and employee satisfaction. This second conclusion is that a mechanism is needed to ensure that interfacing activity is properly recorded and kept up to date with the functional activities to reflect the inevitable, ongoing interface activity changes. There is therefore a clear strategic need for an ongoing interface mapping programme if best practice is to be achieved and maintained. Such an ongoing programme would be consistent with the management principle of being disciplined that is in place in the best organizations in the world (see Chapter 2: the international research revealed that leading organizations had invested in policies, procedures and standards to create a living knowledge platform they then used to manage by).

As a senior manager committed to keeping his interface maps up to date, Tom Lucey of GE Capital, comments:

> Annually we have continued to leverage ongoing measurement through the use of the XeP3 interface mapping tool to determine that the changes we were making through centralization, automation and task obliteration were delivering. It would be easy to think there would be a natural increase into 'Core & Support' activities. This just isn't the case. We needed to understand where staff were allocating their time and through year on year measurement adjust our internal process, job requirements, job design and incentive systems to better align the work effort to drive increased returns and volumes whilst not compromising the engagement and commitment of our team.

Essential features of an ongoing interface mapping programme

The first three features of an interface activity mapping programme are technical requirements we have alluded to before. They arise because the individual interface activities are small – on average less than 2 hours per month per average incidence (see Figure 5.4 on page 106). The first requirement is to be able to map the whole of the organization so that both the causal factors can be identified where they first occur and the 'viral' impact of each causal factor across the business can be accumulated. The second requirement is to be able to reference and accumulate all the occurrences of interface activity noise by causal factor so that priorities can be established and minor incidences discarded. This feature will allow organizations to avoid the ever-present continuous improvement trap of attending to locally obvious but perhaps overall small discontinuities rather than essential needs. The third requirement is to know where each of the activities is located (that is, in which team it occurs), so that the benefits of the changes deployed can be harvested with precision.

In Chapter 3 we first raised the issue that the only people who are fully aware of the nature and resource impact of each of the interfacing activities are the staff who actually do the work in each of the teams. We found that even the team leaders, the first line of management, cannot be relied upon to know even most of the activities that are being conducted under their leadership. The fourth requirement is thus a mechanism that allows everyone in each team, including the team leader, to contribute to, amend and agree the team data. Today this means web-enabled access for everyone in each team. So while we will readily agree that the data could be developed by a more traditional interviewing process carried out, of necessity, with each and every team member in each team across the organization, we would argue that the time frame for this would be inordinately long. We have witnessed many incidences of process mapping by interview taking six months to two years while failing to capture any of the vital interfacing activities. As we have already stated, with the appropriate tools a whole organization of 6,000 staff can be fully interface-mapped in just three weeks.

Using each team to conduct the interface mapping brings the additional benefits of ownership and understanding by everyone in the business. Further, having developed the data for the first time the teams have developed the skills and knowledge to keep it up to date.

Month 1 deliverables

The first deliverable – knowledge

Knowledge is the first deliverable in the three weeks of an interface mapping programme. A quantified, thorough database, accepted by everyone, that will enable a user of it to pinpoint all the gaps and weaknesses in the firm's business processes will result. It will reveal how many activities are missing from existing documentation. Further, because databases can be easily combined to incorporate the interface mapping work from partner organizations, the total end-to-end delivery becomes visible, noise and all.

The information is then ready to be used to ensure that:

- the functional activities called for by the strategy are being done;
- the toxic interface activity noise stands out;
- non-compliance with world best practice principles is evident.

Using in-company work teams to develop the interface maps delivers this benefit with no downside. The team members (that is, all staff and junior managers) own and agree the data and the noise categorization of their work. The consequence is that the data, and the conclusions drawn from it, will rarely, if ever, be challenged. Indeed, we have witnessed many, many instances of junior staff talking openly with senior managers about the high levels of interfacing activity noise in their team and suggesting ways to address it while travelling together in a lift. Everything is exposed to the light of day and openly discussed.

We do recall one of just a handful of challenges. We were working with a large international insurance business. The staff-generated interface activity data revealed an unusually high interfacing activity noise level of 59 per cent – that is, three days of every person's five-day week were spent correcting errors or chasing missing information or dealing with the consequences. One manager who had been absent for a period of weeks before and during the data development challenged, 'How do you know the data is right? It could well have been falsified.' I asked him how he thought it would be falsified. He said, 'Obviously the teams would have underreported the interfacing activity noise.' I refrained from answering – then he realized what he had implied, that his division was wasting more than three days out of every five for every one of his staff. Had he been one of the people who felt there was a need for a crisis to underpin a change programme, he certainly had one now. The 59 per cent noise in his organization marked a record at the time – and the incident underlined the need to make sure everyone participates and absentees are engaged.

The second deliverable – enthusiasm

Widespread enthusiasm for change is engendered well within the first month and this begins to create a change-friendly culture. This comes directly from the participative preparation of the data. Once the teams have documented, quantified and agreed the interface activity noise they always become eager, impatient even, to see this noise fixed quickly. After all, no one enjoys dealing with errors, staying late to catch up or handling angry clients. Understandably, the staff will feel that they have proved in their interface activity documentation that the issues they have wanted to be fixed for years are really there, so they simply will not see why the issues cannot be dealt with immediately. They never even seem to care whether the noise issues were caused by their own actions or the actions of others, they just want them fixed. So the manager's job becomes one of harnessing their enthusiasm. However, this is much easier than trying to herd them unwillingly through a process they do not want to be a part of and then having to check every day whether they have reverted to old practices.

The third deliverable – speed

The mapping is done fast with the support of the right tool. Members of each work team, and we have worked with thousands of teams on every continent in various languages, will document their activity base, quantify it and categorize it by part-time participation in an elapsed time of three weeks. They will then deliver a complete catalogue of everything that is done in the whole business, signed off ready to analyse by business process.

The fourth deliverable – managers' confidence

Managers gain confidence that there are real, tangible opportunities from the immediately available analysis of the data. Some managers talk about knowing what is going on for the first time, others talk about the enthusiasm of staff and others focus on the potential. At this point one can just press a button to know the amount of interfacing activity noise (the wasted time devoted to upsetting customers and staff alike) in the total organization broken down by department and team. It is a very exciting and sobering experience. Even the very best organizations have never been disappointed. From previous chapters you know that interfacing activity noise on average absorbs $1\frac{2}{3}$ days out of every person's five-day week. Browsing through your own business opens a whole new dimension. You can look at every one of the multitude of instances should you so wish – and most do, at least some of them muttering things like, 'I just knew it...', as they flick from team to team, department to department.

The fifth deliverable – a platform for change

The most important deliverable at the end of the first month is the platform for change that has been established. The data describing what is really happening in the business, warts and all, is there ready to be used. The culture will be opening up. The staff will be on side with an expectation that the issues that frustrate them and annoy the customers will, perhaps for the first time, be addressed soon. The business can now pursue the opportunities presented and move from managing projects to delivering the outcomes that really matter – continuously.

Determining change priorities strategically

So how do you use this rich data to plan and implement change on a wide front? Well, the first thing to point out is that you probably do not do it alone. Much of it will be done by groups of staff once the priorities have been agreed. Change can therefore be implemented more quickly and surely as more initiatives can be tackled simultaneously.

The first step is to analyse the data strategically, that is by business process. The key processes in any organization are generally well recognized – the claims process, the mortgage acceptance process, the building maintenance process, the process for operating on a patient, etc. Each major process is likely to have KPIs and these highlight the process performance and therefore indicate process weaknesses. These KPIs could include cost per service request, elapsed time to respond, percentage satisfied first time. All are likely to be related to key strategic issues.

The interface mapping tool you choose to use should have features to enable all of the activities to be dragged and dropped into each business process and this gives an opportunity to obtain complete business process descriptions for the first time. This is because key support activities, that is, support activities that directly contribute to the performance of the process, should be included in the process description and thus the strategic alignment analysis. There is a strong argument for including the support functional activities with the associated interfacing activities because the objective is to achieve end-to-end strategic process alignment, including support from within the organization, to deliver the required outcomes. Including the support activities in the key business process will guarantee that instances of non-compliance with the management principle of integration of effort stand out.

The end-to-end process can now be analysed. The first, and obvious, step is to look at the total interfacing activity noise to examine the productivity opportunities – and the potential will be significant. The individual occurrences of interfacing activity noise then can be allocated to drivers and a Pareto analysis generated to identify the top 10 or 20. Non-compliance with the management principles of being time-based, being disciplined and ensuring integration of effort will be immediately evident and represented in the list, so that implementation priorities can be established. Then align the drivers with any weaknesses shown by the KPIs in the Balanced Scorecard, especially the customer service elements. Priorities for customer service can then be set.

Delivery of the required changes

Having set the priorities for implementation it is now time to re-engage with the people who provided the interface mapping data because these are the people, whatever the nature of the change, who will be affected by it and are likely to be the ones who need to change. For each priority use the process interface map to invite those affected by the selected driver of interfacing activity noise to attend an ideas meeting to decide on the solution and plan the change. Provide the attendees with the relevant parts of the interfacing activity map, discuss various options and work through and plan the changes needed much as would have been the case with a quality circle implementation. There are strong parallels with quality circles at this point. The priorities have been established by management. All the people who are affected by the driver have been invited. The ideas are focused on low-cost or no-cost solutions to eliminating (or reducing the impact) of a particular driver and those affected by the change are present to agree the nature of the change and the interfacing activities that would be eliminated or reduced in their part of the business. A good interface mapping tool will now provide the links and tracking features needed to plan the change and monitor through to implementation. The links between business processes, teams, change initiatives and plans will enable scenario modelling of outcomes.

Locking in the changes – BCIs

At the beginning of the chapter we raised the issue of the amount of time that needs to be devoted by managers involved in change to ensure that the change occurs and that people continue to do their work in the new way. Many managers deny that their job includes auditing adherence to the management principle of being disciplined, but when asked what they do, even on their way into the office, they will tell you they often go via... department to check that.... Or they will stop to see a particular manager to check.... The first thing many managers do when a KPI is trending in the wrong direction is to go and check to ensure that particular things are being done.

What if it were possible to extend the Balanced Scorecard to include indicators to confirm that key tasks were being done? Obviously, to object on practicality grounds, it would dramatically increase the number of measures that would need to be collected and that would involve assembling data from each team because the essential activities would be being done in the teams. But let us turn this argument on its head. If each *team* maintained a number of measures that showed the right input activities were being done, activities that were known to achieve a particular business outcome, then this would be evidence that the management principle of relating the micro to the macro was firmly in place. As the principle states, the staff would know how their particular activities and individual efforts contribute to the 'big picture' of business success and they would have the measures to prove it. Further, it could be argued that the members of each team could easily manage to maintain a dozen measures or so to demonstrate to themselves and the rest of the organization that the essential (core) activities were being done.

Now let's return to the principles underpinning the elimination of interfacing activity noise and its viral impact on the business as a whole. Eliminating a driver of interfacing activity noise usually requires the team receiving the transaction to ensure that it is correct, complete and on time. Interface mapping will allow the major drivers to be defined and then solutions can be designed and implemented to eliminate their cause. This presents two ongoing reporting opportunities. First the number of items received in error, late or incomplete can be monitored to find out whether the issue remains under control. However, more importantly, (core) activities will be initiated that prevent or eradicate the driver of interfacing activity noise. These initiatives include such changes as redesigning the web page or form to make it impossible to miss vital information; educating the sender; ensuring that the information the sender uses is kept up to date; sharpening the cutter after 2,000 operations; servicing the lift after 4,000 cycles; ensuring that all new gas processing equipment is added into the preventative maintenance programme; notifying the buying department of pricing discrepancies, checking the Xray is the right way round, etc. These become the BCIs for each team. The measures show that the new activities have been locked into place.

This enhances the reporting of changes. When each change is initiated the early reports monitor the degree to which the plan is being adhered to and which of the planned steps have been completed. When the change is reported as complete then the team can report on the BCIs. This will accord completely with the management principle of measuring and reporting, and indeed it becomes the systematic implementation of that principle.

The last step

The final step is to decide how frequently to update the interfacing activity database. This depends on the degree of change in your business, including the rate of technological change, length of product life cycles, and the volatility of the market, industry and economy. For example, a mining company that has mature and stable operations, processes and systems, long product life cycles, and low rates of technology change, would answer this question differently from a company such as Google, which is constantly innovating its products and its processes due to the fact that nearly everything changes in its business environment every month. So we would argue that some organizations need to be updating their interfacing activity database every six months, whereas others could survive very well by doing so annually.

Conclusions

A review of what awaits you

Our research has clearly shown that in hundreds of international organizations of all sizes and in all sectors, the average of wasted effort through failure to manage the plethora of interfaces is one-third of the total staff and management time. In many cases it is over 50 per cent. The waste from interfacing activity noise in the better managed organizations is still between around 15 per cent of the total staff and management cost because the level of change organizations have to live with means that new interfacing activity noise is being created all the time. In the worst-run organizations this continual build-up of noise in the interfacing activities has raised the waste of people's time to over 70 per cent – three and a half days out of every five.

In service industries, such as the many public sector departments, where there is little or no plant and equipment, organizations are bearing a burden on average of 50 per cent or more on their service costs. This is because of failure to manage interfacing activity. In addition, this level of interfacing activity noise will ensure that service levels and employee satisfaction will be way below par. This same impact is present in the finance industry – banks, insurance companies and so on. In capital-intensive industries where personnel as a percentage of costs are much lower, the 50 per cent burden on the people cost element of transactions is still there, but the impact on service levels will translate into lower plant utilization, wasted and spoiled product and environmental and occupational health and safety risk. We have found, for instance, that service organizations associated with mining equipment, electricity distribution and transportation surrender up to half of their productive capacity to interfacing activity noise. As an example, let's take Australia – here, in a workforce of 10 million this waste translates to a burden of about A $250 billion per annum of which at least half, $125 billion, is accessible with little or no capital investment.

The best organizations deliver their strategic intent with efficiency and sound service and the worst can hardly deliver at all. Remember the provisional bankruptcies of General Motors and before that Chrysler and National Steel. We have to believe that these organizations had good strategies and certainly had scale, but could not deploy them effectively. And in the public sector, while we do not see bankruptcies as such in the first world, inefficiency and ineffectiveness is rife, and organizations are ready for a large upswing in productivity. The core question is 'How?', and its answer will come from adding a new focus and providing the information to manage the ever-increasingly complex interfacing activities.

So just what is this interfacing activity noise, waste, in organizations and why has it not been attacked before in efficient markets, much less in public sector organizations? As we have explained in the early chapters in the book there are two reasons for it. The first is that until comparatively recently it has been below the radar and received no attention from top managers, business schools and top-tier consultants. The second is that the opportunity lies hidden in plain sight in the interfaces between functional work steps, in interfacing activity noise. Middle managers were left to struggle with something they neither had the support to measure, the tools to analyse nor the ability to harvest the benefits of in the many teams scattered throughout the end-to-end business processes. There was no awareness that these interfacing activities go unrecorded, outnumber documented activities 3:1 or that interfacing activity noise absorbs around US $25,000 per person employed per annum in the average organization.

The 'devil' really 'is in the detail'. Thousands of different irregularities can occur in any transactional system, and do. These cause service systems to slow down, waste large amounts of money and frustrate both staff and customers. But chasing thousands of miniscule discontinuities is impossible. It is only when it is realized that there will be a few drivers of interfacing activity noise that cause most of the damage that it is worthwhile addressing them. The drivers will differ from location to location because of situational factors, so an industry list would not be helpful. Identifying these main drivers means accumulating interfacing activity noise by causal factor across the business or supply chain. Harvesting the benefits means managing all the many teams affected by them so that the resource and wasted effort is released. Whole businesses or whole supply chains need to be interface mapped to capture all the fettling (the work-arounds and other adjustments to work processes) that most employees just have to do to make things work so they can do their job.

When the organization needs to change its strategy, market positioning or introduce new products and services, or address issues in customer service, employee satisfaction, growth, margin, equipment utilization, etc then process capability should be at the top of the agenda. Process capability can become both a competitive weapon and an enabler of new and powerful business strategies not available to managers who still have high levels of interfacing activity noise bouncing around in their firms.

So let's go back to the new role for managers – managing the internal and external interfaces to achieve specific strategic business outcomes and release much of the 33.6 per cent of wasted people time. This means knowing how to use interface mapping and preferably do it in such a way that the best-practice management principles that characterize the best organizations in the world will be gradually implanted in your business. In other words, you will be catching them up to get on par with them without having to spend decades doing it.

We close by listing again the principles of business excellence (in Table 10.1). The table sets out the ability or lack of ability to implement and achieve the benefits the principles promise, when the detailed cartography – in the form of an interfacing map – is present and when it is absent.

Note: The text, figures and tables in this book contain proprietary material. Elements of the methodology such as the collection and recording of interfacing activities, how to analyse them including classifying activities, mechanisms for display and the use of BCI measures are the subject of patents held by companies associated with the authors.

TABLE 10.1

Management principle	Without interface mapping	With interface mapping
Having the desire to be out front	This is a dream	Interface mapping provides the tool and understanding
Ensuring integration of effort	There is no mechanism (noise driver) to uncover non-compliance. Leaders can only hope that managers and staff genuinely are operating to meet the company's goals, not personal ones	All significant non-compliance incidents are revealed. Specific data identifies which goals are affected and where. There is a mechanism to measure compliance through BCIs
Being disciplined	Process maps and procedures are prepared but rarely referred to as they focus on functional activities and are never quantified. Processes are static, rarely updated, add little value and are of little value for reference	Interface mapping provides a catalogue of functional and interfacing activities. Noise is readily identified. Data should be kept up to date. Interface mapping provides information on how to do functional and interfacing activities. Even new staff find it useful and usable. There is automatic generation of procedures
Creating customer value	Surveys quantify the severity and nature of problems. Judgement is used to define solutions. Multiple iterations are usually required	Sophisticated surveys based on activities in interface maps pinpoint the issues strategically. Activity noise drivers are quickly ascertained and addressed. Change is locked in with BCIs
Being time-based	It is impossible to identify two-thirds of the potential benefit so many of the key opportunities are never seen. There is a tendency to identify capital-intensive solutions	Interface activity noise pinpoints and quantifies the opportunities. It enables low-cost solutions to be developed with the staff

TABLE 10.1 (Continued)

Management principle	Without interface mapping	With interface mapping
Creating strategic capabilities	It is impossible to achieve. Creating capabilities is mainly about tuning interfaces to achieve specific business process excellence. This means managing the unrecorded, unmeasured interfacing activities	Fully achievable. It is a key goal from managing the interfacing activities.
Relating the micro to the macro	This is difficult to achieve, impossible to know	Activity coding by the staff themselves and involvement in change locks them into a clear understanding of cause and effect. It is measurable by BCIs on core activity
Establishing a learning culture	There is generic training only	Specific training is targeted on the interfacing activities and core activities to achieve capability needs
Embracing change	This is difficult to achieve. Overcoming resistance from middle managers especially difficult	The culture begins to open up within the first two weeks of interface mapping. There are specific programmes for middle managers
Supporting distributed leadership	This is hard to achieve. If practised, it usually means loss of control over processes	Interface mapping creates a culture for distributed leadership and provides the mechanism (interface maps) to focus effort onto key issues and oversee implementation

(Continued)

TABLE 10.1 (*Continued*)

Management principle	Without interface mapping	With interface mapping
Being up front	This needs a lot of effort. Building trust and ability to tolerate error admission can take years. It can be destroyed in days by the action of a few people in senior positions	Being up front is inherent to interface mapping. Quantified interface activity noise is regarded as an opportunity rather than revealing failure. Staff become proud of revealing high noise levels
Gaining alignment	There are usually high-level workshop outcomes that are difficult to translate into the workplace	Hard wired as change is deployed
Measuring and reporting	High-level lagging KPIs at business and sometimes process level are identified through the Balanced Scorecard implementation	High-level lagging KPIs are linked to team-based leading indicators to drive performance – BCIs
Resourcing for the medium term	There is episodic change	There is continuous realignment

Definitions and an example of an interfacing mapping tool

Definitions

Activity categorization

Activity categorization or strategic activity categorization is a framework that allows organizations to link the micro activity people do to the macro strategic goals of an organization. The four categories are core, support, discretionary and noise.

Business process

A business process is a sequenced list of functional activities an organization wishes to undertake in order to implement its business strategy. It is often presented in the format of a process map (see Figure 3.2 on page 67) or a catalogue of functional activities to be undertaken.

Capability or strategic capability

A strategic capability is a business process in which resources are strategically aligned to deliver the outcomes called for in the organization's business strategy. Creating strategic capabilities requires both functional and interfacing activities to be managed closely.

Core activities

These are the 'DNA' of high-performing processes and, therefore, high-performing organizations. Core activities are the activities that are value adding but in addition are undertaken in organizations to drive or create a particular desired outcome. By definition, devoting more time to carrying out core activities delivers increased business performance. They are the process embodiment of the six management principles focusing on strategic intent, and deliver the strategic outcome. There is an important distinction between the core activities of a profession such as an accountant, which are a measure of the wide range of activities accountants input to businesses, and the core activities of a business, which are the few activities that drive required outcomes.

Discretionary activities

As their name implies, these are activities carried out at a management team's discretion. They are most often associated with risk management and include such activities as checking for errors or omissions and conducting compliance audits. What exactly is checked, how it is checked and where the checking takes place is at management's discretion. Obviously, duplicated specific checks are usually coded as noise. The code is also used to highlight activities not directly related to achieving specific outcomes – such as generic training – for review by management.

Functional activities

The staff in every organization undertake activities to convert an input into a desired output. Functional activities are those activities undertaken using the particular skills of the staff located in a specific organizational function. Examples would include taking an order, entering the order into a computer, preparing a training programme, processing an invoice for payment, picking goods, loading a truck using a fork-lift truck.

Interfacing activity

Interfacing activity consists of the steps needed to prepare data, product, transactions etc to enable them to be accepted to be processed by the next functional activity in the process. Interfacing activity includes chasing, connecting, completing steps and the downstream viral impact of these delays and errors.

Interface mapping

Interface mapping is a technique for documenting business processes. It, like conventional process mapping, records functional activities in the sequence in which they are normally performed. It differs from process mapping in two vital ways. First, it quantifies the resource associated with each activity. This is critical to informed, strategic resource allocation. Second, it records the hidden 80 per cent of activity, the situationally determined interfacing activity.

Interfacing activity is the essential component to aligning business processes strategically. It contains the noise that acts like a virus in an organization because it disrupts customer service, reduces employee satisfaction and unnecessarily increases cost. Noise is a critical provider of free resource for injecting core activity. A key requirement is that this information needs to be collected at a high level of detail quickly. It therefore needs to be collected by team.

Noise

Noise is non-value-adding time, potentially distributed throughout the whole supply chain, that is a direct consequence of not doing the strategically needed core activity earlier in the process. Noise is the consequence of failure to do the job once, right first time and therefore includes chasing, correcting and duplication. Noise is always measured in resource hours.

Support activities

These are value-adding activities that need to be performed routinely to provide a service. Unlike core activities doing more of these (for example re-fuelling and re-arming aircraft, transmitting orders to scramble, maintaining radar installations on line, entering an order, printing a production schedule, setting up a file for a claim or producing salary slips) makes no sense. A business cannot exist without support activities but spending more time doing them will not affect the bottom line or outcome.

Work team

A work team or natural work team is the building block on which all structures are based. It is usually a team of between 2 and 12 people including the first line of management – the team leader. Examples are a sales team, a risk assessment team, a women's health policy team, a northern suburbs help team.

Interface mapping tool

For an example of an interface mapping tool, please see www.xep3.com.

REFERENCES AND LITERATURE RESEARCHED

References

Antony, J and Banuelas, R (2002) 'Key ingredients for the effective implementation of Six Sigma program', *Measuring Business Excellence*, **6** (4), pp 20–27

Bungay, S (2000) *The Most Dangerous Enemy: A history of the Battle of Britain*, Aurum Press, London

Crosby, PB (1979) *Quality is Free*, McGraw-Hill, London

Deming, WF (1986) *Out of the Crisis*, MIT Press, London

Guimaraes, T (1999) 'Field testing of the proposed predictors of BPR success in manufacturing firms' *Journal of Manufacturing Systems*, **18** (1) pp 53–66

Ireland, R and Hitt, M (1999) 'Achieving and maintaining strategic competitiveness in the 21st century: The role of strategic leadership' *The Academy of Management Executive*, **13** (1), pp 43–58

Jones, G and Butler, J (2000) 'Costs, revenue and business level strategy', *The Academy of Management Review*, **13** (2), pp 202–13

Kaplan, RS and Norton, DP (1996) *The Balanced Scorecard: Translating strategy into action*, Harvard Business School Publishing

Porter, M (1990) *The Competitive Advantage of Nations*, Free Press, New York

Rice, R and Cooper, S (2010) *Organizations and Unusual Routines*, Cambridge University Press

Samson, D and Challis, D (1999) *Patterns of Excellence: The new principles of corporate success*, Pearson Education, London

Samson, D and Terziovski, M (1999) 'The relationship between total quality management practices and operational performance', *Journal of Operations Management*, **17**, pp 393–409

Simon, D, Gove, S and Hitt, M (2008) 'Resource management in dyadic competitive rivalry: the effects of resource bundling and deployment', *The Academy of Management Journal*, **51** (5), pp 919–35

Slack, N et al (2006) *Operations and process management, principles and practice for strategic impact*, Pearson Education, London

Slater, R (1999) Jack Welch and the GE Way, McGraw-Hill, New York

Smith, M (2003) 'Changing an organisation's culture: correlates of success and failure, *Leadership & Organization Development Journal*, **24** (5/6), pp 249–62

Smith, MF (2003) 'Business process design: Correlates of success and failure', *The Quality Management Journal*, **10** (2), pp 38–50

Stalk, G and Hout, T (1990) *Competing Against Time: How time-based competition is reshaping global markets*, Collier Macmillan Publishers, London

Tranfield, D and Smith, S (1998) 'The strategic regeneration of manufacturing by changing routines', *International Journal of Operations and Production Management*, **18** (2) pp 114–127

Wernerfelt, B (1984)) 'A resource-based view of the firm', *Strategic Management Journal*, **5** (2), pp 171–181

Literature Researched

Ahadi, H R (2004) 'An examination of the role of organizational enablers in business process reengineering and the impact of information technology', *Information Resources Management Journal*, **17** (4), pp 1–19

Ahire, S, Golhar, D and Waller, M (1996) 'Development and validation of TQM implementation constructs', *Decision Sciences*, **27** (1), pp 23–56

Anderson, J C, Rungtusanatham, M, Schroeder, R G and Deveraj, S (1995) 'A path analytic model of a theory of quality management underlying the Demming Management Method: Preliminary empirical findings', *Decision Sciences*, **26**, pp 637–58

Anjard, R (1996) 'Applying re-engineering', *Work Study*, **45** (7), p 9

Antony, J and Banuelas, R (2002) 'Key ingredients for the effective implementation of Six Sigma program', *Measuring Business Excellence*, **6** (4), pp 20–27

Amundson, S D (1998) 'Relationships between theory-driven empirical research in operations management and other disciplines', *Journal of Operations Management*, **16**, pp 341–59

Banker, R D, Lee, S, Potter, G and Srinivasan, D (1996) 'Contextual analysis of performance impacts of outcome-based incentive compensation', *Academy of Management Journal*, **39** (4), pp 920–49

Barney, J B (1986) 'Organization culture: Can it be a source of sustained competitive advantage?' *Academy of Management Review*, **13**, pp 656–65

Barney, J B (1991) 'Firm resource and sustained competitive advantage', *Journal of Management*, **17**, pp 99–120

Becker, B and Gerhart, B (1996) 'The impact of human resource management on organizational performance: Progress and prospects', *The Academy of Management Journal*, **39** (4), pp 779–801

Beer, M (2003) 'Why quality management programs do not persist: The role of management quality and implications for leading a TQM transformation', *Decision Sciences*, **34** (4), 623–43

Biazzo, S (1998) 'A critical examination of the business process re-engineering phenomenon', *International Journal of Operations and Production Management*, **18** (9/10), pp 1000–1013

Brandon, B and Guimaraes, T (1999) 'Empirically assessing the impact of BPR on banking firms', *The Journal of Bank Cost and Management Accounting*, **12** (2), pp 26–59

Buffa, E S (1981) 'Commentary on production/operations management: agenda for the 80's', *Decision Sciences*, **12** (4), pp 572–73

Bullington, Stanley F E, John, Y, Greenwood, A G, Bullington, K E (2002) 'Success factors in initiating versus maintaining a quality improvement process', *Engineering Management Journal*, **14** (3), pp 8–15

Burnes, B and James, H (1995) 'Culture, cognitive dissonance and the management of change', *International Journal of Operations and Production Management*, **15** (8), pp 14–34

Capon, N, Farley, J, and Hoenig, S (1990) 'Determinants of financial performance: a meta analysis', *Management Science*, **36** (10), pp 1143–59

Chendall, R H (1997) 'Reliance on manufacturing performance, total quality management and organizational performance', *Management Accounting Research*, **8**, pp 187–206

Choi, T Y and Eboch, K (1998) 'The TQM paradox: relations among TQM practices, plant performance and customer satisfaction', *Journal of Operations Management*, **17**, pp 59–75

Crosby, P B (1979) *Quality is Free*, McGraw-Hill, New York

Das, A, Handfield, R B, Calantone, R J, Ghosh, S (2000) 'A contingent view of quality management – the impact of international competition on quality', *Decision Sciences*, **31**, pp 649–90

Davis, R A and Stading, G L (2005) 'Linking Firm Performance to the Malcolm Baldrige National Quality Implementation Effort Using Multi-attribute Utility Theory', *Managerial Finance*, **31** (3), pp 19–35

Davenport, T and Short, J (1990) 'The new industrial engineering: Information Technology and Business Process Re-design', *Sloan Management Review*, Summer, pp 11–27

Day, G S and Reibstein, D J with Gunther, R (1997) *Wharton on Dynamic Competitive Strategy*, John Wiley and Sons, New York

Denis, J-L, Lamothe, L and Langley, A (2001) 'The dynamics of collective leadership and strategic change in pluralistic organisations', *Academy of Management Journal*, **44** (4), pp 809–38

Douglas, T J and Judge Jr, WQ, (2001) 'Total quality management implementation and competitive advantage: the role of structural control and exploration', *Academy of Management Journal*, **44**, pp 158–69

Dow, D, Samson, D, Ford, S (1999) 'Exploding the myth: do all quality management practices contribute to superior quality performance?', *Production and Operations Management*, **8**, pp 1–27

Drew, S A W (1996) 'Accelerating change: financial industry experience with BPR', *The International Journal of Bank Marketing*, **14** (6), pp 23–26

Droge, C, Jararam, J and Vickery, S K (2004) 'The effects of internal versus external integration practices on time-based performance and overall firm performance', *Journal of Operations Management*, **22**, pp 557–73

Easton, G S and Jarrell, S L (1998) 'The effects of total quality management on corporate performance: an empirical investigation', *Journal of Business*, **72** (2), pp 253–307

Fullerton, R R, McWatters, C S and Fawson, C (2003) 'An examination of the relationship between JIT and financial performance', *Journal of Operations Management*, **21** (4), pp 383–404

Garvin, D (1987) 'Competing on the eight dimensions of quality', *Harvard Business Review*, **65**, pp 202–209

Gersick, C J G (1991) 'Revolutionary change theories: a multilevel exploration of the punctuated equilibrium paradigm', *The Academy of Management Review*, **16** (1), pp 10–36

Goleman, D (1998) *Working with Emotional Intelligence*, Bloomsbury Publishing, London

Grover, V and Malhotra, M K (1997) 'Business Process Reengineering: a tutorial on the concept, evolution, method, technology and application', *Journal of Operations Management*, **15**, pp 193–213

Guimaraes, T (1999) 'Field testing of the proposed predictors of BPR success in manufacturing firms', *Journal of Manufacturing Systems*, **18** (1), pp 53–66

Hamel, G and Prahalad, C K (1994) *Competing for the Future*, Harvard Business School Press, Boston, MA

Hamel, G (2000) *Leading the Revolution*, Harvard Business School Press, Boston, MA

Hamid, R A (2004) 'An examination of the role of organizational enablers in business process reengineering and the impact of information technology', *Information Resources Management Journal*, **17** (4) pp 1–19

Hammer, M (1990) 'Reengineering work: Don't automate, obliterate', *Harvard Business Review* (July–August), pp 104–112

Hammer, M and Champy, J (1993) *Reengineering the Corporation: A Manifesto for Business Revolution*, Harper Business, New York, NY

Hammer, M and Stanton, S A (1995) *The Reengineering Revolution: A Handbook*, Harper Business, New York, NY

Hammer, M (1996) *Beyond Reengineering*, Harper Business, New York, NY.

Handfield, R B and Melnyk, S A (1998) 'The scientific theory-building process: a primer using the case of TQM', *Journal of Operations Management*, **16**, pp 321–39

Hax, A C (1981) 'Commentary on production/operations management: agenda for the 80's', *Decision Sciences*, **12** (4) pp 574–77

Hendricks, K B and Singhal, V R (1996) 'Quality awards and the market value of the firm: an empirical investigation', *Management Science*, **42**, pp 415–36.

Hendricks, K B and Singhal, V R (1997) 'Does implementing an effective TQM program actually improve operating performance? Empirical evidence from firms that have won quality awards', *Management Science*, **43**, pp 1258–74

Hill, T J (1985) *Manufacturing Strategy: The Strategic Management of the Manufacturing Function*, MacMillan, London

Ireland, D R and Hitt, M A (1999) 'Achieving and maintaining strategic competitiveness in the 21st century: The role of strategic leadership', *The Academy of Management Executive*, **13** (1), pp 43–58

Jacob, R, Madu, C N and Tang, C (2004) 'Quality and reliability corner: An empirical assessment of the financial performance of Malcolm Baldrige Award winners', *International Journal of Quality and Reliability*, **21** (8), p 897

Jarrar, Y F and Aspinwall, E M (1999) 'Business process re-engineering: Learning from organizational experience', *Total Quality Management*, **10** (2), p 173–87

Jones, G R and Butler, J E (2000) 'Costs, Revenue and Business Level Strategy', *The Academy of Management Review*, **13** (2) pp 202–13

Juran, J M (1979) *Quality Control Handbook*, 3rd Edition, McGraw-Hill, New York

Kanter, R M, Stein, B A and Jick, T D (1992) *The Challenge of Organizational Change*, The Free Press, Toronto, Canada

Kaynak, H (2003) 'The relationship between total quality management practices and their effects on firm performance', *Journal of Operations Management*, **21** (24), pp 405–35

Kotter, J P (1996) *Leading Change*, Harvard Business School Press, Boston, MA

Lillrank, P and Kano, N (1989) *Continuous Improvement: Quality Control Circles in Japanese Industry*, Center for Japanese Studies, University of Michigan, Ann Arbor

Machiavelli, N (1961) *The Prince* (first published in 1513), New York, Penguin

MacIntosh, R and MacLean, D (2001) 'Conditioned emergence: Researching change and changing research' *International Journal of Operations and Production Management*, **21** (9/10), pp 1343–58.

Maani, K, Putterill, M and Sluti, D (1994) 'Empirical analysis of quality improvement in manufacturing', *International Journal of Quality and Reliability Management*, **11** (7), pp 19–37

Malhotra, M K and Grover, V (1998) 'An assessment of survey research in POM: from constructs to theory', *Journal of Operations Management*, **14** (4), pp 406–25

Marshak, R J (2004) 'Morphing: The Leading Edge of Organizational Change in the Twenty-first Century', *Organization Development Journal*, **22** (3), pp 8–22

Maskell, B 'The age of agile manufacturing', *Supply Chain Management*, **6** (1), pp 5–12

Maull, R S, Weaver, A M, Childe, S J, Smart, P A and Bennett, J (1995) 'Current issues in business process reengineering', *International Journal of Operations and Production Management*, **15** (11), pp 37–53

Meredith, J (1998) 'Building operations management theory through case and field research', *Journal of Operations Management*, **16**, pp 441–54

Miller, J G and Graham, M B W (1981) 'Commentary on production/operations management: agenda for the 80's', *Decision Sciences*, **12** (4), pp 547–71

NIST (2002) National Institute of Standards and Technology, 'Frequently asked questions about the Malcolm Baldrige National Quality Award'

O'Leary-Kelly, S W and Vokurka, R J (1998) 'The empirical assessment of construct validity', *Journal of Operations Management*, **16** (4), pp 387–405

O'Neill, P and Sohal, A S (1998) 'Business process re-engineering: application and success – an Australian study', *International Journal of Operations and Production Management*, **18** (9/11), pp 832

Pande, Peter S, Neuman, Robert P and Cavanagh, Roland R (2000) *The Six Sigma Way*, McGraw-Hill, New York

Papke-Shields, K E and Malhotra, M K (2001) 'Assessing the impact of the manufacturing executives role on business performance through strategic alignment', *Journal of Operations Management*, **19** (1), pp 5–22

Penrose, E T (1959) *The theory of the growth of the firm*, Oxford, Blackwell

Peteraf, Margaret A (1993) 'The cornerstones of competitive advantage: A resource based view', *Strategic Management Journal*, **14** (3), pp 179–91

Porter, M E (1980) *Competitive Strategy, Techniques for Analysing Industries and Competitors*, The Free Press, New York

Porter, M E (1990) *The Competitive Advantage of Nations*, Free Press, New York

Powell, T C (1995) 'Total quality management as competitive advantage: a review and empirical study', *Management Journal*, **16**, pp 15–37

Priem, R L and Butler, J E (2001) 'Is the resource-based "view" a useful perspective for strategic management research?' *Academy of Management Review*, **26**, pp 22–40

Rajagopalan, N and Spreitzer, G M (1997) 'Towards a theory of strategic change: A multi-lens perspective and integrative framework', *The Academy of Management Review*, **22** (1), pp 48–80

Rindova, V P and Kotha, S (2001) 'Continuous "Morphing": Competing through dynamic capabilities, form, and function', *The Academy of Management Journal*, **44** (6), pp 1263–81

Rummler, Garry A and Brache, Alan P (1990) *Improving Performance: How to Manage the White Space on the Organization Chart*, Josse-Bass Inc, San Francisco, California

Samson, D (1991) *Manufacturing and Operations Strategy*, Prentice Hall of Australia, Melbourne

Samson, D and Challis, D (1999) *Patterns of Excellence: The New Principles of Corporate Success Driving Success*, Prentice Hall

Samson, D and Terziovski, M (1999) 'The relationship between total quality management practices and operational performance', *Journal of Operations Management*, **17**, pp 393–409

Saraph, J, Benson, P and Schroeder, R (1989) 'An instrument for measuring the critical factors of quality management', *Decision Sciences*, **4**, pp 810–29

Schroeder, R (1983) 'Operations strategy: A perspective on productivity and Quality', *Research paper*, University of Minnesota, December 1983

Shewhart, W A (1931) *Economic Control of Quality of Manufactured Products*, Van Nostrand, New York, NY

Sirkin, H L, Keenan, P and Jackson, A (2005) 'The hard side of change management', *Harvard Business Review*, **83** (10), p 108

Slack, N, Chambers, S, Johnston, R. and Betts, A (2006) *Operations and Process Management*, Prentice Hall

Slater, R (1999) *Jack Welch and the GE Way*, McGraw Hill, New York

Smith, M E (2003a) 'Business process design: Correlates of success and failure', *The Quality Management Journal*, **10** (2), pp 38–50

Smith, M E (2003b) 'Changing an organisation's culture: Correlates of success and failure', *Leadership & Organization Development Journal*, **24** (5/6), pp 249–62

Smith, H and Fingar, P (2002) *Business Process Management, the Third Wave*, Meghan-Kiffer Press

Smith, T M and Reece, J S (1999) 'The relationship of strategy, fit, productivity, and business performance in a services setting', *Journal of Operations Management*, **17** (2), pp 145–61

Sousa, R and Voss, C A (2002) 'Quality management revisited: a reflective review and agenda for future research', *Journal of Operations Management*, **20**, pp 91–109

Stalk, G and Hout, T M (1990) *Competing Against Time: How Time Based Competition is Reshaping Global Markets*, Collier Macmillan Publishers, London

Tapinos, E, Dyson, R G and Meadows, M (2005) 'The impact of performance measurement in strategic planning', *The Journal of Productivity and Performance Management*, **54** (5/6), pp 370–85

Tranfield, D and Smith, S (1998) 'The strategic regeneration of manufacturing by changing routines', *International Journal of Operations and Production Management*, **18** (2), p 114–27

Treacy, M and Wiersema, F (1995) *The Discipline of Market Leaders*, Harper Collins, London

Vakola, M and Wilson, I E (2004) 'The challenge of virtual organization: critical success factors in dealing with constant change', *Team Performance Management*, **10** (5/6), pp 112–21

Wacker, John G (1998) 'A definition of theory: research guidelines for different theory-building research methods in operations management', *Journal of Operations Management*, **16**, pp 361–85

Wacker, John G (2004). "A theory of formal conceptual definitions: developing theory-building measurement instruments", *Journal of Operations Management*, **22** (6), pp 629–50

Wernerfelt, B (1984) 'A resource based view of the firm', *Strategic Management Journal*, **5** (2), pp 171–81

White, G (1996) 'A meta-analysis model of manufacturing capabilities', *Journal of Operations Management*, **14**, pp 315–31

Wilson, D D and Collier, D A (2000) 'An empirical investigation of the Malcolm Baldrige National Quality award causal model', *Decision Sciences*, **31**, pp 361–90

York, K M and Miree, C E (2004) 'Causation or covariation: an empirical re-examination of the link between TQM and financial performance', *Journal of Operations Management*, **22** (3), pp 291–311

INDEX

NB: page numbers in *italic* indicate figures or tables
introductions to, objectives and summaries of chapters are indexed as such